Understanding and Treating Adolescent Substance Abuse

Philip P. Muisener

Sage Sourcebooks for

S|S|≡|S|

the Human Services Series

27

SAGE Publications

International Educational and Professional Publisher

Thousand Oaks   London   New Delhi

For information address:

 SAGE Publications, Inc.
2455 Teller Road
Thousand Oaks, California 91320

SAGE Publications Ltd.
6 Bonhill Street
London EC2A 4PU
United Kingdom

SAGE Publications India Pvt. Ltd.
M-32 Market
Greater Kailash I
New Delhi 110 048 India

Printed in the United States of America

Library of Congress Cataloging-in-Publication Data

Muisener, Philip P.
    Understanding and treating adolescent substance abuse / Philip P. Muisener.
        p.   cm.—(Sage sourcebook for the human services series; v. 27)
    Includes bibliographical references and indexes.
    ISBN 0-8039-4275-3.—ISBN 0-8039-4276-1 (pbk.)
    1. Teenagers—United States—Drug use. 2. Teenagers—United States—Drug use—Prevention. 3. Teenagers—United States—Alcohol use. 4. Teenagers—United States—Alcohol use—Prevention. 5. Drug abuse—Treatment—United States. 6. Alcoholism—Treatment—United States. I. Title. II. Series.
    HV5824.Y68M85   1994
    362.29′0835—dc20   93-32463

94 95 96 97   10 9 8 7 6 5 4 3 2 1

Sage Production Editor: Diane S. Foster

This book is dedicated with hope
to today's young people and their families.

CONTENTS

FOREWORD

While there is a substantial amount of research about various aspects of adult alcohol and substance abuse problems, only recently has attention been given to comprehensive and thorough evaluation in the adolescent population. The need for research and thoughtful comment focusing on adolescent substance abuse became evident as the proliferation of drugs and alcohol use by teens reached epidemic proportions in the 1970s and 1980s. Early studies tended to take adult models and merely apply them to the adolescent population. While these studies were not without merit, the subtle and more overt differences between adults and adolescents were often overlooked. As research in this area became more sophisticated, the value of the commentary and depth of understanding increased significantly.

The present work succeeds in integrating the varied and complex elements that impact the initiation, maintenance, and treatment of adolescent substance abuse. To achieve this, a progressive and illuminating approach, the biopsychosocial model, is used to conceptualize the problem and develop creative treatment alternatives.

It is clear that the problem cannot be viewed as simply adult substance abuse issues in adolescents, nor will a linear line of thinking adequately address this dynamic and pervasive problem. Rather, it is the complex interaction of biological, psychological, and social variables with individual personality traits of adolescents as a distinct population that must be considered when trying to fathom the possible causes and effective treatment options for addressing this issue.

The first section of the book sets the tone for the entire work by its focus on current issues, definitions, and perspectives on adolescent substance abuse. Adolescents are presented as a clearly defined group with unique needs and concerns, a population requiring the most sophisticated evaluation possible. Adolescent specific concerns are discussed from conceptual and treatment perspectives. The author presents the biopsychosocial premise and proceeds to consider the various interactive elements that comprise the model.

The biopsychosocial model as it applies specifically to adolescent substance abuse is examined in greater detail in Part II. Salient issues in the biological, psychological, and social (peers and family) realm of experience for adolescents are thoroughly addressed. These vital areas are discussed in terms of the normative issues for adolescents and how impairment in these areas can cause, or be the result of, substance abuse. Understanding the interaction of adolescence as a developmental process and the impact of drugs during this time is vital to accurately assess the scope of the problem and make relevant treatment choices.

The third section, however, is the crux of the book. The biopsychosocial model as a specific yet dynamic guide to implementing treatment is offered. Using the model as a starting point, "real life" treatment issues such as assessment, treatment planning, service provision, and the adolescent (as well as family/peer) recovery process are examined. Finally, consideration is given to adolescents who have multiple areas of impairment and subsequently require additional therapeutic understanding and skill to create the best opportunity for improvement.

The overriding focus of the work is to guide the reader to a more accurate and useful understanding of adolescent substance abuse. By engaging the biopsychosocial model, a sophisticated integration of complex and dynamic variables is made possible. It provides a comprehensive understanding of the problem, and the greatest opportunity for treatment.

This book takes on a formidable task. In doing so, it stimulates a provocative and progressive dialogue in an attempt to create a reality-based, integrated, conceptual model for understanding and treating this pervasive problem. It is what the field needs to move us to a more enlightened, efficient and effective position.

Thomas M. Doolittle, Ph.D.
Clinical Director,
Parkview Counseling Center

ACKNOWLEDGMENTS

I would like to offer special thanks to Tom Doolittle, Ph.D., for his insights and encouragement in the writing of this book. His expertise was invaluable in the shaping of the manuscript, and his good will and humor helped me in dealing with the "loneliness of the long distance writer." I would also like to express my gratitude to a number of colleagues for their support and for their influence in the evolution of my thoughts about how to help young people. In particular, I want to thank my colleagues at Glastonbury Youth and Family Services over the past several years, and especially Carol E. Gammell, M.A., M.Ed., for consistently reminding me of the richness and integrity of working with adolescents and their families. I owe a debt of gratitude to my former colleagues at the Child and Adolescent Psychiatric Services at Mount Sinai Hospital, especially Len Kupec, C.I.S.W., for fueling my curiosity and sense of wonder about how to encourage healthy development in young people. I also want to thank Bob Sinkewicz, M.S.W., for his imaginative ideas about young people and growing up. And I owe special thanks to Cliff H. for showing me the very human face of recovery.

In addition, I want to extend my appreciation to those people responsible for giving my book a chance. My thanks to Charles Garvin at the University of Michigan School of Social Work for his faith in this writing project at an embryonic stage, and to Marquita Flemming at Sage Publications for her enthusiasm while this writing project developed.

I would also like to offer special recognition to Sofia Striffler and Beryl Glover for their work on the preparation and typing of my manuscript. I could not have done it without their skillful assistance.

Finally, my heartfelt gratitude to my parents, and my sisters and their families, and to my friends for understanding about my periods of semiseclusion while I created this book. You have my love.

INTRODUCTION

Substance abuse has proliferated as a national health problem over the past quarter century. The reasons for this social cancer have been well documented (Musto, 1987). Suffice it to say that such a national epidemic often strikes hardest the most vulnerable segments of society. The elderly, the poor, the psychologically impaired, the culturally disenfranchised, and the young are among those populations that live in the shadows of society. This book is concerned with how the problem of substance abuse relates to one of these vulnerable groups—adolescents in society.

Much as the problem of adolescent substance abuse has grown over the latter part of the 20th century, so also have the ways of understanding and treating this problem grown. Throughout the 1980s the trend was toward the expansion of treatment programs for adolescent substance abusers (Nakken, 1989). New understanding about the treatment of adolescent substance abuse, including the importance of family treatment, evolved and became incorporated into these expanding programs. Further contributing to these newer understandings and treatment approaches was the cross-fertilization of perspectives created by those involved with treating adolescent substance abusers. The walls were lowered among the different mental health disciplines and between the mental health disciplines and advocates of 12-step recovery. Bridges of collaboration began being built around how to best understand and treat adolescent substance abusers. It has been imperative that this spirit of cooperation among professionals treating adolescent substance abusers continue into the 1990s. Due to the changing nature of health care reimbursement, treatment providers and programs have had to reorganize around how to treat drug-involved teenagers. Creativity has been the underpinning of evolving approaches to treatment and will need to be in the future.

As we move toward a new century, innovation will continue to be the driving force behind emerging models for dealing with teenage drug problems. Practitioners dealing with adolescent substance abuse will need to continue to cull together sometimes diverse and complex concepts and translate these concepts into practical treatment applications. Treatment approaches will need to continue being functionally eclectic with focused, yet flexible, treatment interventions.

This book presents a biopsychosocial model for understanding and treating adolescent substance abuse. This paradigm is offered as one way of addressing the treatment community's need for comprehensive and useful models during these times of increasingly austere health care resources.

The search for new and more helpful understandings about health and illness is a constant quest for the scientific community. Implicit in this quest is the recognition that such understandings come from the merging of ideas, often between disciplines. As Schwartz (1982) asserts,

> It is within this broad scientific context that biopsychosocial approaches to health and illness have been formulated. Stimulated by the realization that the boundaries separating disciplines were becoming less rigid, that new connections were becoming possible between disparate disciplines, and that complex problems of health and illness were turning out to be inherently multidimensional in nature, researchers and clinicians from diverse disciplines have become motivated to seek better ways of building bridges between disciplines and establishing a common set of terms and principles. (p. 1041)

Biopsychosocial approaches are neither orthogonal nor integrative in scope. These approaches embrace the major paradigm shifts of disciplines toward multiple factorial and interacting systems. Addressing a health problem from a viewpoint of multiple and interacting understandings develops an appreciation for the many and complex factors that can contribute to an illness. At the same time, treatment of a health problem that incorporates multiple and interactive approaches respects varied and sometimes complicated treatment strategies being used as well as the different systems that need to be involved in treatment. A biopsychosocial approach to a disorder is not "the perspective" but rather "a perspective" that allows for a range of ideas and efforts to be considered.

An addiction is a multifaceted disorder with a diverse course of manifestation. Consequently, there is a value to adopting a paradigm that addresses this multifaceted nature and diversity. A biopsychosocial model is such a paradigm. According to Donovan (1988), "The biopsychosocial model represents an emergent paradigm within the field of addictions" (p. 13). Zucker and Lisansky Gomberg (1986) have developed a biopsychosocial model applicable to the prototype of chemical addictions—adult alcoholism. Lawson (1992) has suggested a biopsychosocial paradigm of adolescent substance abusers, and Chatlos (1989) has provided a biopsychosocial model for dealing with adolescent substance abusers concurrently afflicted with a psychological disorder.

The biopsychosocial model of adolescent substance abuse presented in this book approaches adolescent substance abusers as a heterogeneous group. Teenagers with drug problems vary in gender, psychological make-up, family background, peer affiliation, ethnicity, and socioeconomic status among other factors. Due to this heterogeneity there is a need for diversity in ways of understanding adolescent substance abuse, and a need for translating these diverse understandings into relevant treatment approaches.

Part I of this book identifies some dilemmas encountered by treatment professionals who work with adolescent substance abusers. Chapter 1 looks at some current issues being dealt with in defining and understanding adolescent substance abuse. Chapter 2 covers some contemporary issues in treating adolescent substance abusers. These chapters suggest how a biopsychosocial model of adolescent substance abuse can help to address these issues of defining, understanding, and treating teenage drug problems.

Part II encompasses the biopsychosocial model for understanding adolescent substance abuse that is presented in this book. Chapter 3 introduces this model and provides an overview of biological, psychological, family, peer, community, and societal components in this paradigm. Chapter 4 focuses on one of the three primary factors—adolescent psychological development—in this biopsychosocial model. Chapter 5 discusses the remaining two factors—family functioning and peer relationships—in the triad of primary factors from this model.

Part III is concerned with the biopsychosocial model for treating adolescent substance abuse that is offered in this book. Chapter 6 provides an overview of this biopsychosocial model of treatment looking at different systems—biological, adolescent psychological development, family, peer relationships, community, and society—involved in treatment, as well as therapeutic systems used in treatment. Chapter 7 details assessment issues, and dovetails with the treatment planning considerations discussed in Chapter 8. One of the three primary recovering systems in this biopsychosocial treatment model—the adolescent's psychological recovery—is the subject of Chapter 9. In Chapter 10 the remaining two primary recovering systems—the recovering family and the adolescent's peer relationships in recovery—are the focus. Finally, Chapter 11 explores how substance abuse treatment can be provided to three different high risk populations of adolescents—those with concurrent psychological disorders, those who are victims of physical or sexual abuse, or those who grew up with substance-abusing parents.

This book has been developed and written with the needs of helping professionals and students from different orientations in mind. It is intended for mental health professionals grounded in psychological theory and a systems approach who are searching for a model that helps to integrate their knowledge with current understandings about addiction and recovery with adolescents. It is also designed for substance abuse treatment professionals familiar with traditional substance abuse treatment approaches and 12-step recovery programs who are seeking a clinically useful model for working with teenage substance abusers. In addition, this book is intended for students who are preparing to work with adolescent substance abusers and are interested in a model that promotes an inclusiveness of theoretical ideas and a diversity of treatment approaches. The overriding hope is that the breadth and depth of the model presented in this book will prove useful to any helping professional or student involved in the very challenging work of treating young people with drug problems.

One premise accepted throughout this book is the concept of the unity of addictive disorders (Doweiko, 1990). The implication of this concept for substance use disorders is that the emphasis is on the addiction process itself, not on the substance of choice. Except where distinctions are noted, an adolescent's abuse of alcohol, marijuana, cocaine, or any other psychoactive substance is not differentiated in this book. The focus is on the adolescent's process of addiction to psychoactive substances in general.

It is further assumed in this book that the terms substance abuse, drug addiction, and chemical dependency all mean the same thing. They are terms that represent the addiction process. Throughout this book these terms are used interchangeably for the sake of variety in language.

Part I

CURRENT ISSUES IN ADOLESCENT SUBSTANCE ABUSE

Chapter 1

DEFINING AND UNDERSTANDING ADOLESCENT SUBSTANCE USE AND ABUSE

INTRODUCTION

It is very useful for those who help individuals with substance abuse problems to consider how they have arrived at their definitions and understandings of these problems. A clinician's definitions and understandings not only reflect the "reality" of a given person's drug problem but can also contribute to creating the clinician's own "reality" of how to be helpful with this individual's drug problem.

The terms and concepts used by those who treat adolescent substance abusers can sometimes seem entangled in a knot of opinions, perspectives, and judgements. Loosening this knot and viewing each strand can be an enlightening process.

Among professionals who treat adolescent substance abusers, there are currently various dilemmas about ways of defining and understanding substance use and abuse. One dilemma pertains to delineating the different stages of adolescent chemical use. Another involves how to distinguish between substance use and abuse, and how to determine what truly is a "drug problem" with a given young person. Yet another dilemma is how to best explain adolescent chemical use throughout different stages. There are also problems comprehending addiction and the disease concept of addiction.

This chapter seeks to address these dilemmas and to clarify definitions and understandings about adolescent substance abuse. It is hoped that clearer terms and explanations can yield more potent treatment interventions for young chemical users and their families.

DEFINING THE STAGES
OF ADOLESCENT SUBSTANCE USE

Adolescent chemical use can be construed as occurring in different stages along a continuum. Young persons progress, regress through, or stay at different stages according to varied biological, psychological, and social factors. In addition, their course may be affected by factors endemic to specific drugs.

Jellinek (1960) and Johnson (1973) were two of the pioneers in explaining alcoholism, and they both developed stages-of-use models of conceptualizing alcoholism. Their respective models have been combined and adapted as constructs for representing the different stages of chemical dependency. Macdonald (1984), Newton (1981), and Macdonald and Newton (1981) modified Johnson's stages-of-use model for adult alcoholism into a useful tool for comprehending the stages of adolescent drug use. Presented in this book is the Adolescent Chemical Use Experience (ACUE) continuum (Figure 1.1), derived from Macdonald and Newton's model for defining the stages of teenage chemical use.

The Adolescent Chemical Use Experience Continuum

A conceptual model representing the stages of adolescent chemical use is just that—a model. This model is not reality, but an abstraction of reality to aid in understanding the problem of teenage drug use. Stages of use overlap, and specific cut-off points from one stage to another are basically arbitrary. Nonetheless, it is necessary to make distinctions among the kinds of experiences that adolescents have along a continuum of chemical use (Muldoon & Crowley, 1986).

The adolescent chemical use experience (ACUE) continuum is a four-stage model of teenage substance use that is presented in this book. The central characteristic for defining the four stages is the adolescent's experience of a chemically induced mood swing in each stage. In this context a mood swing refers to the effect of taking a psychoactive substance on the adolescent's internal subjective state. Summarizing

Macdonald and Newton (1981), the four stages of teenage drug use are (a) learning the mood swing, (b) seeking the mood swing, (c) preoccupation with the mood swing, and (d) doing drugs to feel normal.

The ACUE continuum incorporates four stages of experiencing the chemically created mood swing, as well as other features of adolescent substance use that are manifest in these respective stages. Although a small portion of teenagers do not try or use any substances during their adolescent years (Weiner, 1992), this "no use" stage will not be considered along the ACUE continuum.

Stage 1: Experimental Use (Learning the Mood Swing)

The first stage of adolescent chemical use relates to the young person's discovery of the potential of chemicals to create a change in feeling state. The teenager learns that ingesting a chemical can change her mood and emotions. An example of a Stage 1 experimental user is a 14-year-old female who, along with her girlfriend, got caught drinking by her girlfriend's parents. Both girls shared about a half of a bottle of wine. They reported that this was their first experience of trying alcohol and that they did so out of "curiosity."

This is the stage of experimentation and exploration with drugs. "Drug experimentation is best defined as the use of one drug—usually not more than four or five times—to seek an intoxicant effect and to gain a sense of mastery over the experience" (Miller, 1986, p. 200). The experience of experimentation is relatively developmentally adaptive and corresponds to the adolescent's developmental strivings.

A majority of teenagers probably try out drugs the way they try out all sorts of sensual and frightening experiences, in effect, to see what it is like—to find out what all the talk is about and whether it is true; to see if they will be scared; to see if they can master it." (Noshpitz & King, 1991, p.404)

For many adolescents, this experience of trial and error with chemicals leads into a second stage of drug use.

Stage 2: Social Use (Seeking the Mood Swing)

The second stage of adolescent chemical use pertains to the young person exhibiting a pattern of chemically altering his emotional state, particularly in a social setting. The teenager's behavior occurs with peers who are also seeking this mood swing. Labeling this stage the social stage is not meant to imply that the adolescent's chemical use is socially acceptable but is intended to identify the context within which the adolescent is seeking the mood swing.

An illustration of a Stage 2 social user is the case of a 17-year-old male who has been drinking beer on occasion during the past year. His use has been confined to weekends and takes place when he is with his friends. He is aware of the effects of alcohol, as he had one episode of intoxication about 6 months ago. Since then he has limited the amount of beer he drinks on the occasions when he drinks.

Although some adolescents do become more vulnerable to experiencing this chemically modified mood swing and traverse into substance abuse, the social stage is fairly adaptive and normative for many adolescents. As Ungerleider and Siegel (1990, p. 437) observe, "Drug and alcohol use have become quasi-normal" behaviors in the adolescent subculture of the United States, at least on an experimental or recreational level. This is not to say that teenagers in the social stages do not have episodes of misuse or intoxication. But with most adolescents in this stage these episodes are transient and highly intermittent. The quality of over-indulgence with a substance in this stage differs from intoxication in Stages 3 and 4, where the young person's life is becoming organized around regular episodes of getting drunk or high. Although adolescents in the second stage have not and may not progress to the next stage, there are serious risks with using drugs at this social stage.

Stage 3: Operational Use (Preoccupation With the Mood Swing)

The third stage of adolescent chemical use signifies the young person's entry into substance abuse, with the gradual grip of addiction becoming more manifest. The adolescent is actively engaging the mood swing effects of psychoactive substances. In short, she is "acting out" with drugs as a way to have drugs "act on" her internal affective state.

Any chemical use in this stage can be considered to be self-medication. The teenager has become a junior pharmacist and is self-prescribing drugs to operate on her feelings. The adolescent may subjectively experience this self-medication as adaptive, but in reality it is quite developmentally maladaptive.

Medicinal drug use consists of taking drugs to relieve anxiety or tension or to enjoy a drug experience for its own sake. Because of the purposes it serves, medicinal drug use is primarily an individual experience. Two or more medicinal users may take drugs in each others' company, but they are likely in doing so to be concerned more with their own mental state than with facilitating any personal interaction. (Weiner, 1992, p. 391)

There are two types of adolescent operational users of chemicals. The first type is the teenager whose use is pleasure pursuant or "hedonistic use" (Nowinski, 1990). These adolescents seek the euphoric effect of chemicals as an end in itself. These pleasure-pursuant users can appear a lot like social users, but the truth is that their hedonistic use is motivated by an incessant need to chemically intensify pleasurable feeling states. The second type of operational users are the pain-avoidant types or the "compensatory users" (Nowinski, 1990). These young persons use drugs to treat dysphoria or other painful feeling states. Adolescents who are operational users of chemicals can have characteristics of both pleasure-pursuant and pain-avoidant types of use.

An example of a Stage 3 operational user is a 15-year-old female who began using chemicals about 1 1/2 years ago, about the time of her mother's remarriage. She manifested symptoms of depression following her parents' divorce 4 years ago, and these symptoms became more pronounced over time. She currently smokes marijuana approximately 3 to 5 times weekly and drinks alcohol about 2 times per week. This girl experiences a temporary sense of relief when she is "high," yet her lingering dysphoric mood returns once the effects of the chemicals have worn off.

This third stage of adolescent chemical use represents a point along the ACUE continuum at which an adolescent may meet the criteria for a DSM-III-R psychoactive substance use disorder (American Psychiatric Association, 1987).

> The DSM-III-R criteria for psychoactive substance use disorders do not change with age. The continuum of adolescent substance use ranges from nonusers, through experimental and casual users, to compulsive users. The line between use and abuse is crossed more easily by young persons than by adults. (Dulcan & Popper, 1991, p. 96)

In this third stage of adolescent chemical use it is more likely that the teenager will meet the DSM-III-R criteria for psychoactive substance abuse, rather than the more problematic psychoactive substance dependence.

Stage 4: Dependent Use (Using to Feel Normal)

The forth stage of adolescent chemical use is the stage in which addiction is maintaining a firm hold on the young person's life. The adolescent is compulsively consumed with urges to experience the mood swing from drugs. This chemically altered internal state is experienced as "normal" by adolescents in this fourth stage. Coping style, affect regulation, sense of self, identity, and drugs are inextricably intertwined for the chemically dependent adolescent.

An illustration of a Stage 4 dependent user is the example of a 16-year-old male who uses drugs as often as he can obtain them. Along with a 5-year pattern of alcohol use and a 3-year pattern of marijuana use, he reports to having "tried just about every drug possible except for heroin." Over the past 6 months he has been taking LSD at least once a week. His voracious appetite for chemicals is tied to his reported desire to "feel together with himself."

It is often difficult for therapists to distinguish between the dependent stage and the operational stage. "There is no definitive means of discriminating severe chemical abuse from dependency in adolescents" (Wheeler & Malmquist, 1987, p. 439).

An adolescent in this fourth stage of chemical use inevitably meets the criteria of a DSM-III-R psychoactive substance use disorder. Minimally the adolescent can be diagnosed as presenting with psychoactive substance abuse, but many in this stage will likely meet the criteria for psychoactive substance dependence.

Movement Along the ACUE Continuum

Based on various biological, psychological and social factors, and factors indigenous to certain drugs, any given adolescent can experience different movement through the stages of the ACUE Continuum. Considering the effects of these different factors, a teenager might progress from one stage to a more advanced stage, possibly regress from one stage to a less advanced stage, or might maintain himself at a given stage of chemical use for a period of time.

Most adolescents who use chemicals maintain their use at Stage 1 and Stage 2. "The vast majority of adolescents who have tried drugs appear to be experimental or social users, inasmuch as only a small minority of them show the pattern of current, regular drug-taking that characterizes medicinal or addictive use" (Weiner, 1992, p.392).

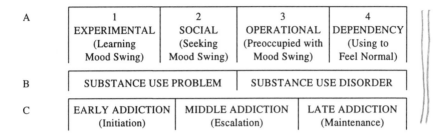

	1	2	3	4
A	EXPERIMENTAL (Learning Mood Swing)	SOCIAL (Seeking Mood Swing)	OPERATIONAL (Preoccupied with Mood Swing)	DEPENDENCY (Using to Feel Normal)

B	SUBSTANCE USE PROBLEM	SUBSTANCE USE DISORDER

C	EARLY ADDICTION (Initiation)	MIDDLE ADDICTION (Escalation)	LATE ADDICTION (Maintenance)

Figure 1.1. Three Ways of Defining Substance Abuse

A. Adolescent Chemical Use Experience Continuum (ACUE); B. types of problems; C. stages of adolescent addiction.

Of the adolescents who try or use chemicals in Stages 1 or 2, only a fraction progress to the extreme stage of dependency. As Wheeler & Malmquist (1987) note, "A relatively low portion of chemical-using adolescents are seen as meeting the criteria for dependence (6-10 percent is the estimate)" (p. 439). Nevertheless, this is still an unacceptable percentage of young people who are experiencing chemically induced atrophy rather than growth during the teen years.

Those adolescents who progress to substance abuse and then regress to a less problematic stage, or cease using altogether, have usually been impacted by some external intervention. For an adolescent substance abuser to experience a spontaneous remission or practice self-prescribed abstinence for any length of time is a rarity.

DEFINING PROBLEMS WITH ADOLESCENT SUBSTANCE USE AND ABUSE

Overview

Trying to identify what exactly is problematic about an adolescent's chemical use can be highly subjective. Some parents and professionals may identify the actual event of using a drug to be the problem, while others may consider the effects of the drug use (for example, becoming aggressive and getting into fights) as the problem. Still others may consider the underlying spread of an addiction to be the problem.

Striving toward consensually developed definitions of adolescent substance use and abuse involves discussion within and among the disciplines of medicine, psychiatry, psychology, social work, and the professionals who treat addiction in the adolescent population. Working toward clear clinical definitions can be all the more difficult when legal and moral definitions of adolescent drug problems are added to the discussion. Although legal and moral perspectives have their own definitional classifications with teenage drug problems, such perspectives tend to muddy the definitional waters for clinicians.

Distinguishing between adolescent substance use problems and substance abuse disorders is an essential task in defining adolescent drug problems. This differentiating between "use problem" and "use disorder" can be difficult, but it serves a necessary purpose. As Chassin (1984) remarks, "There is a need to distinguish patterns and determinants of substance use that is relatively benign from those types of use that are problematic" (0. 132).

It can be helpful to have some functional guidelines for distinguishing teenage substance use from abuse. The Adolescent Chemical Use Problem (ACUP) Index (Table 1.1) is presented in this book as a tool to assist in differentiating an adolescent substance use problem from a substance abuse disorder. The ACUP Index identifies various difficulties a young person might experience from his or her chemical use. The acute or cumulative nature of these difficulties can help in clarifying an adolescent's experience as being a substance use problem or a substance use disorder.

The Adolescent Chemical Use Problem Index

The Adolescent Chemical Use Problem (ACUP) Index includes six domains of problems—chemical use effects, physical health, psychological health, behavioral functioning, social functioning, and interpersonal functioning—and two categories of problems for each domain, acute problems and cumulative use problems. This index represents possible acute use and cumulative biopsychosocial effects for adolescents.

In general, three assumptions can be made about the types of problems experienced throughout the different stages of the adolescent chemical use continuum. One assumption is that acute chemical use problems can occur throughout all four of the continuum stages. An adolescent can have an episode of intoxication in any stage, and thus possibly experience any of the acute adverse effects from any of the six domains of the ACUP Index. A second assumption is that cumulative chemical use problems occur, for the most part, in the latter two stages of the continuum. If a teenager is experiencing cumulative use problems from any of the six problem domains, it is most likely the result of an operational or dependency pattern of use rather than experimental or social use. A third assumption is that as a young person progresses further along the ACUE continuum, there will be an increase in both the range of and intensity of acute and cumulative use problems. More and complicated problems are experienced by the teenager who becomes entangled in operational or dependent use, than by one whose use is at an experimental or social level.

Adolescent Substance Use Problems

In terms of the ACUP Index, adolescent substance use problems involve, for the most part, acute chemical use problems rather than cumulative use problems. These acute chemical use problems can be thought of as "problems related to use" rather than as problems of "substance abuse" (Muldoon & Crowley, 1986).

In spite of possible occasional episodes of intoxication, most teenagers who consume chemicals are relatively adaptive in this use. As mentioned earlier in this chapter, most adolescent experimental and social users do not progress into substance abuse. The problems experienced by teenagers in Stages 1 or 2 should be recognized as substance use problems (Figure 1.1), and not evidence of a substance use disorder.

However, despite many instances of teenage overindulgence and chemical misuse being indicative of "youthful indiscretion," there may be other problems possibly churning beneath the surface of such chemical misuse. Occasional and transient episodes of intoxication can possibly be: (a) symptomatic of possible psychological disorder, family dysfunction, or other stressful condition in the young person's life; (b) reflective of symptomatic or "early stage" of a substance use disorder; or (c) both symptomatic of another difficulty and reflective of early addiction. Careful monitoring of the young person's chemical use pattern, as well as a thorough assessment of his or her overall functioning, is necessary for identifying whether episodes of intoxication are indicative of youthful misuse or a sign of some trouble in his or her life.

Adolescents with substance use problems do not meet the DSM-III-R's criteria for a psychoactive substance use disorder. However, the substance use problem might reflect some other condition classified in the DSM-III-R as a disorder of childhood or adolescence.

Adolescent Substance Use Disorder

In terms of the ACUP Index, adolescent substance use disorders involve both acute use and cumulative use problems. In cases of substance use disorders, teenagers are not simply acting out with chemicals or exhibiting symptoms of some troublesome condition in their lives. In these cases adolescents are demonstrating the problems that go hand-in-hand with having a primary substance use disorder.

Substance use disorders are maladaptive patterns of chemical use that are impairing the young person's functioning and compromising his development. Stages 3 and 4 of the ACUE continuum, the operational and dependent stages respectively, are the stages in which substance use disorders become more fully manifest (Figure 1.1).

Teenagers with substance use disorders meet the DSM-III-R criteria for a psychoactive substance use disorder. Some of these adolescents will only meet the criteria for psychoactive substance abuse, while others with more progressed features in their use will meet the criteria for psychoactive substance dependence. The young person who meets the criteria for psychoactive substance dependence can be further differentiated in this DSM-III-R category according to whether the substance dependence is mild, moderate, or severe.

The primary qualitative difference between adolescents with substance use problems and those with substance use disorders is that adolescents with substance use disorders continue to abuse chemicals in spite of the adverse consequences of their abuse. Problems become cumulative because the adolescent experiences these adverse consequences as more tolerable than discontinuing his chemical use.

To illustrate the differences between an adolescent with a substance use problem and one with a substance use disorder, a comparison between two adolescents can be made. One adolescent, a 16-year-old male, began drinking alcohol approximately a year ago. He and his friends were modeling a pattern of drinking for one another. Until 3 months ago, this teenager experienced no adverse consequences from his occasional episodes of drinking during the weekend. This adolescent first became intoxicated at a school dance 3 months ago. He experienced the acute use problems of being physically sick from overdosing on alcohol, violating school rules about drinking, and violating family rules about drinking. After being disciplined by both the school and his parents for this drinking episode, he made and has kept an agreement to be chemically free. Although raising some cause for concern, this teenager demonstrated a substance use problem, not a substance use disorder.

Another adolescent, a 15-year-old male whose chemical use commenced 3 years ago, is manifesting a substance use disorder. He began drinking when he was 12, progressed to marijuana when he was 14, and recently has become involved in cocaine use. Despite a compounded history of acute use and cumulative problems (including escalation of arguments with his parents, a steady deterioration of academic performance at school, confining his friendships to chemical-using peers, total withdrawal from extracurricular activities at school, an arrest for possession of alcohol by a minor, and numerous hangovers and adverse physical side effects), this teenager continues to use substances. He is clearly manifesting evidence of a substance use disorder.

Distinguishing between adolescent substance use problems and substance use disorders is more than an exercise in semantics. The benefit of delineating different types of teenage chemical use problems is that it can help in making the most effective treatment interventions. The biopsychosocial model presented in Parts II and III of this book pertains primarily to understanding and treating adolescent substance use disorders.

UNDERSTANDING ADOLESCENT SUBSTANCE USE AND ABUSE

Overview

Along with defining the stages of adolescent chemical use and distinguishing between substance use and abuse, there exist differences among treatment professionals as to how to best explain the range of adolescent chemical use experiences. Among the differences are which factors should be emphasized in trying to understand adolescent drug use at different stages and which perspectives or theoretical models best explain these factors and combination of determinants at different stages.

There are splits among different disciplines about how to understand addictive disorders and which factors should be underscored for understanding.

Pharmacologists, for example, understand the addictions as a set of pharmacological problems involving such pharmacological categories as

Table 1.1
Adolescent Chemical Use Problem Index
(Possible Problems Related to Chemical Use)

Domain # 1—Chemical Use Effects

Acute Problems	*Cumulative Problems*
Learns chemical effects	Becoming preoccupied with chemical
Developing a pattern of using chemicals	effects
Beginning to develop initial tolerance	Developing a maladaptive pattern of
	using chemicals
	Increasing tolerance to chemical effects
	Intensifying frequency of use
	Expanding range of chemicals for use
	Growth of addiction dynamics

Domain # 2—Physical Health

Acute Problems	*Cumulative Problems*
Withdrawal or abstinence syndrome	Repeated withdrawal episodes
Overdose	Complicates preexisting biomedical
Toxic reactions to dilutents used with	condition
chemical preparations	Higher risk for range of biomedical
Exacerbating preexisting biomedical	conditions
condition	Effects from route of chemical
Medical complications unique to a	administration (complications specific
specific chemical's pharmacological	to smoking, intranasal use, or
action	intravenous use)
	Impedes adolescent's physiological
	development with some systems
	Increase in sickness (headaches, virus, etc.)
	Weight loss or gain
	Decline in physical appearance
	Malnutrition
	Sleep Deprivation

Domain # 3—Psychological Health

Acute Problems	*Cumulative Problems*
Chemically-induced psychosis	Complicates preexisting psychological
Chemically-induced panic attacks	vulnerability
Chemically-induced flashbacks	Psychological regression and
Chemically-induced suicidal ideation	disorganization with intrapsychic
Exacerbates pre-existing psychological	functioning
vulnerability	Impeded with development of adaptive
Impaired judgement	coping resources during adolescence
	Cognitive and learning impairments
	Anti-social pattern becoming part
	personality

continued

Table 1.1
Continued

Domain # 4—Behavioral Functioning

Acute Problems	*Cumulative Problems*
Impulsive reactions	Increase in high risk behavior (such as
Aggressive/violent behavior	aggressive behavior, suicidal behavior,
Suicide attempts	accident proneness, sexual
Increased risk of accidents	promiscuity, etc.)
Driving under the influence	Developing an antisocial lifestyle
Unprotected sexual intercourse and accompanying risks	
Decreased compliance with social controls and laws	

Domain # 5—Social Functioning

Acute Problems	*Cumulative Problems*
Violates school rules about chemical use	Deterioration in school attendance, performance, and behavior
Violates work rules about chemical use	Deterioration in work attendance, performance, and behavior
Violates community standards about use	Leisure activity centered around chemical use
Arrest for intoxication	Illegal activity to support chemical use
Arrest for unlawful possession of chemicals	Decline in involvement in religious/church activities
Arrest for chemically-induced behavior	

Domain # 6—Interpersonal Environment

Acute Problems	*Cumulative Problems*
Conflict with family/family members about chemical use episode	Increased family disorganization associated with adolescent's chemical use
Conflict with peer(s) about chemical use episode	Adolescent's chemical use becoming the center of family's functioning
	Running away from home
	Associating primarily with chemical using peers
	Becoming enabling of peers chemical use
	Rejected by "mainstream" peers

drugs, tolerance or binding sites. Psychologists and psychiatrists are typically willing to read into the phenomenon of addiction the problems of learning, compulsion or ego function. Physiologists posit problems of withdrawal, metabolism or target organ effects. Sociologists see processes of social regulation, peer pressure and/or environmental forces. Politicians, lawyers and law enforcement agents view addiction problems as involving controlled substances, criminals and/or deterrence. At present, no single theory dominates thinking in the field of addictive behavior or directs clinical interventions comprehensively. (Shaffer, 1985, p. 66)

There are even splits within disciplines that treat addicted populations as to which theories or perspectives can best explain crucial etiological factors. For example, psychiatrists and psychologists—focusing on psychological variables contributing to a drug problem—may range from holding a classic psychodynamic perspective (emphasizing unresolved unconscious processes) in viewing the problem to a position that incorporates such contemporary perspectives as behaviorism, interpersonal theory, trauma theory, role theory, family and general systems theory, and the group-therapy movement, among other perspectives (Rivinus, 1991b).

To understand the spectrum of adolescent chemical use, it is essential to move beyond the myopia that can occur when clinging to a specific perspective toward a lens that can offer a comprehensive view. Such a lens would have a wide angle to include the range of factors that can contribute to adolescent substance use and abuse, be kaleidoscopic to account for the interactive nature of these factors, and have the capacity to be finely tuned for focusing on those primary factors most critical for viewing adolescent chemical use.

Toward a Model of Multiple and Interactive Factors

Understanding the spectrum of teenage drug use necessitates identifying a range of possible contributing factors as well as considering the complexity of the interaction of these factors. Lettieri (1985) has provided a comprehensive summary of 43 theoretical perspectives relevant to adolescent substance abuse. In garnering this collection of theoretical positions, Lettieri highlights the multiplicity of factors essential for understanding teenage drug abuse: "We must be cognizant of the need to incorporate variables from diverse scientific disciplines in order to fully understand the drug dependence process. No one discipline or viewpoint, alone, has successfully accounted for the multifaceted phenomenon of drug dependence" (p.12).

At the same time, Lettieri expounds upon the significance of the interaction of different factors for understanding the spectrum of adolescent chemical use:

If one wishes to account for why persons continue in their use of drugs, then biomedical disciplines are probably best; in contrast, however, if one wishes to explain the initiation of drug using behavior, then social psychological explanations seem most pertinent. Sociological elements in combination with biomedical factors may be ideally suited to understanding the escalation of drug use to drug abuse, while psychological and even political and economic elements are essential to an understanding of the cessation of use. (p.12)

Within this framework of multiple and interacting factors contributing to the different stages of adolescent chemical use there can be a further refinement for understanding adolescent substance abuse. Weiner (1992), in referring to the work of Brook and colleagues (Brook, Nomura, & Cohen, 1989; Brook, Whiteman, & Gordon, 1983), posits that personality, family, and peer determinants are the essential factors for understanding adolescent substance abuse. According to Weiner (1992), focusing on this triad of primary factors has three important implications:

- There is a greater likelihood of an adolescent using substances, or developing a substance abuse disorder, if all three factors—personality, family, and peers are operating as a negative influence to a significant degree.
- One factor exerting a particularly strong influence can be sufficient enough for a young person to become drug-involved, even though the other two factors are minimal.
- Strong positive influences from one or more of these factors can shield an otherwise high-risk adolescent from developing a serious drug problem.

This triad of primary factors—adolescent psychological development, family functioning, and peer relationships—serves as the centerpiece of the biopsychosocial model of adolescent substance abuse presented in this book.

A Biopsychosocial Model as a Multi-Factorial Interactive Model

A biopsychosocial model is a cogent perspective from which to think of drug problems. This integrated perspective is inclusive of multiple etiological factors, while not exclusively endorsing any single factor. Also, the interplay of these varied factors attests to the axiom that the whole is greater than the sum of the parts.

The specifics of the model are discussed in Chapter 3, but the fundamental strength of the model is that it encompasses the multifactorial and interactive perspective that is important for understanding teenage drug abuse. Five levels of possible causative variables—biological, adolescent psychological development, interpersonal environment (family and peer factors), community, and societal—and the synergy of these variables is identified. In addition, the triad of primary variables—adolescent psychological development, family functioning, and peer relationships—within this model are highlighted.

This biopsychosocial model is "adolescent sensitive." As teenagers can develop substance abuse disorders 7 times faster than adults (Myers & Anderson, 1991), those factors unique to adolescent substance abuse need to be isolated. In addition, treatment interventions need to be targeted at those systems—the teenager, as well as his family and friends—that correspond with those unique factors.

UNDERSTANDING ADDICTION
WITH ADOLESCENTS

Like many of the terms in the chemical dependency field, the term *addiction* has come to mean different things to different people. What is key in having a working definition of addiction is to identify the essential addiction dynamics. Understanding addiction for adolescents also involves an awareness of the stages of adolescent drug addiction. Also, no discussion about addiction can be complete without some examination of the disease concept of addiction.

A Working Definition of Addiction

For a number of years the accepted definition of addiction included the criterion of the addict being physically dependent on a drug (O'Brien & Cohen, 1984). However, by 1965 the definition of addiction/drug dependence, as articulated by the World Health Organization (WHO), did not emphasize being physically dependent on a drug as a necessary condition for addiction.

A state, psychic and sometimes also physical, resulting from the interaction between a living organism and a drug, characterized by behavioral and other responses that always include a compulsion to take the drug on a continuous or periodic basis in order to experience its psychic effects, and sometimes to avoid the discomfort of its absence. Tolerance may or may not be present. A person may be dependent on more than one drug. (O'Brien & Cohen, 1984, p. 6)

What this definition of addiction by the WHO does emphasize is the dynamic of compulsion to use a drug. This criteria of compulsion is the foundation for defining addiction. More recent suggestions for defining addiction emphasize other addiction dynamics, along with compulsion. The tendency to relapse following discontinued drug use is one additional dynamic that is stressed (Blum, 1984; Donovan, 1988), and the "phenomenon of denial" is another dynamic that is emphasized (Miller & Gold, 1989).

An operative definition of addiction, which applies to adolescent substance abusers and shall be used in this book, incorporates the addiction dynamics of relapse and denial with the essential dynamic of compulsion to use a drug. Each of these three addiction dynamics— compulsion, relapse proneness, and denial—can be manifest in biological, psychological, and social ways. In this sense the addiction process can be construed as a biopsychosocial process involving these three dynamics. The biopsychosocial addiction process and the biopsychosocial expression of these addiction dynamics are detailed in Chapter 3.

Stages of Adolescent Addiction

Addiction is most overtly manifest in the fourth stage of the ACUE continuum. But adolescent addiction also has its own sequence of stages—an initiation stage, an escalation stage, and a maintenance stage (Coombs & Coombs, 1988). Although these stages of addiction can overlap the stages of adolescent chemical use experience (Figure 1.1), this is not to assume that these two series of stages are necessarily linked together. The earlier stages of adolescent addiction can only be diagnosed in hindsight, after the teenager has progressed to the later stages of addiction. In other words, most young persons in the experimental use or social use stages are not in the early stages of addiction and will not progress into operational use or dependency use stages, in which addiction becomes entrenched. However, for those unfortunate teenagers who—for whatever combination of biological, psychological, or social factors, or factors intrinsic with specific drugs—progress to the latter stages of the ACUE continuum, their experimental or social stages of use can be diagnosed "after-the-fact" as having been early addiction.

These three stages of adolescent addiction can be likened to a progressive slide down a chute into the abyss of chemical dependency. As the young person slides further down this chute, she gathers increasing momentum before "hitting the bottom." Substance abuse treatment represents the hope for interrupting this developmentally crippling tumble down the chute of addiction.

The Addictive Disease Concept

History of Disease Concept

Alcoholism is the prototype of the addictive disease. Although some support for the disease concept of alcoholism dates as far back as 19th-century Europe (Jellinek, 1960), the modern era of the disease concept of alcoholism as advanced by the medical community in the United States, can be attributed to the mid-20th century (Anderson & Henderson, 1984). In identifying alcoholism as a disease, this disorder meets the disease characteristics of being a primary, progressive, chronic, and fatal condition (Johnson, 1973).

As knowledge grew about addiction to chemicals other than alcohol, the disease model of alcoholism was applied to these other chemical addictions. The current disease concept of chemical dependency is the result of the extrapolation of the disease model to other drug addictions.

Challenges to the Disease Concept

There has been criticism of the addictive disease concept for as long as a disease concept has been applied to the addictions. These criticisms seem to fall into four general categories: (a) debates about the nature and definition of disease, and whether addictions correspond with these definitions; (b) indictments about the absence of conclusive biological evidence for addictions; (c) criticism of Alcoholics Anonymous and other 12-step recovery programs, which are central to the disease model of treatment; and (d) dismissing the disease concept as more metaphor than science.

The following arguments support the disease concept of addiction in response to the aforementioned challenges to this model.

Addictions Correspond With the Nature of Disease. Among the arguments put forth by addictive disease critics is that "real diseases" are inextricably connected to physical functioning and disorder and that addictions do not meet this criterion (Peele, 1989). However, there is no agreement on what exactly constitutes a disease (Campbell, Scadding & Roberts, 1979).

There has come to be growing acceptance of behavioral disorders and addictions as diseases by the medical community, specifically, and by society in general. As Dupont & McGovern (1991) observe, "The change from the threat of infectious diseases to the threat of behavior disorders is the central reality of the evolution of diseases from the first decades to the last decades of the twentieth century" (p. 326).

Evolution From Classic to Contemporary Disease Concept. In keeping with the real-disease-is-biological-disease line of thinking, disease critics also contend that without conclusive genetic markers for an addiction the disease model does not apply. In short, without genetic proof there is no disease.

Genetics and other biological research are just beginning to be explored and are truly on the frontier of addiction research. Although a conclusive genetic link for alcoholism, the prototype of addiction, has yet to be found, promising discoveries have occurred (Chapter 3).

However, a concern about the absence of a genetic marker is that it confines addictive disease to reductionistic thinking. Such reductionism was applied with the original disease concept of alcoholism (Robak, 1991). But this classic disease concept has since evolved to a contemporary disease model that is inclusive of genetic and other biological factors, yet not confined to these factors. "At present the concept views the condition as a highly complex illness of multi-factorial etiology, characterized by progressive physical and psychosocial impairment and/or dependence" (Anderson & Henderson, 1984, p. 80).

Twelve Step Recovery Useful in Addiction Treatment. Another challenge to the disease concept of addiction arises from its often corresponding model of treatment, 12-step recovery. These self-help fellowships are under fire for a variety of reasons. A detailed listing of the criticisms and responses to the criticisms of 12-step recovery is contained in the next chapter.

In spite of the arguments against 12-step recovery, "the program," when used in conjunction with appropriate mental health treatment approaches, can be a powerful therapeutic force in the treatment of addictions.

Where Metaphor Meets Science. As Shaffer (1985) states, "The disease concept is, on certain occasions, a useful metaphor for the natural history of drug-related human problems. It is not, however, an accurate scientific representation of the evidence that surrounds drug dependencies" (p. 73). Thus the disease concept of addiction is also criticized as being more symbolic than truly substantive.

Yet the benefits of the "addictive disease metaphor" need not be dismissed as unscientific. For research purposes the disease metaphor can serve as a heuristic device for communicating about addiction, "Calling a behavior a disease is only a way of talking about it, which may or may not be useful; it is not a truth that can be proved or disproved" (Neuhaus, 1991, p. 88). For treatment purposes the disease metaphor can be a potent therapeutic analog, providing the map for therapy,"The important question to answer here is whether saying that addiction is a disease allows treatment personnel to make useful interventions, and with which patients" (Neuhaus, 1991, p. 88).

The Biopsychosocial Perspective and the Contemporary Addictive Disease Model

The disease model of alcoholism has evolved from its original disease concept to the contemporary disease model. This contemporary disease model of alcoholism can be understood from a biopsychosocial perspective (Wallace, 1989).

As alcoholism has historically been the prototype addictive disease model, alcoholism viewed from a biopsychosocial perspective can represent the prototype of the contemporary addictive disease model. This biopsychosocial alcoholism model paves the way for understanding chemical dependency in general, with both adults and adolescents, as a biopsychosocial disease.

By viewing addictive diseases from a biopsychosocial perspective it can be asserted that they fit the criteria for a biopsychosocial model. Addictive diseases are both multifactorial and factorial interactive in their etiology, and treatments are multisystematic and interactive.

SUMMARY

Professionals who treat adolescents with drug problems should be open to examining their conceptualizations of these problems. There is integrity to broadening one's conceptual framework by integrating new and relevant knowledge.

This chapter discussed some current dilemmas among treatment professionals regarding definitions of and understandings of adolescent substance use and abuse. A synthesis of different perspectives was offered in an attempt to address these dilemmas: delineating the stages of adolescent chemical use, distinguishing between adolescent substance use problems and substance abuse disorders, possible ways of explaining adolescent chemical use throughout the different stages, and how to comprehend addiction and addictive disease.

Helping to treat teenagers with drug problems begins with having cogent clinical definitions of and understandings of these problems. Working toward such useful definitions and understandings requires informed and conscientious efforts by those entrusted with aiding these young people and their families.

Chapter 2

TREATING ADOLESCENT SUBSTANCE USE AND ABUSE

INTRODUCTION

Adolescent drug problems can run the gamut from relatively minor difficulties intertwined with growing up to devastating addiction that ravages the adolescent's functioning, family life, and future. The treatment response throughout this spectrum of problems is fraught with disagreements among professionals who work with adolescents.

Among the differences currently debated are: (a) whether or not treatment of adolescent chemical users is truly helpful; (b) if treatment is helpful, then should it be qualitatively different throughout the four stages of adolescent chemical use; and (c) can the major treatment approaches (the mental health approach and the 12-step recovery approach) work together for the benefit of those adolescents who experience the most serious drug problems—substance abuse disorders—and their families and, if so, how?

This chapter seeks to address these differences as they exist among professionals who treat adolescent substance abusers. In addition, there are suggestions for some resolution of these differences, so that they do not impede the work of being helpful to teenagers with drug problems.

THE VALUE OF TREATMENT

A pressing issue among professionals treating chemically involved adolescents is the dispute, both inside and outside the chemical dependency field, over the benefit of treatment. The central premise is that a good number of teenagers with drug-related problems who do not receive treatment will "outgrow" their problems (Peele, 1989). This faith in the spontaneous remission and natural recovery of myriad drug-involved teenagers is a specious clinical position for several reasons.

First, some adolescents simply will not outgrow their drug problems. This is particularly true with teenagers who have progressed to the third or fourth stages of adolescent chemical use (see Chapter 1) and with those who also present various high-risk factors for continued use. Rather than maturing out of their substance problem in adulthood, many adolescents instead will carry their drug problem into their adult years, experiencing a deeper deterioration of functioning.

> The treatment of compulsive drug use is nearly always related to the issues of adolescence and early adulthood, even if chronologically the patient may be far beyond that period. In most instances substance abuse had its inception in the middle or the late teens; there it is where the emotional development got stuck because of the drugs' stifling effect upon further emotional growth. (Wurmser, 1987, p. 157)

Second, although some teenagers will be fortunate enough to outgrow their difficulties with chemicals, there is often a personal price to be paid for "learning the hard way." Although some young people—most probably those in the experimental and social stages—will find a path away from problem drug use in their adult years, the risks are substantial.

> Cessation of drug use may be a consequence of the extent to which individuals relinquish participation in deviant, nonconforming activities and assume the roles of adulthood. With maturation and the assumption of adult responsibilities and roles there is disengagement from adolescent activities and behaviors. (Kandel & Raveis, 1989, p. 115)

But prior to finding this path in adulthood, many young persons may experience adverse and long-lasting effects upon their development, social functioning, and family life that are related to their teenage drug odyssey (Sarri, 1991).

Third, some adolescents will not have the opportunity to outgrow their drug-related problems as they will die from some experience related to their chemical use. Overdoses, diseases and physical disorders resulting from taking drugs, and accidents are among the more common tragedies that claim the lives of countless chemical-using teenagers every year.

Treatment is necessary and beneficial. What is important in addressing the hyperbole of spontaneous remission and natural recovery with adolescents is to not reduce treatment to an "all-or-nothing" experience. There are and should be varieties and gradations of treatment for teenagers all along the spectrum of adolescent chemical use. Treatment for a social stage young person dealing with a substance use problem should be both qualitatively and quantitatively different from treatment for a dependent stage adolescent with a substance abuse disorder. For example, putting a social stage user in a residential program would be highly "overtreating" this adolescent, and treating a dependent stage user on a once-a-week basis in a therapist's office would be severe undertreatment. It is essential for therapists to articulate what systems—the adolescent, his family, and/or his peers—should be intervened with, as well as what approaches should be used in treating these respective systems throughout the stages of adolescent chemical use. In addition, it is crucial for therapists to identify those systems, and treatment approaches with those systems, that should be focused on with the more problematic teenage drug problems—substance abuse disorders. The biopsychosocial model presented in Parts II and III of this book pertains primarily to understanding and treating adolescent substance abuse disorders.

TREATING ADOLESCENT
SUBSTANCE USE AND ABUSE

Systems for Intervention

Much as multiple factors should be considered as possible determinants of drug problems along the adolescent chemical use experience (ACUE) continuum, multiple systems should be evaluated for possible treatment interventions with these problems. The adolescent's physical functioning (biological system), psychological development, family and peer relationships (interpersonal system), and community, as well as the larger society, are all systems meriting different levels of attention with adolescent substance abuse treatment. However, just as a triad of primary causative factors can be identified for understanding adolescent chemical use, so then a triad of primary systems can be delineated for treating this chemical use.

The adolescent's psychological development, his family functioning, and his peer relationships are the three systems that necessitate the focused therapeutic interventions throughout the four stages of adolescent chemical use. Which particular systems, or combination of systems, should be the target of therapy for any given case is a matter of clinical judgement.

In addition, biomedical interventions for both acute and ongoing physical conditions can indeed be critical for the drug-involved teenager. As the goal of interventions with the triad of primary systems is to facilitate interruption of the drug use cycle, biomedical interventions are intended to treat the physical effects from this cycle.

Community and societal interventions, essential for permitting treatment delivery systems to be accessible to adolescents and their families, are outside the purview of a clinical intervention for a specific case. Influencing treatment availability at community and societal levels involves community organization, lobbying, and policy making among other macro-systemic interventions.

Treatment Approaches

The triad of primary systems—adolescent, family, and peers—is the major focus of treatment interventions along the ACUE continuum. In addition, consideration needs to be given to biomedical interventions along the four stages of the continuum. Given this, consideration to what approaches are most therapeutic with the three primary systems becomes paramount.

There are two major approaches for treating substance abusers—the mental health approach and the 12-step recovery approach. Both approaches have rich traditions of helping both adult and adolescent drug abusers, and both approaches have different treatment indications for the four stages of adolescent chemical use.

Brief History of Mental Health
and 12-Step Recovery Approaches

Mental Health Approaches With Adolescent Substance Abusers. Mental health therapeutic approaches with drug-involved teenagers began receiving attention in the professional literature in the late 1960s, during the initial proliferation of adolescent substance use. Approaches at that time focused on individual psychotherapeutic approaches and resolution of unconscious psychodynamic processes related to drug use (Hartman, 1969; Wieder & Kaplan, 1969).

In the 1970s both group therapy approaches with substance abusing adolescents (Bratter, 1971; Raubolt & Bratter, 1974) and family therapy approaches with families of drug-involved teenagers (Kaufman, 1980; Stanton, Todd, Heard, Kirschner, Kleiman, Mowatt, Riley, Scott, & van Deusen, 1978) began receiving increased acceptance by therapists working with this population. These group therapy and family therapy approaches concentrated on the interpersonal environment of the teenage drug abusers.

This expansion of treatment approaches and systems targeted for treatment laid the foundation for the multiple levels of treatment offered by chemical dependency programs in the 1980s. While having a broader repertoire of therapeutic approaches available to them, mental health practitioners examined if and how to incorporate the therapeutic elements of 12-step recovery with these mental health treatment strategies.

Twelve-Step Recovery Approaches with Adolescent Substance Abusers. Alcoholics Anonymous (AA) is the parent of 12-step recovery programs. Founded in 1935 in Ohio, AA has been a source of hope and healing for millions of alcoholics for over half a century. In 1948, the sister organization to AA, Al-Anon, was founded to respond to the needs of family members of alcoholics (Doweiko, 1990). By 1957, Al-Anon recognized the special needs of teenagers with alcoholic parents and caretakers, and created Al-Ateen to respond to their needs (Doweiko, 1990).

The AA program contains four basic therapeutic elements: (a) group membership, (b) a 12-step map of recovery (see Appendix), (c) applying particular "cognitive-behavioral" tools of the program, and (d) having a sponsor serve as a mentor in recovery. Both Al-Anon and Al-Ateen modified these four therapeutic elements for their respective programs.

In 1953, another 12-step self-help program, created along the lines of AA, was founded as a source of healing for those suffering from chemical addictions not confined to alcohol. Narcotics Anonymous (NA) has been in existence for almost 40 years, but it first published its recovery manifesto—the NA "Big Book"—in 1982 (Narcotics Anonymous, 1982). From 1983 to 1988, NA experienced a 600% increase in groups nationwide (Coleman, 1989). Chemically Dependent Anonymous (CDA), a self-help program with a mission very similar to NA's, also grew in availability in the 1980s (Chemically Dependent Anonymous, 1990).

During the 1970s parents with drug-abusing sons and daughters began to empower themselves as helping resources to their addicted children through self-help programs designed for their needs. Families Anonymous (FA), fashioned after Al-Anon, originated in California in 1971 (LaFountain, 1987). Tough Love was founded in Pennsylvania during this period and has been responsible for advocating its own "Ten Beliefs" of effective parenting with troubled teenagers (York, York, & Wachtel, 1982).

Just as therapists with a mental health orientation have been slowly but steadily working to form alliances with the recovery fellowships in recent years, advocates of these 12-step self-help programs have also been striving to forge effective linkages with the professional treatment community.

Indications for Mental Health Approaches and 12-Step Recovery Approaches

The reality is that neither mental health approaches nor 12-step recovery approaches are the be-all and end-all in helping chemical-using adolescents. Each approach has distinct contributions to make within the matrix of treatment interventions throughout the four stages of adolescent chemical use.

Many seem to think that in Stages 1 and 2, in which substance use problems are the main concern, the therapeutic efforts from a mental health approach are indicated. Individual psychotherapy, family therapy, and group therapy, either separately or in some combination, are regularly the treatments of choice. Twelve-step recovery programs are not usually indicated for teenage experimental and social users. However, some adolescents in these initial stages may benefit from aspects of 12-step programs, such as relating with and being a part of a group of sober peers.

During Stages 3 and 4, in which a substance use disorder is manifest, a mental health approach alone is not sufficient. Treatment that is informed by a mental health approach in conjunction with a 12-step recovery approach is indicated for these adolescents in the grip of addiction. This conjunctive treatment approach—"recovery-oriented" treatment (Zweben, 1989)—is elaborated on in the remaining section of this chapter.

RECOVERY-ORIENTED TREATMENT WITH ADOLESCENTS FOR SUBSTANCE USE DISORDERS

Overview

Recovery-oriented treatment is a comprehensive treatment approach for chemically dependent adolescents. This treatment approach is a hybrid model that seeks to integrate the therapeutic modalities of the mental health approach with the therapeutic elements of 12-step recovery.

The joining together of these two approaches over the years has not been, and still is not, an easily congruent process. Historically, there have been misperceptions of self-help programs by mental health professionals as well as misunderstandings about mental health treatment by members of 12-step fellowships. Nonetheless, these two approaches do share a lot of common ground and can work compatibly in treating young drug abusers. In addition, this hybrid recovery-oriented approach can meet the test of being a biopsychosocial model of treatment.

Integrating Mental Health and 12-Step Recovery Approaches

Mental health professionals and 12-step fellowship members have harbored differences with one another for years. Dupont and McGovern (1991) characterize this rift as follows:

> There are still conflicts between the 12-step programs and health-care professionals. Too frequently, the professionals are seen as patronizing and ill-informed by the members of mutual-aid groups. On the other hand, the mutual-aid program members are seen as poorly educated about the latest in scientific medicine and hostile to the use of this knowledge for the betterment of chemically dependent people. Unfortunately, both points of view are often legitimate. (p. 323)

Much of the misunderstanding between the professional and the self-help communities have stemmed from their respective misconceptions of each other's stance on the nature of addiction and the nature of "kicking" an addiction. The following is a review of the misconceptions of each community, as well as some discussion on how efforts have been made and can continue to be made for bridging these differences.

Misconceptions of 12-Step Recovery

Misconceptions of AA. Being the parent of the 12-step recovery movement, Alcoholics Anonymous has endured criticism by mental health professionals for years. Misconceptions about AA and its philosophy are at the root of this criticism.

Flores (1988, p. 212) has summarized Wallace's (1984) listing of the more common misconceptions of AA. These misconceptions are as follows:

- AA endorses a simplistic and naive disease concept of alcoholism.
- AA dismisses psychological factors as determinants of alcoholism.
- AA is a substitute dependency.
- AA coerces members to admitting to be alcoholics.
- AA categorically rejects controlled use of alcohol.
- AA is a religious organization.

Each of these misconceptions of AA is just that—an inaccurate interpretation of some part of the AA program. Flores (1988) disputes each of these criticisms in examining the professional biases underlying these misunderstandings. These criticisms of AA by mental health practitioners can be extrapolated to other 12-step recovery programs that are patterned after AA. The challenging of 12-step self-help programs is even more strident when these programs are advocated for on behalf of adolescent substance abusers (Peele, 1989).

Misconceptions of 12-Step Recovery With Adolescents. As most self-help fellowships have been conceived by and for adults, there is much questioning by mental health professionals about their applicability to teenagers. Their contention—that many of the principles of 12-step recovery are not relevant to the developmental needs of adolescents—is well intended but much too rigid. The basic principles of 12-step recovery can be made salient for teenagers. The basic tenets of the 12-step programs can be maintained, while their application can be modified to make the programs more "adolescent-friendly."

One example of a question of 12-step recovery for adolescents pertains to a teenager's developmental limitations with being able to be genuinely empathic and caretaking toward other teenagers—an essential ingredient in 12-step recovery. Echoing this concern, King and Meeks (1988) observe:

Adolescents do not usually have the capacity to reciprocate the dependency position—even with peers—as much as do adults. The patients are encouraged to support and help new patients. They are told, "You can only keep it (sobriety and good mental health) by giving it away." They do make a genuine and successful effort to follow these directions. However, treatment or no treatment, they remain adolescents with a legitimate developmental right to be partially dependent on available adults. (pp. 525-526)

Yet "program wisdom" also suggests that you have to crawl before you can walk. In other words, it should be acceptable for adolescents—developmentally lagging due to the impairment of substance abuse—to rely on adults or stable adolescents for an appreciable period of time in recovery in order to internalize the psychological resources of others and cultivate their own caretaking capacities. The supportive environment of 12-step recovery programs can be an excellent setting for the young person to be surrounded by role models of empathy and nurturance.

Another example of mental health practitioners questioning the appropriateness of 12-step recovery for teenagers has to do with working the 12 steps. A central premise for a person working these steps is a self-admission of powerlessness and unmanageability in regard to chemical use. As Wheeler and Malmquist (1987) write:

The admission is doubly foreign to the teenage alcoholic; it requires not only the "surrender" of the denial and delusion that shields all chemically dependent people from clear realization of their addiction, but a relative retreat from the developmental ethic of individuality and independence. (p. 440)

But it is possible to do "modified stepwork" (Evans & Sullivan, 1990). Modified stepwork in this instance means reframing the messages of the steps to make them concrete and receivable for adolescents.

These are just two examples of how arguments about the inappropriateness of 12-step recovery can be refuted by demonstrating how 12-step recovery principles can be adopted for the developmental needs of recovering young people. Therapists' flexibility and resourcefulness can help to make 12-step recovery "adolescent-friendly."

In spite of some mental health professionals' general misunderstandings about 12-step recovery and specific questions about the appropriateness of these self-help programs for adolescents, the fellowships have much to offer adolescent substance abusers and their families.

This new reality in medicine, which we see as a largely unrecognized revolution in our midst, is the emergence of "mutual aid," most often in the form of one of the 12-step programs, as a dominant force in contemporary American culture. (Dupont & McGovern, 1991, p. 314)

This "force" is more compatible with, rather than competitive with, the aims of mental health professionals in treating teenage drug abusers.

Misconceptions of Mental Health Approaches

Advocates of 12-step recovery programs have also had misconceptions about mental health approaches to chemical dependency treatment. For the most part these misconceptions have been based on limited understanding of mental health perspectives or the etiology of addictions, as well as their therapeutic strategies with treating addictions.

Among the more common misconceptions about mental health approaches to chemical dependency treatment are:

- Mental health professionals view chemical dependency as symptomatic of some underlying psychological disorder rather than as a primary disorder in its own right.
- Mental health professionals overlook the larger addiction process with an addict and focus on the psychodynamic or interpersonal process of the addict.
- Mental health professionals believe that "controlled use" of drugs is possible with many addicts, promote controlled use as an acceptable therapeutic goal, and in doing so "enable" the addict's further progression into chemical dependency.
- Mental health professionals dismiss the role of spirituality in an addict's recovery.

These misconceptions are primarily distortions of the mental health position toward addiction. As pertains to adolescent substance abuse, the first three misconceptions—"only a symptom," "addressing underlying psychological issues," and "promoting controlled use"—are criticisms that are particularly invalid when applied to teenagers in beginning stages of chemical use. Adolescent experimental and social users should not be viewed as having a primary substance use disorder, nor should the focus be on an addiction process, where any break from abstinence indicates addiction. However, many mental health professionals have come around to the thinking that adolescents with substance use disorders need to have their substance abuse treated as a primary disorder. Inherent in this thinking is that attention must be paid to the addiction process, and that abstinence is a necessary therapeutic goal.

The role of spirituality in an addict's recovery is a more intricate issue for mental health practitioners to reconcile. Suffice it to say that some therapists' discomfort with integrating spiritual issues into a young person's overall substance abuse treatment is rooted in the more historical exclusion of spirituality from psychological or psychiatric approaches to treatment (Nowinski, 1990).

Bridging the Differences Between Mental Health and 12-Step Recovery Approaches

The competitiveness and suspiciousness that has marked the tension between traditional mental health approaches to treatment and 12-step recovery programs has lessened in recent years. A growing spirit of cooperation and collaboration between these two communities continues to evolve.

In general, mental health practitioners have become more accepting of the value of 12-step recovery programs with adolescent substance abusers.

> Often, family and individual therapists alike believe that substance abuse can be solved through insight therapy for the individual and family therapy for the entire family. Their professional bias leads them to believe that drug problems fade away when other problems are dealt with. That's incorrect. For a potential drug abuse problem, you begin with the drug experts. Psychotherapy, psychiatric help, and family counseling are simply not enough for battling substance abuse. A 12-step program combined with a drug rehab program as well as individual or group counseling is the treatment of choice; perhaps family therapy may be useful, too. But the addiction or abuse must be controlled before the other forms of therapy can even begin to work. (Levine, 1991, p. 159)

At the same time, the 12-step fellowships have grown in recognizing the vital contribution that mental health approaches can make in the recovery of young chemical abusers. They have more and more come to realize the detriment in practicing such a narrow view of helpfulness. "It is important that the therapist avoids suggesting that all the important recovery elements can only be gotten from 12-step programs" (Zweben, 1987, p. 249).

The truth is that both mental health professionals who treat teenage drug abusers and 12-step recovery programs need each other. They may not form a perfectly congruent match for helping adolescent substance abusers. But they can combine to form a hybrid treatment model—recovery-oriented treatment—that can be a workable integration for the benefit of adolescent substance abusers and their families.

Recovery-Oriented Treatment as a Biopsychosocial Approach

Recovery-oriented treatment with adolescent substance abusers can be considered a biopsychosocial approach to treatment. Multiple systems—with emphasis on the primary triad of the adolescent, his family, and his peers, as well as consideration for necessary biomedical interventions—are the focus of treatment interventions. Also, these multiple systems are treated with multiple approaches, the therapeutic strategies from the integration of mental health approaches and 12-step recovery. This biopsychosocial treatment approach is eclectic, with multiple approaches, rather than eso-teric with a single approach. Finally, these multiple systems and multiple approaches interact. "Another assumption of the biopsychosocial model is that treatments will interact with each other as well as with the person and his or her environment" (Donovan, 1988, p. 14).

A biopsychosocial approach to treating adolescents with substance abuse disorders can also be adolescent-relevant. Due to adolescents' developmental fluidity, their treatment needs are different from those of their adult counterparts, and this biopsychosocial model reflects that difference.

There are usually ego strength differences between substance-abusing adults and substance-abusing adolescents. Most adults have found some psychological baseline that has served them, at least partially, as young adults or adults to provide successful experiences. Most adolescents are searching for that psychological baseline whether they are substance abusers or not. (King & Meeks, 1988, p. 525)

SUMMARY

Differences about treatment exist among professionals involved in helping adolescents with drug-related problems. These differences can be fueled from individual sources, such as one's own philosophical biases, or be driven by larger societal forces, including current changes in health care reimbursement. Treatment professionals bridging these differences must keep in mind the overall best interests of the adolescents during this critical period of development. Young substance abusers do need those entrusted with helping them to be advocates for their needs—to assert that there is value in treatment, to consider an appropriate level of treatment according to the adolescent's stage of chemical use, and, for teenagers in the most trouble with drugs (those with substance abuse disorders), to be provided with the most comprehensive treatment possible beyond professional parochialism or missionary myopia.

If the recent and current trends among treatment professionals are any indication, the future holds continued promise for creative ways of responding to the various treatment needs of teenagers with drug problems. Therapists' openness to integrating treatment approaches and developing new methods of being helpful bodes well for the future of substance abuse treatment with adolescents and their families.

Part II

A BIOPSYCHOSOCIAL MODEL
FOR UNDERSTANDING
ADOLESCENT SUBSTANCE ABUSE

Chapter 3

ESSENTIAL CONNECTIONS FOR UNDERSTANDING ADOLESCENT SUBSTANCE ABUSE
A Biopsychosocial Perspective

INTRODUCTION

In the introduction to this book a biopsychosocial perspective toward health problems in general, and specifically to addictions, is summarized. This perspective entails a multi-factorial and interactive understanding of a given disorder.

The biopsychosocial model for understanding adolescent substance abuse presented in this book encompasses five possible levels of causal factors. These levels are: biological factors, adolescent psychological development variables, interpersonal determinants (both family functioning factors and peer relationship factors), community variables, and societal factors (Figure 3.1). These five levels of factors can be viewed as contained within each other, much like a set of Chinese boxes. The levels also interact with each other (Todd, 1985). In addition, the toxic agent in this model—psychoactive substances—penetrates all five levels with the ensuing result—adolescent substance abuse disorder—being manifest at all five levels.

Although this model of adolescent substance abuse presents a broad range of possible contributory factors, the emphasis in this biopsychosocial model is on the triad of primary factors: adolescent psychological development, family functioning, and peer relationships. Within this triad of primary factors, adolescent psychological development serves as the central factor circularly interacting with both family functioning and peer relationship determinants.

Underscoring this triad of factors does not invalidate the influence of biological, community, or societal variables. This emphasis serves to delineate the factors that are the most useful for a clinical understanding of adolescent substance abuse.

THE TOXIC AGENT:
PSYCHOACTIVE SUBSTANCES

Figure 3.1 illustrates how psychoactive substances serve as the toxic agent in this biopsychosocial model of understanding adolescent substance abuse. However, all drugs are not created equal. Different drugs used by adolescents induce different pharmacological effects, some of which may be desired and some of which may not be desired. Along with having a variety of chemicals available to use, teenagers may also display varied sequences by which they select their drugs of choice during their periods of chemical use.

Psychoactive Substances
Used by Adolescents

Substances of Use

Adolescents use the same chemicals as adults. The DSM-III-R identifies 10 classes of psychoactive substances (American Psychiatric Association, 1987). These 10 classes of drugs are: alcohol, amphetamine or similar acting substances, cannabis (marijuana), cocaine, hallucinogens, inhalants (including solvents and aerosols, and the nitrates), nicotine (both smoking and chewing tobacco), opiates (from synthetic opiates to major opiates such as heroin), phencyclidine (PCP) or similar acting substances, and sedatives or hypnotics. In addition, over the past decade look-alikes, drugs of deception, and designer drugs—chemicals that are psychoactively similar to but molecularly different than known substances—have emerged (Seymour, Smith, Inaba, & Landry, 1989, p. 1). Schuckit (1989) is among those who have provided a detailed discussion of the psychoactive effects of chemicals in these 10 classes.

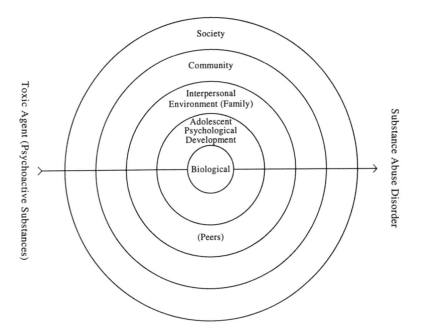

Figure 3.1. Biopsychosocial Model of Adolescent Substance Abuse Etiology

The actual pharmacological action of any given substance is affected by the strength of the dosage, the purity of the chemical (the extent to which the chemical is diluted), and the route of administration (whether swallowed, smoked, inhaled, or injected). Adolescents, due to naivete or a sense of adventure or both, are prone to experimenting with dosages, purity, and routes of administration.

Multiple Substance Use

Adolescent substance users can concoct different drug combinations. This is even more the case with teenagers who are abusers of multiple chemicals, "Multiple drug use is the rule, not the exception, for the overwhelming majority of substance-using adolescents" (Bailey, 1989, p. 152).

Among the reasons that an adolescent might engage in multiple substance use are: (a) using a secondary drug to offset the noxious effects of a primary drug (such as using alcohol to diminish the effect of stimulant use), (b) using two drugs simultaneously to amplify the effects of both drugs (such as combining an episode of cocaine use with an instance of heroin use to alter the effects of both drugs), and (c) using a secondary drug as a substitute for a primary drug not immediately available (such as taking sedatives to relax if alcohol cannot be readily obtained) (Inaba, 1990).

Multiple substance use can cloud the assessment and treatment picture with teenage substance abusers. For example, one multiple-substance-abusing female adolescent was identified by her therapist as having a "problem with alcohol." This therapist developed a treatment plan that included a strict no-drinking contract, as well as parental involvement to monitor this contract. Although no evidence of ongoing drinking was detected, this girl continued to use marijuana unbeknownst to both her therapist and her parents. Her marijuana use had an ongoing adverse effect on her moods, her performance in school, and her relationship with her parents.

Incidence of Use

One of the more reliable sources on the epidemiology of adolescent substance use is the National High School Survey (University of Michigan Institute for Social Research, 1992), which annually tracks trends in adolescent chemical use. According to this survey, alcohol is the chemical most commonly used by teenagers (88% have tried alcohol by their senior year). Marijuana (36.7%) is the next most common for high school seniors, followed by inhalants (17.6%), hallucinogens (9.6%), cocaine (7.8%), sedatives (7.2%), and opiates (overall 6.6%; heroin 0.9%). The reality is that the incidence of use may be even higher than these figures, as the 15% of adolescents nationwide who drop out before the 12th grade are not taken into account in this survey (Ungerleider & Siegel, 1990).

During the past decade, this survey has been reporting a gradual decline in adolescent substance use in general, as well as a decline in use of specific substances. What cannot be forecast with any certainty is if this trend of declining use will continue, if it will plateau at current levels, if use may decline for some substances but rise for others, or if a nationwide increase in adolescent substance use might recur.

Who, in 1962, could have predicted the upsurge in illegal drug taking among middle-class Caucasian youth during the last half of the 1960s?

Who, in the midst of the counterculture's boom, would have predicted its sudden demise and the growing self-centeredness and eventual conservatism of young people? (Mandel & Feldman, 1986, p. 39)

Sequences of Psychoactive Substance Use by Adolescents

Kandel (1975) was one of the first to identify a pattern by which adolescents choose different drugs to use. Simply stated, Kandel postulated that teenage drug use usually proceeds according to four stages of chemical choice: (a) drinking beer and wine; (b) smoking cigarettes and drinking hard liquor; (c) smoking marijuana; and (d) using other illicit drugs, including cocaine, sedatives, hallucinogens, and opiates.

The value of Kandel's model is that it does illustrate how an adolescent at an advanced stage of chemical choice is more likely to select a chemical at that stage if he has used chemicals from a previous stage. For example, a teenager who drinks hard liquor and smokes cigarettes is more likely to try marijuana than a teenager who drinks only beer and does not smoke cigarettes.

Among the limitations of Kandel's model is that it does not account for the variety of substance use choice patterns by adolescents. For a number of young persons, inhalants, not alcohol, are the first psychoactive substances sampled (McHugh, 1987). Some teenagers will develop a chemical dependency with only beer and wine. For other teenagers, using an illicit substance—such as marijuana—may precede alcohol use.

Another limitation of Kandel's model is that it can be misconstrued as resembling the "stepping stone theory"—using one drug automatically leads to using another drug. As Weiner states, "Adolescents who drink are not inevitably drawn to smoking marijuana, nor are those who smoke marijuana destined to become hard drug users" (Weiner, 1992, p. 390).

LEVELS OF BIOPSYCHOSOCIAL FACTORS IN ADOLESCENT SUBSTANCE ABUSE

There are five levels of possible determining factors in this model of adolescent substance abuse. These levels are: biological factors, adolescent psychological development factors, interpersonal factors (family functioning and peer relationship factors), community factors, and societal factors. Adolescent psychological development variables, family functioning determinants, and peer relationship factors comprise the triad of primary factors in this biopsychosocial model for understanding adolescent substance abuse.

Biological Factors:
The Biology of Substance Abuse

An adolescent's susceptibility to developing a substance abuse disorder may, in part, be determined by certain biological factors. When it comes to drug addiction, biology may not necessarily be destiny, but it cannot be overlooked in understanding and treating addictive disorders.

> The biological predisposition to addictions is strong, and any attempts at treatment and personal recovery need to take this fact into account. Our bodies themselves are chemical entities, and they have strong tendencies toward the abuse of certain chemicals. Chemical imbalances and certain chemicals have large and lasting effects on mood, awareness, and behavior. To ignore these facts is to make lasting recovery less likely—facts with important implications for individuals in treatment and recovery. (Robak, 1991, p. 110)

In many ways understanding about the biology of addictive disorders is a new frontier in the addictions field. More has been learned about the human brain and consciousness in the past several years than was known in all previous history (Seymour et al., 1989), and much of this knowledge has significant applications to understanding the biological underpinnings of substance abuse.

Biological factors for substance abuse disorders can be categorized by three types of factors: (a) genetic factors, (b) neurological factors, and (c) idiosyncratic physiological factors.

Genetic Factors

Current understandings about the genetics of substance abuse are predominantly based on research into alcoholism. The sources of this research are primarily family studies, adoptive studies, and twin studies (Goodwin, 1983).

Researchers seemed to be finally identifying a genetic marker for alcoholism (Blum, Noble, Sheridan, Montgomery, Ritchie, Jagadeswaran, Nogami, Briggs, & Cohn, 1990), only to have this discovery sharply challenged (Adler, 1990). With the addictions research community divided on the conclusiveness of a genetic link for alcoholism, Wallace offers an observation on the mounting evidence tilting towards a genetic marker for alcoholism, "Multiple pathways into alcoholism probably exist with a pure genetic pathway constituting only one of several routes into the disease" (Wallace, 1989, p. 12).

As alcoholism is the prototypical chemical dependency model, a relevant issue is to what extent the genetics of alcoholism can be extrapolated to other chemical addictions. Basically the genetic understanding of chemical dependencies other than alcoholism is more at the hypothesized stage than the empirical stage. The current dearth of "hard" scientific data for genetic links with other chemical addictions should not, however, invalidate these hypotheses. "Most of the solid research data has come in the specific area of alcoholism, but clinical experience suggests that similar experience will hold for all abused substances" (Meeks, 1988, p. 512).

Neurological Factors

Neurological understandings about addictions can be divided according to: (a) neurochemical transmission processes and (b) new brain-old brain distinctions.

Neurochemical Processes. The transmission of neural messages in the brain is an electrochemical process, and psychoactive substances introduced into the brain can easily disrupt this process (Robak, 1991). Cohen (1988) and Sunderwirth (1990) are among those who have detailed these neurochemical transmission processes and the disruptive role of psychoactive substance use with these processes. Sunderwirth (1990) offers a metaphor that succinctly illustrates how drug use interferes in the neurochemical activity of the brain.

The relationships that exist between the brain, endogenous chemicals produced through activities, and powerful mind-altering drugs may be understood using an analogy of a computer and two different brands of software. In the analogy, consider the brain as the hardware, which can be programmed to achieve various moods depending on the type of software used. A person may program his or her brain by using compatible software, such as those molecules produced by activities. Alternatively, a person may choose to use software that is not completely compatible. Although the incompatible software (amphetamine, cocaine, or heroin) will run certain programs (various mood changes), extended use of this software has the potential to cause serious damage to the hardware (brain). (p. 28)

The actual quality and extent of brain chemistry aberrations experienced by the substance user will differ according to a collection of variables. These variables include the endemic neurochemical make-up of the person, the types of substances used, and the amount and frequency of substances used.

New Brain-Old Brain. Another possible contribution of neurological factors in understanding addictions is with current ideas about which region of the brain controls drug use. It has been hypothesized that substance abuse is "mediated" in the cerebral cortex or new part of the brain, which oversees such functions as memory and cognition (Heaslip, Van Dyke, Hogenson, & Vedders, 1989). However, addiction is actually "mediated" in the hypothalamus or old part of the brain, which manages basic survival needs like breathing and hunger (Heaslip et al., 1989). This distinction helps to portray the addict's compulsive cravings to use drugs as comparable to essential human survival instincts.

Idiosyncratic Physiological Factors

Some adolescents may be biologically vulnerable to substance abuse because of their psychological functioning, the biological aspect of this psychological functioning, and the self-medicating effects of their chemical use with their psychological functioning.

> There is evidence that drug abuse has a significant physiological cause when it is used to self-medicate mood disorders, schizophrenia, and the helplessness produced by attention deficit disorders. In some types of alcoholism, and perhaps with marijuana, there may be a specific reinforcing response to the drug that is physiologically produced in the genetically vulnerable drug taker. (Miller, 1986, p. 60)

Different chemicals provide different "bio-psychological" reinforcement for these vulnerable teenagers.

The Triad of Primary Factors: Adolescent Psychological Development, Family Functioning, and Peer Relationships

The three primary factors contributing to adolescent substance abuse are the young person's psychological development, factors related to his family's functioning, and variables pertaining to his peer relationships. Adolescent psychological development factors are the focus of

Chapter 4, and family and peer factors combining to create the teen-ager's interpersonal environment are the subject of Chapter 5.

As mentioned in Chapter 1, any of these primary factors can singu-larly contribute to a teenager's drug problem. In addition, the more primary factors there are influencing the young person's substance use, the greater the likelihood that this use will result in a substance abuse disorder.

The biopsychosocial model of adolescent substance abuse stresses the interactive nature of the variables contributing to the problem. The triad of primary factors can all interact together to form a synergistic, multi-factorial collection of variables, or dyads of these primary factors can combine to dominate the clinical picture.

There is a circular causality between adolescent psychological devel-opment and family functioning, with the family's emotional climate influencing the teenager's handling of the changes of adolescence and the young person's developmental transformation influencing the tenor of family life. The adolescent and his peers are mutually influential, as both the teenager and his friends are coexperiencing new and myriad developmental strivings during this phase of life. The adolescent's family and peers also have a reciprocal interplay (which in turn interacts with the adolescent's interaction with them) by either being an allied interpersonal environment or a conflictual interpersonal environment for the teenager.

Adolescent Psychological Development Factors

Adolescence is a period of life marked by significant shifts in intrapsychic structure. Internal structures become loosened, a norma-tive regression to recapture intrapsychic structures of early childhood ensues, and an eventual tightening of a more "mature" intrapsychic structure emerges. Parents (as well as other family members) and friends are vital external resources for the adolescent experiencing these internal changes. These natural psychological changes render the young person vulnerable to various maladaptive responses—including the abuse of drugs.

There are arguably many ways of classifying factors that influence adolescent psychological development. Four categories of pertinent factors drawn from a psychodynamic focus are identified in this book. The categories are: (a) the major changes of adolescence (physical and sexual changes, cognitive and moral development, and adjustment with

experiences from childhood); (b) the subphases of adolescent development (early, middle, and late adolescence); (c) developmental crises of
adolescence (separation, narcissistic, and identity crises); and (d) impaired psychological development during adolescence (teenagers with
psychological disorders, those who are victims of physical or sexual
abuse, or who are children of substance-abusing parents). These four
categories of adolescent psychological development and their subcategories overlap and mutually interact with one another. How each of
these subcategories of factors may play a part in a teenager's drug
problem is the basis of Chapter 4.

The Interpersonal Environment:
Family Functioning and Peer Relationship Factors

The adolescent's interpersonal environment—family and peers—provides the emotional and relational climate that facilitates the young person's developmental changes. In regard to substance abuse, family and peer
environments can either: (a) align to coprotect the teenager from having a
problem with drugs, (b) align to coinfluence the young person's drug
problem, or (c) conflict in attempting to buffer the adolescent from the
drug-influencing behaviors of the other environment.

Family Functioning. The family is the primary environment for
facilitating the adolescent's psychological growth. It can operate as a
climate for promoting non-substance-abusing development or as a climate for enabling the substance-abusing development of the teenager.

Four categories of factors related to family functioning are identified
in this book. These categories are: (a) the major family life factors
(changes in family structure, family composition, geography, ethnicity,
socioeconomic status, and the family in the postmodern age); (b) family
dynamics (leadership, boundaries, affectivity, communication, and task/
goal performance); (c) family crises of adolescence (structural crises,
developmental crises, and dramatic crises); and (d) family dysfunction
(with particular attention to the family with a substance-abusing parent).
These four categories of family factors and their subcategories overlap
and are reciprocally influential with one another. The ways in which
each of these categories and subcategories could be a determinant in a
young person's substance abuse disorder is elaborated on in Chapter 5.

Peer Relationships. The adolescent's peer relationships are her "second family"—the secondary environment for facilitating her traversing
of developmental passages. Just as with the family environment, the

teenager's peer relationships form a climate that may either encourage nonsubstance-abusing development or enable the adolescent's substance abuse.

Two categories of peer relationship factors associated with substance abuse are identified in this book. These categories are: (a) peer crises of adolescence (crises of exclusion, betrayal, and disillusionment) and (b) the dysfunctional peer group (with specific emphasis on the substance-abusing peer group). These two categories of peer relationship factors and their subcategories share much in common and interact with one another. How they might have a contributing role with an adolescent's chemical abuse problem are detailed in Chapter 5.

Community Factors: The Immediate Social Environment and Adolescent Substance Abuse

The biological, adolescent developmental, and interpersonal environmental levels of biopsychosocial factors are experienced in the immediate social environment, the community. The community is composed of those systems—schools, churches, community organizations, police departments and criminal justice systems, and other local government institutions and services—that support the adolescent and his family and peers throughout his development.

A community is a factor in adolescent substance abuse in relation to its success in providing the services and programs of primary, secondary, and tertiary prevention. In this context primary prevention consists of the organized activities intended to prevent any adolescent substance use problems, secondary prevention pertains to planned programs designed to assist with intervening in the early stages when an adolescent has a substance abuse problem, and tertiary prevention refers to specific efforts to promote recovery in teenagers with substance abuse disorders (Suski, 1992).

Primary prevention programs focusing on strict proscriptions against any chemical use and promotion of healthy lifestyles are not considered by some to be particularly effective for adolescents (Carroll, 1986). Such programs, when effectively implemented, are more useful for the substance abuse prevention needs of preadolescents and younger children.

Secondary prevention programs are vital community resources for teenagers, their families, and their friends. The three major objectives of a secondary prevention program are: (a) helping the teenager to be aware of the stages of adolescent chemical use; (b) helping teenagers to identify their own possible chemical-use problem or the chemical-use problem of a friend; and (c) helping teenagers, their families, and their friends to access resources for assistance with a chemical use problem (Carroll, 1986).

Tertiary prevention programs are concerned with assisting the recovering adolescent and family to thrive in recovery. This can be done through sponsoring AA, NA, and Families Anonymous (FA) meetings in the community and through creating greater access to individual, family, and group therapy services, which are essential in recovery.

When a community is not successful in providing primary, secondary, and tertiary prevention programs to its young people and families, then the community can be engaged in a kind of community enabling of adolescent substance abuse. For a community (and different systems within a community) to ignore, blame, or collude with adolescent substance abusers, their families, and their peers is, in essence, to collaborate with this substance abuse. A community that provides successful prevention programs is being a part of the solution, not a part of the problem, with teenage drug abuse.

Societal Factors: The Larger Social Environment and Adolescent Substance Abuse

Enveloping all of the other levels of biopsychosocial factors is the larger social environment—society. In the context of the biopsychosocial model of adolescent substance abuse, society is delineated as: (a) the federal government and its public policy toward substance abuse and (b) the media (including the entertainment industry) and its communication of attitudes and values about drugs.

Substance abuse by adults and adolescents is, in part, a function of the loosening of social controls in this country.

> Not only have traditional social controls on drug and alcohol use been relaxed in America over the last two decades, but so have social controls over eating and sexual behavior. It is no accident that the drug and alcohol epidemic from which the U.S. suffers is part of a larger epidemic of pleasure-driven behaviors. (DuPont, 1988, p. 49)

In some ways this loosening of social controls represents enabling on a national level. Both the federal government, with its mostly ineffective public policy towards substance abuse in this country, and the media, with their ambiguous messages about drug use, have taken an active part in enabling the substance abuse problem of this country.

Government Policy and Substance Abuse

The federal government's current policy on substance abuse is manifested in its ongoing War on Drugs. The current war shares some common themes with other wars on drugs waged in this country over the past century (Morgan, Wallack, and Buchanan, 1989):

- One of the most common characteristics of drug wars is the notion of a new public menace.
- Drug wars serve the interests of politicians, often by the introduction of new legislation with hidden political agendas.
- Drug wars are characterized by increased criminal justice involvement.
- A dramatic increase in media coverage usually shifts the image of the problem to fit the needs of the drug war.
- Undefined concepts of addiction and disease are used to characterize the problem.
- Youth and women are portrayed as victims.

There is much controversy over the effectiveness of the federal government's policy on substance abuse. Among the ways in which the War on Drugs policy is controversial is its punishment-oriented philosophy. The greater emphasis of this policy is on the "supply side"—international interdiction and coercive social control. The "demand side" of the problem—education, prevention, and treatment—is underemphasized. Such a punishment-oriented philosophy can take the complexity of adolescent substance abuse and reduce this national health problem to simplistic issues of right-wrong or good-bad.

Another way in which the drug war policy proves contentious is when it tries to address the demand side of substance abuse, particularly with adolescents. Often such demand-side initiatives are ineffective.

Current efforts at drug "education" seem flawed on two counts. First, they are alarmist, pathologizing normative adolescent experimentation and limit-testing, and perhaps frightening parents and educators unnecessarily. Second, and of far greater concern, they trivialize the factors underlying drug abuse, implicitly denying their depth and pervasiveness. (Shedler & Block, 1990, p. 628)

Still another way in which the War on Drugs represents questionable public policy is in overlooking the role of alcohol with the nation's drug problem. The United States has a historically duplicitous relationship with alcohol, and sidestepping the "alcohol problem" within the War on Drugs only mirrors this ongoing ambivalence. Such governmental duplicity can be construed as hypocrisy by adolescents, who are highly sensitive to false images cast by authorities and institutions.

Media Messages and Substance Abuse

The mass media and the entertainment industry together form an information complex that is a powerful force in communicating attitudes and values in this country. This transmission of ideas and images can be particularly powerful by inculcating attitudes and values in adolescents, who are in a period of life when they are forming and internalizing their own moral codes and value systems. The media's messages about drugs can influence a young person's developing attitudes and values about chemical use.

The dilemma with the media communicating values about drugs, especially for teenagers, is that the overall message of "responsible decision making" is fraught with contradictions. On the one hand there is an attempt to promote responsible decision making about chemical use through public service campaigns and the entertainment industry's efforts in "drug-sensitive" television programs and movies. On the other hand, all this is offset by the seductive messages of the advertising industry (especially as relates to alcohol), the "medicalization of the human condition" by the pharmaceutical industry, and the glamorizing and sensationalizing of the drug lifestyle (although this seems to have subsided during the lowered national tolerance with illicit substance use of recent years) (Coombs, Paulson & Palley, 1988).

The result of transmitting these contradictory messages to adolescents is that the media present a picture of national ambiguity over drug use to young people. Assimilating such equivocal messages about drugs can be extremely disconcerting for teenagers in the midst of trying to clarify their attitudes and values about chemicals.

BIOPSYCHOSOCIAL EXPRESSIONS
OF ADDICTION DYNAMICS

The interaction of psychoactive substance use with the adolescent's biological, psychological, and social systems can culminate in an addiction process. This addiction process simultaneously infiltrates every aspect of the young person's life. As discussed in Chapter 1, addiction can be thought of as unfolding across three stages—initiation, escalation, and maintenance—and is composed of three dynamics: compulsion, relapse, and denial. These three addiction dynamics can be understood as having biopsychosocial expressions.

Compulsion

Compulsion—the driving urge to obtain, use, and continue using drugs—is the central addiction dynamic. Compulsion can be understood as having biological, psychological, and social manifestations with adolescents.

As previously discussed in this chapter (The Biology of Addiction), true addiction is mediated in the hypothalamus or "old brain." This is the same brain center that regulates urges to breathe, eat, have sex, and survive. When an adolescent's substance abuse progresses to addiction, the urge to use chemicals is qualitatively similar to other basic biological urges. This is the biological side of compulsion.

Compulsion also has a psychological component to it. The teenager whose thoughts and psychological life are preoccupied with obsessive ideation of drug use is manifesting compulsion. Such ruminating over how, where, and when substances will be obtained and used is a common sign associated with addiction.

Compulsion and loss of control are two sides of the same coin. If a young person is experiencing a driving compulsion to use substances and then acts on this compulsion in the social world, then she is in effect demonstrating loss of control. Loss of control represents the social side of compulsion—violating interpersonal boundaries as well as violating the social norms and standards as the result of substance abuse.

Relapse

Relapse is a process within the larger addiction process. Adapting Marlatt and Gordon's (1985) model, relapse can be thought of as occurring along four stages: (a) immediate determinants stage, (b) crossroads stage, (c) breaking of abstinence stage, and (d) abstinence violation coping stage. A biopsychosocial perspective can be applied to understand an adolescent substance abuser's experience with relapse during each of these four stages.

The *immediate determinants stage* involves those stressors that might serve as precipitants to the teenager's relapse. These stressors may be biological, such as the physiological changes of adolescence, or overall poor health. In addition, they might be psychological, including developmental crises of adolescence, or even social, such as conflicts with friends or family members.

The *crossroads stage* entails those resources that the teenager may rely on to cope with the stressors from the previous relapse stage. Such resources may be biological, including adequate acceptance of evolving physiological changes and promoting positive physical health. These resources may also be psychological, such as the teenager's overall coping and adaptation capacities, or social—for example, relying on friends and family as a support system.

The *breaking of abstinence stage* is concerned with the actual effects of the young person's resumed chemical use following a period of abstinence. As discussed in Chapter 1 with the Adolescent Chemical Use Problem (ACUP) Index, chemical use effects for the adolescent can be acute or cumulative and can be manifest in biological, psychological, or social ways.

The *abstinence violation coping stage,* much like the crossroads stage, involves what resources the young person accesses to cope with his or her resumed chemical use. Depending on how successful he or she uses his or her biological, psychological, or social resources, he or she may adaptively cope and discontinue further drug use, or he or she may maladaptively cope and plunge deeper into relapse.

Denial

The denial system of adolescent substance abusers involves those systems and processes that most immediately and directly diminish their awareness of their chemical use and the effects of this use. This blunted awareness contributes to continued, and often escalating, chemical use by teenagers.

Denial is a process that has biopsychosocial aspects to it (Rivinus, 1991b). Denial can be viewed as operating at biological, psychological, and social levels with adolescent substance abusers.

At the biological level, denial can be manifest as blackouts, repressions, and euphoric recall (Johnson, 1973). Blackouts are periods of chemically induced memory impairment that are often confused with unconsciousness. A person in a blackout is consciously functioning while in the blackout. Once the blackout wears off, however, there is no memory of this functioning. While blackouts involve no recall of behavior while intoxicated, euphoric recall and repression work in tandem to distort recall of behavior while intoxicated. Euphoric recall is remembering only the more pleasurable experiences of being intoxicated, while repression serves to keep unpleasant memories inaccessible to consciousness. These three biological functions of denial contribute to the young person's overall delusion with her substance abuse problem.

At the psychological level, denial can be experienced as different addiction defenses—denial, projection, rationalization, and splitting—working to insulate the adolescent from the psychological impact of her drug use. Intrapsychic defenses are fluidly forming, and, when a substance abuse problem develops, these defenses become more regressed and rigid to protect the teenager from both the emotional pain associated with the chemical use as well as an emotional understanding of the need to discontinue using drugs.

At the social level, denial is enacted through the enabling behaviors of family, friends, and other significant persons in the adolescent's life. Enabling processes (Chapter 5) essentially involve a person or persons colluding, unconsciously or consciously, with the adolescent to protect her from experiencing undesirable consequences of her substance use. In effect enablers knit a cloak of delusion for the young person to wear and shield herself from the reality of her involvement with drugs.

The biological, psychological, and social expression of the addiction dynamics of compulsion, relapse, and denial are illustrated in the following example. An 18-year-old male had a 5-year history of multiple substance abuse, had twice been admitted for treatment, and both times had left treatment without successfully completing his program. His compulsion to use chemicals is experienced as a physical craving to "get high" daily, as a psychological need to self-medicate the emotional pain he feels about himself and his life, and as socially out-of-control behaviors (including dealing drugs, committing burglaries, and spending large amounts of money on drugs). His relapsing from prior, although brief, periods of abstinence is demonstrated physically by an overall deterioration in his health, psychologically by a plummeting of his self-esteem and sense of despair, and socially by emotional estrangement from both his parents. His denial is physically manifest through his impaired recall of what he has done while under the influence of chemicals, psychologically demonstrated by his steadfast refusal to acknowledge a drug problem, even in the face of overwhelming evidence, and socially exhibited through his collusion with his older sister who is enabling his use by allowing him to live with her. His addiction is currently the core of his life.

SUMMARY

This chapter presented a biopsychosocial model for understanding adolescent substance abuse. Briefly stated this model encompasses five levels of factors—biological, adolescent psychological development, interpersonal environment (family and peers), community, and society—that can play a part in a young person's substance abuse. At the same time, this model underscores a triad of primary factors—adolescent psychological development, family functioning, and peer relationships—that carry the most weight in a teenager's development of a drug problem. In portraying this range of factors, while emphasizing particular factors, the biopsychosocial model advocates a balanced perspective: appreciating the breadth of factors contributing to this complex problem while delineating in depth those factors that are most highly contributory to this problem.

The following is a metaphor that symbolizes the biopsychosocial model of adolescent substance abuse presented in this chapter. The growing teenager is represented by an apple tree in an orchard. This tree is in the season of blossoming and is on the threshold of bearing fruit. A fire, like the toxic agent drugs, becomes a predator of the maturing tree. The origin of this fire—whether matches, or heat friction, or some random synergy of elements—cannot be easily determined. How this sprouting tree resists or succumbs to the fire is, in part, reflective of its overall combustibility—analogous to the adolescent's intrapsychic structure. Depending on this young tree's overall combustibility, it may be able to withstand the fire or be susceptible to severe burns. The endogenous constitution of the wood of the tree—similar to the biological factors of addiction—may, in part, contribute to the flourishing of the fire. The cluster of other trees surrounding the apple tree is similar to the teenager's interpersonal environment of family and peers. By fueling the fire, this cluster of surrounding trees may enable the fire to continue much in the way that family and peers can enable an adolescent's continued substance abuse. Larger environmental elements within and beyond the orchard—climate and weather conditions—can encourage or impede the burning of the tree, just as community and society factors can enable the teenager's continued chemical abuse. The addiction dynamics of compulsion, relapse, and denial also resemble some dynamics of this fire. Compulsion is akin to the driving symbiosis between the burning fire and the apple tree, relapse is analogous to smoldering roots of the tree that can reignite a later fire, and denial is similar to the smoke that billows from the fire, engulfing the tree so as to obscure awareness of the extent of the fire. The interplay of all of these factors will determine if the apple tree experiences only minor charring, much like a substance use problem, or suffers extensive fire damage, similar to a substance abuse disorder.

Chapter 4

ADOLESCENT PSYCHOLOGICAL DEVELOPMENT AND SUBSTANCE ABUSE

INTRODUCTION

Adolescence is a period of psychological development unique from other developmental phases. Adolescent psychological development spans the period of time from puberty—often generalized as beginning around age 12—to incorporation of an adult identity, which occurs somewhere between the late teens into the 20s. This period of psychological life, in essence a recapitulation of the first 5 years of development, abounds with a rate of internal change not experienced since one's early childhood and not to be experienced in adulthood.

The nature of the adolescent years is change. The crux of the psychological changes—the reorganizing of personality structure replete with new and intense affective states, a reordering of how one experiences internal representations of parents and peers, and an expanded sense of one's self—has been the source of much discussion and debate by child development theorists. For years the concept of *sturm and drang*—adolescence as a period of deep emotional turmoil—dominated the thinking in adolescent development. In more recent years, the emphasis on the normal aspects of adolescent psychological development has gained much acceptance (Offer, Ostrov, & Howard, 1981). Yet even this recent emphasis toward thinking of adolescent development as more chaos-free has been met by challenging voices.

The traditional view of normal adolescence as a time of sturm and drang has been so thoroughly discredited that there is now a real danger of overstatement in the opposite direction—by denying that adolescent behavior is significantly different from that of adults. While most adolescents are not disturbed (their incidence of mental illness is no higher than that of adults), objective indexes do suggest that adolescence is not a time of utter stability. (Hodgman, 1983, p. 515).

As adolescents are a psychologically heterogeneous group, the psychological changes that teenagers undergo fall along a widely variable range. For many young persons these changes are an opportunity for challenge and growth. These adolescents discover new and adaptive ways of dealing with their feelings, with other people, and with the world. For some teenagers, however, the psychological changes of adolescence are perceived as a threat to inner stability. These adolescents are overwhelmed by the stress of psychological changes and rendered vulnerable to more maladaptive ways of coping, including substance abuse. This maladaption through substance abuse may be viewed by the outside world as a problem, but, for the teenager with a fragile sense of self, this use of chemicals may indeed be experienced as adaptive self-protection.

The changes of adolescence that affect psychological development can be looked at in many different ways but are considered here according to four categories of changes. These four categories are: (a) the major changes of adolescence, (b) the subphase of adolescent psychological development, (c) developmental crises of adolescent psychological development, and (d) impaired development and adolescent psychological development. Adolescent psychological development and the related changes are discussed in this book from a predominantly psychodynamic perspective.

There are differences in the psychological development of adolescent males and adolescent females. However, the discussion in this chapter is centered on a more general paradigm of adolescent psychological development and its possible role in substance abuse.

Adolescent psychological development is the central factor in the triad of primary factors from this book's biopsychosocial model for understanding substance abuse. The other two primary factors, the adolescent's family and peer relationships, are considered together in the next chapter.

MAJOR CHANGES OF ADOLESCENCE AND ADOLESCENT PSYCHOLOGICAL DEVELOPMENT

This book identifies five major changes experienced during adolescence that can influence intrapsychic evolution. These five changes are: (a) physical changes, (b) sexual emergence, (c) cognitive development, (d) moral development, and (e) adjustment from early childhood experiences.

A teenager may negotiate changes in these five areas in ways that are fairly adaptive with his psychological development, or he may deal with changes in these five areas in ways that are maladaptive and developmentally impairing. Substance abuse is among the problems to which psychologically vulnerable adolescent may fall prey.

Physical Changes

One factor that affects the adolescent's psychological development is physical change during this period of life. This physiological metamorphosis ushers in often-dramatic changes in weight and height, the emergence of secondary sexual characteristics, and a growing consciousness of an overall body image.

How well an adolescent accepts and integrates these changes as a natural part of growing up contributes to his or her evolving sense of self. Difficulty in accepting and integrating these physiological changes may be disruptive to his or her psychological development. For example, O'Connell (1989) has discussed how dramatic variations in the maturational timetable can be psychologically impairing to some adolescents, contributing to their involvement with drugs.

> Late maturing boys and early maturing girls experience significant psychological pain during early adolescence. During this developmental phase they are egocentric and self-absorbed with their body image. For some of these children the psychological scars incurred in this developmental period will be carried on into late adolescence and adulthood. (O'Connell, 1989, pp. 50-51).

Adolescents need to feel supported as their bodies change. Self-respect rather than self-shame needs to be encouraged with this often awkward and uncontrollable aspect of growing up.

Sexual Emergence

The adolescent's sexual emergence is precipitated by the physical and psychological changes brought on by puberty. As explained by Sarrell and Sarrell (1990):

> Sexual unfolding is defined as a process made up of innumerable experiences during adolescence through which a person becomes aware of himself or herself as a sexual being—male or female—who relates to oneself and others sexually in some characteristic ways. (p. 19)

The young person's sexual emergence can impact on his psychological development by: (a) his feelings about having sexual feeling and a growing sexual self, (b) his feelings about sexual performance, and (c) his feelings about his sexual identity. These feelings can range from exhilarating and exciting to anxious and shameful. Some of these feelings may be indicative of considerable intrapsychic pain, possibly leaving the teenager susceptible to substance abuse. "Drugs may be used as a substitute for sexual intercourse or to allay anxiety about sexual competence, to facilitate masturbation, or to resolve conflicts about sexual identity" (Miller, 1986, p. 209).

Adolescents need empathy as they grow to understand the "normalness" of the emerging sexual self. It is through this self-understanding and self-acceptance of sexual feelings that the teenager can be assisted with developing a mature, and chemically free sexual self.

Cognitive Development

While physiological changes and sexual maturation are being integrated with psychological development, the cognitive world of the adolescent is rapidly growing and exerting influence on psychological development. Among the ways in which cognitive development can affect psychological development are: (a) through the emergence of formal operations thinking and (b) with adolescents who have a learning disability, making cognitive adjustments during this period of new intellectual demands.

As initially theorized by Piaget (1975), formal operations thinking empowers the adolescent with capabilities for abstract thought, more complex constructs of logic, moral reasoning, philosophical and ethical musings, more intricate modes of problem solving, and tendencies to futurize. The extent to which an adolescent develops formal operations thinking capacities (some people remain at a concrete operational stage for their entire lives) will be influential with his overall psychological development. However, involvement with chemicals can disrupt a young person's attainment of formal operations thought processes, "Adolescent involvement with drugs may impede progress from concrete to formal operations, or introduce greater instability in the exercise of incompletely consolidated formal operations schemes" (Baumrind & Moselle, 1985, p. 53).

Learning disabilities—difficulties with attention, language, spatial orientation, memory, fine motor control, or sequencing—are other cognitive variables that might influence adolescent psychological development.

> The relationship between learning disabilities and psychological development is a complex and ongoing intrapsychic and psychosocial process. It is interwoven with the concerns, conflicts, strengths, weaknesses, coping strategies, dreams, wishes, and various psycho-social factors of each developmental stage. (Cohen, 1985, p. 186)

Undetected learning disabilities can result in the young person attempting various compensatory strategies, underachieving as the result of these strategies, and internalizing a sense of failure and lowered self-esteem. A decline in self-esteem can put the adolescent at a greater risk for the perceived self-bolstering effects of chemicals. "Adolescents with severe chemical dependency also have an unusually frequent history of learning disabilities, attention deficit disorders, and other evidences of subtle brain dysfunction" (Meeks, 1988, p. 512).

Moral Development

Moral development goes hand in hand with the teenager's cognitive development. "The adolescent's acquisition of formal thought, combined with the new experiences of the secondary school years, i.e., diverse attitudes, greater possibilities, and wider perspectives, provide the opportunity for advancing moral reasoning" (Shelton, 1989, p. 50).

If cognitive development becomes fixed at a concrete level, it might interfere with the growth of the teenager's mature moral reasoning. Consequently, immature moral development can compromise a young person's sense of ethics and personal responsibilities—factors that may contribute to choosing to use drugs (Nowinski, 1990). This becomes a vicious cycle as substance abuse, and the often antisocial values associated with it, can further undermine the young person's development of more mature moral reasoning.

Adjustment From Early Childhood

Another set of factors influencing how an adolescent might contend with psychological changes during this phase of development is his or her legacy from early childhood. If adolescence is a recapitulation of one's first 5 years of psychological development, then psychological adaptations and deficits from early childhood, combined with other layers of adaptations and deficits from the latency years, is the psychological apparatus with which the child enters adolescence. How well the young person has negotiated the developmental process in the earlier stages of life, particularly during the first 3 years, determines to a large extent the psychological resources and liabilities that he or she brings into the adolescent development process (Prall, 1990).

If a child has enjoyed a relatively adaptive and developmentally stable early childhood, then he or she possesses a measure of psychological resources necessary for negotiating a more stable path through the psychological changes of the teenage years. But if a child has endured an early childhood with significant developmental deficits— for example, growing up in a dysfunctional family environment—then he or she is not likely to possess adequate psychological resources for dealing with the psychological demands of adolescence.

Traversing adolescence with inadequate psychological resources can leave a young person susceptible to compensating for such deficits through chemical use. "The prognosis for those adolescents who abuse drugs as a result of developmental difficulties is considerably better than for those who, because of earlier characterological difficulties, have become physically pubertal but not psychologically adolescent" (Miller, 1986, p. 60).

SUBPHASES OF ADOLESCENT PSYCHOLOGICAL DEVELOPMENT

Adolescent psychological development can be divided into three subphases: early, middle, and late adolescence.

Naturally, any division of phases remains an abstraction; there is no such neat compartmentalization in actual development. The value of this kind of formulation about phases lies in the fact that it focuses our attention on orderly developmental sequences; the phases also make it easier to see the essential psychological modifications and tasks that characterize each phase, as they roughly follow the epigenetic principle of development. (Blos, 1962, pp. 72-73)

These three subphases can be conceptualized according to different developmental tasks represented by the following six developmental lines: (a) psychological separation from parents, (b) heightened and differentiated attachment to peers, (c) increase in range of self-management capabilities, (d) greater propensity toward a cohesive sense of self, (e) formation of an integrated identity, (f) an increase in the capacity for genuine, nonexploitive intimacy. In actuality, the term *developmental line* is a misnomer for describing the process of psychological development, especially with adolescents. With adolescents the lines of development are more like coils of development, interconnected and intersecting, spiraling their way through the fits and starts of regression and progression in psychological development.

Six Developmental Lines and the Three Subphases of Adolescent Psychological Development

Psychological separation from parents is a developmental line that runs from psychological undifferentiation to psychological autonomy. The developmental line representing peer attachment ranges from egocentric preoccupation with one's self to successful companionship with peers. These two developmental lines are summed up by Blos (1967) in his explanation of adolescence as the second individuation process, "The disengagement from internalized objects—love and hate objects— opens the way in adolescence to the finding of external and extra-familial love and hate objects" (p. 157). The need to rebel and the need for affiliation with friends is the teenager's living out of these two developmental lines.

The writings of Kohut (1971, 1987) have brought much understanding to the developmental lines of self-management and cohesive sense of self during adolescence. Self-management capabilities can be construed as a constellation of competencies including, but not limited to, self-esteem regulation, self-control, and self-soothing of affective states. The developmental lines of self-management can be illustrated as extending from dependence on more external resources for self-management to reliance on more internal resources for self-management. The adolescent's need to feel empowered is strongly linked to his self-management. The adolescent's developmental line of self-cohesion represents the young person's evolving sense of "I." The developmental line characterizing this sense of one's self spans from self-fragmentation to self-cohesion. The need for individuality is an expression of this evolving self-cohesion of the teenager.

Erickson's (1956, 1968) contribution to understanding adolescent development has included conceptualizations about the latter two developmental lines—identity formation and engaging in a mutually empathic relationship. Identity formation can be characterized by a developmental line ranging from identity diffusion to identity consolidation.

> The transition from adolescent to adult involves becoming a person in one's own right, not simply someone's son or daughter, and a person who is recognized by the community in such terms. It involves the drawing together and resynthesis of a process that has been going on since birth and the crystallization out of an individual who will tend to preserve his or her identity despite the vicissitudes of life that are yet to come. The individual has passed through a series of developmental phases, and at each level there has been an identity and there has been a relatedness between the identities at each phase. (Lidz, 1983, p. 356)

An increase in the capacity for empathic intimacy is the psychological task of adolescent development depicted as a developmental line extending from narcissistic preoccupation with one's self to engagement of one's self in the give-and-take of mature relationships. To be able to both give and receive love, as well as to express and deal with one another's anger responsibly, are signs of psychological maturity with adolescents.

Some of these developmental lines are more significant during certain subphases of adolescent psychological development. However, all six of these lines do overlap throughout the course of adolescent development. Separation and peer attachment are highly charged inner experiences during early adolescence; enhancing self-management capabilities and deepening a cohesive sense of self are highly critical during middle adolescence; and identity formation and intimacy with others are essential experiences of late adolescence. Succinctly put, early adolescence is a time of searching for one's self, middle adolescence is a stage of discovering one's self, and later adolescence is a period of more fully integrating one's self.

The Subphases of Adolescent Psychological Development and Substance Abuse

Each subphase of adolescent psychological development, with its own distinctive developmental demands, poses different stresses for the fledgling self of the teenager. These stresses may surpass the young person's capacity to deal with them, allowing maladaptive behaviors—such as drug use—to serve as a substitute, albeit an unsuccessful one, for the teenager's further development of his own inner capacities.

Early Adolescence

Early adolescence seems to be the subphase in which teenagers are the most vulnerable to substance abuse. According to Zarek, Hawkins, and Rogers (1987), "Beginning to drink or use drugs at an early age increases the risk of drug problems. Using drugs before the age of 15 years greatly increases the risk of later drug use" (p. 291). The reason for this heightened risk is the vulnerability of the early adolescent's transient and disorganized psychological structure, which is detaching from parents as psychological resources and attaching to peers as psychological resources.

One 13-year-old girl, the oldest of three children in the family, began associating with older drug-involved adolescents and using drugs herself when in junior high school. Being the oldest child she was used to being perceived as "more mature than her age." At the onset of adolescence she underwent a premature and an accelerated separation process from her parents and formed friendships with primarily older teenagers. Her drug use became intertwined with her separation process and her peer attachments.

For the even more developmentally vulnerable adolescent, the psychological upheaval of early adolescence presents a greater risk for problems with drugs.

> Early adolescent experimentation thus not only imitates adults' regressive drug taking but also the drug abuse of older peers. In those early adolescents in whom the struggle for autonomy is intense, their experimentation usually has a defiant quality, and they may become even more rebellious and destructive. . . . Those who are even more vulnerable probably will move to regular drug abuse. (Miller, 1986, p. 202)

Middle Adolescence

A teenager who experiences a drug problem during early adolescence is likely to enter middle adolescence with some drug-induced developmental deficits that compromise the ensuing psychological work of middle adolescence. Even if an adolescent successfully negotiates the passages of early adolescence, developmental stresses of middle adolescence can pose enough of a psychological threat to place the middle adolescent at high risk for problems with drugs.

Drug use in middle adolescence has much to do with attempts at gaining mastery—mastery over one's inner life and mastery with one's drug habit. As middle adolescence is a period of moving from the chaotic inner states of earlier adolescence to more calmer states, adolescents often experience a budding self-confidence with this growth in self-management. But for those teenagers who frequently experience their feelings, impulses, and sensations as unbearably threatening, self-management through chemical use may seem like a viable solution (Rinsley, 1988). For example, a 16-year-old male, who had previously tried but didn't like alcohol, began to use marijuana regularly. He had a lot of normal anxieties about dating, succeeding at school, competitiveness in athletics, and conflicts about pleasing his parents or "being his own person." This teenager, however, experienced his anxieties as overwhelming. He felt that marijuana sedated his anxieties, and he felt overall more "in control" of his feelings with marijuana. In using chemicals to manage his feelings of anxiety he was bypassing learning appropriate coping skills in his life.

The paradox of chemically-anchored self-management is that this often becomes unmanageable. Affective states become more intolerable as the young person becomes more immersed into drug use, thus prompting the urge for even greater self-management through chemical use.

Late Adolescence

If the late adolescent has not heretofore had any problems with drugs, then she is more likely to be better prepared psychologically for the challenges of this subphase than her substance-involved counterpart. But even if a young person has not experienced chemical use problems prior to late adolescence, she is not yet "out of the woods." Developmental stresses of late adolescence, often understood as an identity crisis, can induce the psychological vulnerability that opens the door for substance abuse problems commencing in late adolescence. For instance, an 18-year-old female, who had previously drunk alcohol on occasion without any significant adverse effects, became increasingly involved with alcohol during the 6 months after graduating from high school. She was feeling lost and confused about her future plans—whether to continue working, go to vocational school or college, or enter military service. In addition, she felt very alone, as most of her friends were already acting on their plans for the future. Compounding her circumstances was a sense of obligation to take care of her recently divorced father, who himself was manifesting signs of a drinking problem. This adolescent became more reliant on alcohol as a way of dealing with the many stresses during this passage in her development.

DEVELOPMENTAL CRISES OF ADOLESCENT PSYCHOLOGICAL DEVELOPMENT

Developmental crises are concomitant with the psychological changes during the adolescent years. Developmental crises seem to be strongly associated with adolescent drug problems.

> There are a number of reasons to suggest that a state of stress or crisis precedes the significant period of involvement with a substance. . . . A great deal has been written about the adolescent drug user, and indeed adolescence appears to be a period of special vulnerability for drug use for all the reasons that it marks a developmental crisis at the same time that opportunities for drugs present themselves. (Treece & Khantzian, 1986, pp. 406-407)

A developmental crisis in this context shall be defined as the adolescent's psychological functioning when emotional states are experienced as overwhelming or threatening. Such a crisis may be more endemic to the young person's psychological make up, or may be triggered by either a family crisis, a peer crisis, or both (see Chapter 5).

Adolescent developmental crises can be conceptualized in a number of ways, but the discussion here will center on three specific developmental crises: separation, narcissistic crisis, and identity crisis. All three of these crises are experienced to some extent by all teenagers. They seem to be more acute and complicated in those teenagers who develop substance abuse problems. In addition, this relationship between adolescent developmental crisis and substance abuse is more circular than linear. As an adolescent becomes more reliant on chemicals to manage the crisis precipitated by a subjective sense of inner distress, this very reliance on chemicals further diminishes the adolescent's capacity to develop coping abilities to deal with this crisis. This creates an even deeper experience of distress and failure, including an intensified crisis, and fosters a stronger reliance on chemicals to manage the ongoing crisis.

Separation Crisis

A separation crisis is the young person's experiencing of the natural mourning process over detaching from parents and parental figures. Intrapsychic reorganization accompanies this detachment process. Other losses experienced during adolescence—such as a break-up with a boyfriend or girlfriend—can replicate this primary detachment and also initiate a separation crisis. Feelings of sadness and anxiety predominate during this crisis.

Adolescents whose substance abuse grows out of a separation crisis are circumventing the normal mourning process. Their substance abuse is a defense against the anxiety and sadness stemming from the separation (Greenspan, 1977). As Weidman (1983) points out,

> Adolescent substance abusers have never fully achieved independence and separation from their parents with whom they are still in a dependent and fused relationship. There is little differentiation of adolescent and parent egos. Substance abuse becomes a play at separation—a pseudo-separation. (p. 48)

Narcissistic Crisis

A narcissistic crisis is a "sudden plummeting of self-esteem" related to some kind of disappointment, real or imagined, over one's expectations of one's self (Wurmser, 1977, p. 44). Feelings of shame are at the heart of an adolescent's narcissistic crisis.

With deflated self-esteem a young person can be at greater risk to become involved with drugs. Drugs may provide a sense of inflated, although false, self-esteem to the acutely wounded self of the teenager. For example, one 13-year-old girl was experiencing a particularly severe emotional upheaval during her early adolescence and was extremely sensitive to any message from family members or friends that seemed the slightest bit critical. She was very self-blameful about her fluctuating feeling states and protected her experience of being emotionally wounded by externalizing her attention away from herself and onto others. One way in which this externalizing was manifest was through her argumentative pattern with others. She experienced responses to her arguing, especially from her parents, as belittling and consequently internalized an even deeper sense of shame. Her eventual involvement with drugs and a drug-abusing lifestyle soothed, albeit artificially and with adverse consequences, her relentless sense of being "wounded and defective."

Identity Crisis

Adolescents who experience a profound lack of direction in their lives, often coupled with the sense that life is passing them by, may be in the midst of an identity crisis. Among the signs of an adolescent identity crisis are the young person's perception that peers are moving on with their lives while he or she remains mired in confusion, beset by feelings of being paralyzed by indecision, and the sense that independent choice is more despairing than liberating (Lidz, 1983). A young person in this crisis must grapple with depression, anxiety, and a profound sense of loneliness.

Older adolescents seem particularly vulnerable to an identity crisis and to the maladaptive choice of chemicals as a means of coping with this crisis (Page & Cole, 1991). As Miller (1973) states, "Adolescents who are in an acute identity crisis become introduced to drugs and may deteriorate because of the drugs rather than because of their fundamental emotional instability" (p. 87).

IMPAIRED DEVELOPMENT AND ADOLESCENT PSYCHOLOGICAL DEVELOPMENT

Impaired psychological development during adolescence can be another collection of factors contributing to psychological vulnerability and a subsequent greater risk for substance abuse. This impaired development can be thought of as resulting from early childhood developmental deficits that become compounded in adolescence, or adolescent psychological development that becomes complicated due to the stresses of the teenage passage.

These developmentally impaired adolescents are at a high risk for a number of maladaptive behaviors, including problems with drugs. According to Wieder and Kaplan (1969), "The individuals who either start drugs in early adolescence or who perpetuate conflict resolution with them have already manifested greater regressive disorganization in the course of the adolescent process because of structural deficits originating in early childhood" (p. 351).

Although impaired development can be categorized in many different ways, three particular populations of adolescents with impaired psychological development are discussed here: adolescents with psychological disorders, adolescents who are victims or physical or sexual abuse, and adolescents who are children of substance-abusing parents. Substance abuse treatment considerations with these three vulnerable populations are covered in Chapter 11.

Adolescents With Psychological Disorders

Teenagers with psychological disorders can be susceptible to the effects of self-administered chemicals. Gregorius and Smith (1991) suggest that "sensitive dependence" is the common trait among psychologically disordered adolescents who also have a drug problem.

Sensitive dependence in adolescence is the vulnerability of adolescents to extreme feelings and to labile behavior—instability and turbulence is produced by fluctuations in one or another environment in which development proceeds—physiological, psychological, and interpersonal. In effect, small fluctuations get amplified out of proportion to their size, as they are transmitted from one system to another. (Gregorius & Smith, 1991, p. 85).

Problems in adolescent development that become exacerbated by sensitive dependence can induce painful affective states. These can lead the teenager to seek relief from this pain through self-medication.

The relationship between adolescent psychopathology and substance abuse, however, is not a simple one of cause and effect. There is a chicken-or-the-egg quality to the etiology of dual disorders. Meyer (1986) has suggested some possible correlations between psychological disorders and substance abuse:

- Psychological disorders as a risk factor for developing substance abuse
- Psychological disorders altering the course of substance abuse
- Psychological symptoms may develop as the result of ongoing substance abuse
- Psychological disorders emerging as the result of substance abuse and persist following abstinence

- Psychopathology and substance abuse originating from some common vulnerability
- With some individuals there being no specific relationship between psychopathology and substance abuse

Among the major psychological disorders that teenagers can have are anxiety disorders, mood disorders, eating disorders, personality disorders, and schizophrenia. Diagnostic criteria for these five categories of disorders and corresponding sub-types can be found in the DSM-III-R (American Psychiatric Association, 1987). Each of these particular disorders can have correlations to adolescent substance abuse.

The relationship between adolescent substance abuse and adolescent anxiety disorders is not fully understood, "The existence of anxiety disorders and substance abuse in adolescence has not been carefully studied except for some family studies" (Gregorius & Smith, 1991, p. 91). However, in discussing adolescent substance abusers with anxiety disorders, O'Connell (1989) suggests, "These adolescents are very prone to the use of alcohol/sedative medication to offset the often debilitating anxiety and distress they experience" (p. 63).

Currently there is sparse research to clarify the interactive relationship between adolescent depression and chemical use (Joshi and Scott, 1988). Famularo, Stone, and Popper (1985) suggest some correlation between early-onset alcohol abuse and the development of major affective disorders in adolescence.

The link between adolescent eating disorders, both anorexia nervosa and bulimia, and substance abuse has not yet received much attention from researchers (Stolberg and DeValve, 1991). There are some commonalities between substance abuse and eating disorders in that, "In general, the substance, whether food or other substances, is said to be used to repress feelings, block emotional pain, and fill the feelings of emptiness" (Stolberg & DeValve, 1991, p. 58).

The relationship between adolescents with personality disorders and substance abuse has undergone some clinical investigation. In particular, substance-abusing adolescents with borderline personality disorders have been hypothesized to use chemicals to self-medicate and regulate the volatile feelings—intense anger, overwhelming boredom, and emptiness—that are intrinsic to this disorder (Gregorius & Smith, 1991; Masterson & Strodbleck, 1972).

A correlation between substance abuse and schizophrenia is that adolescents with schizophrenia have likely used chemicals to "hold in abeyance the more ominously regressive fragmentation of the self that would otherwise bring them face to face with frank psychosis" (Rinsley, 1988, p. 5). However, such self-medicating is truly a "double-edged sword," as chemical efforts to fend off regressive thought processes can indeed induce such regressed thought processes.

A disruption of the thinking process can be produced by many substances of abuse including marijuana, amphetamines, and the hallucinogens. Symptoms of a drug-induced thought disorder can be indistinguishable from those caused by primary schizophrenic illness. A drug-induced thought disorder may be superimposed on a preexisting schizophrenic syndrome or may produce a persistent defect in the thinking process. (Easson, 1979, p. 474)

All in all, psychopathology and chemical abuse is a combustible combination for the adolescent's psychological development. There does seem to be some relationship between specific psychological disorders and adolescent substance abuse. Further research is needed to more fully understand the complexity of these correlations.

Adolescents Who Are Victims of Physical or Sexual Abuse

Adolescents who are victims of physical or sexual abuse—either occurring in earlier childhood, beginning in adolescence, or continuing from early childhood through adolescence—are also at great risk for suffering psychological impairments. The impairments from being physically or sexually abused may increase the likelihood of the young person becoming involved with drugs (Dembo, Williams, Wish, Dertke, Berry, Getreu, Washburn, & Schmeidler, 1988).

Physically traumatized adolescents are victims of physical aggression that contributes to an impaired sense of self. The sense of degradation and low self-worth stemming from the victimization can be a determinant in the teenager's involvement with drugs (Schiff and Cavaiola, 1989).

This is illustrated by the case of a male adolescent who had been physically abused by his father since the age of 3. The chronic physical abuse while he was growing up contributed to his core experience of being a "damaged person." Even though he was physically abused by his father, his identity as a male became patterned after his father, and violent behavior grew to become a primary way for him to handle his

anger toward others. When he began drinking alcohol during his adolescence, alcohol use became intertwined with his violent outbursts. His
drinking both decreased his ability to control his anger and chemically
bolstered his deeper sense of low self-worth.

Adolescents who are victims of sexual abuse represent a continuum
of possible trauma. They may be survivors of childhood sexual abuse,
adolescent victims of sexual abuse, or both (Everstine & Everstine,
1989). Among the psychological reverberations for young victims of
sexual trauma are a deep sense of shame and evolving dissociative
phenomena, which can be contributing factors in the development of a
chemical abuse problem with sexually traumatized adolescents.

The psychological echoes from childhood trauma can include painful
affective states combined with a diminished capacity for managing
these threatening feelings. This can overtax the tenuous sense of self of
the victimized adolescent. Chemicals can serve to soothe the painful
feeling states for these teenagers while offering the illusion of solidifying one's sense of self.

Children of Substance-Abusing Parents

Families with substance-abusing parents are one type of dysfunctional family environment. Children who grow up in a chemically
dependent family can experience both environmental and developmental vulnerability, with the latter manifest as the *children of substance
abusing parents* (COSAP) syndrome (Rivinus, 1991a).

> By the time puberty and adolescence arrive, the COSAP may have little
> internalized sense of self, considerable practice in a pathological role
> vis-à-vis family and social systems, little sense of trust in the predict-
> ability of anything but traumatic or psychologically upsetting circum-
> stances, a well-developed idea that he or she is in fact the cause of those
> events, and a behavioral style that tends to reinforce this hypothesis.
> (Levoy, Rivinus, Matzko, & McGuire, 1991, p. 157)

One common manifestation of the COSAP syndrome is the role—
hero, scapegoat, lost child, or mascot—that a child might play in such
a family (Wegscheider, 1981). The hero is the role of the parentified or
high achieving child, being the primary focus of concentrated blame
within the family is the scapegoat role, functioning in a withdrawn or
alienated manner is the lost child role, and the mascot is the role of
distracting the family from primary concerns. Operating in any of these

roles serves as a protection for the COSAP. Although such a role can serve an adaptive function with a child for a while, often it exacts a psychological price later in the child's development.

The overall intrapsychic stress experienced by COSAPs can eventually catch up with them, weakening their psychological resolve for coping, and resulting in their falling into a number of problem behaviors. Following in the footsteps of their substance-abusing parent is but one problematic route taken by some COSAPs.

SUMMARY

Adolescence is a period of many psychological changes. A variety of factors that might affect the rate of change, the quality of change, and the young person's overall adaptiveness to this change were discussed in this chapter. These factors include the major changes of adolescence, the subphases of adolescent psychological development, developmental crises of adolescent psychological development, and impaired development and adolescent psychological development.

The psychological changes undergone during this time of life—personality reorganization, fresh and intense affective states, and an enlarged sense of self—can bring both growth and stress. The stress may be overwhelming to some teenagers, disrupting their psychological stability, and leaving them prone to maladaptive behaviors—including substance abuse.

Substance abuse often leads to regression in development and intrapsychic fragmentation of the adolescent. However, the adolescent substance abuser's psychological damage need not be irreversible.

The crux of treatment with substance-abusing adolescents is reparative developmental work. For a teenager to be in substance abuse recovery amounts to being actively engaged in reapproaching the tasks of adolescence. This is done not through relying on chemicals but through developing their own internal resources and through their interdependence with others. Recovery is pursuing a path of chemically free authentic development, not chemically drenched pseudo-development. The path of recovery for the adolescent is the subject of Chapter 9.

Chapter 5

FAMILY AND PEER RELATIONSHIP FACTORS
The Adolescent's Interpersonal Environment

INTRODUCTION

The adolescent's interpersonal environment is the "holding environment" (Winnicott, 1965) for her psychological development. Holding environment in this context shall be thought of as the clusters of overlapping relationships that provide emotional safety and support for nurturing healthy psychological development.

The adolescent's holding environment can be thought of as having two parts: her family and her peer relationships. Family and friends serve as both a context for the teenager's psychological changes and are co-participants in change during this time of life.

As a context within which change happens, the adolescent's family and peer relationships interact with each other, "The family system and the peer system are seen as operating synergistically during adolescence" (Botvin & Tortu, 1988, p. 255). The teenager's family and peer relationships can interact in four different ways in relation to chemical use: (a) both family and friends can collaborate to co-protect the teenager from developing a problem with drugs, (b) both family and friends can combine to co-influence a teenager's drug use (they can both serve as precipitating and perpetuating environments for the teenager's drug use), (c) the family may conflict with the teenager's peers and attempt to act as a buffer against peers' influence towards drug involvement, or (d) peers may conflict with the family and try to be a buffer against the family's influence toward drug invovement.

As co-participants in change, both the adolescent's family and peers are undergoing changes of their own during this period of life. Families have their own life cycles and the adolescent phase of this life cycle is rife with shifts in family dynamics. Friends are co-journeyers with the adolescent on the path of change-filled intrapsychic development.

Family functioning and peer relationships are the immediate social environment in the biopsychosocial model of adolescent substance abuse discussed in this book. These two factors in the triad of primary factors in this model are discussed separately in this chapter.

FAMILY FACTORS WITH ADOLESCENT SUBSTANCE ABUSE

Overview

The family is the primary holding environment for supporting the adolescent's development. When a family is functioning as an adequate holding environment, the teenager will experience the continuous safety and support of a firm but flexible family environment, encouragement for appropriate expression of a wide range of feelings, and a clear sense of proactively dealing with issues that arise in family life. As Barnes and Windle (1987) note, "A high degree of parental nurturance along with low coercive punishment and clear expectations for adolescent behavior appear to be salient factors for the prevention of alcohol and drug abuse, and other deviant behaviors in adolescence" (p. 17).

If a family becomes overwhelmed by stress from forces outside or inside the family, it runs the risk of functioning as a less-than-adequate holding environment for the adolescent's developmental needs. Such a predicament might adversely impact the young person's ability to sustain adaptive emotional growth. Ensuing maladaptive behavior could be manifest in a number of ways, including drug abuse. It is through the incapacitation of the holding environment that a family might serve as a precipitating environment for a young person's drug problems.

A family becomes a perpetuating environment for a child's substance abuse through its denial of the problem and its enabling behavior. Enabling is essentially the unwitting collusion by significant others of the drug abuser's ongoing use of chemicals. Four types of family enabling of adolescent substance abuse are identified here: (a) uninformed and unaware enabling, (b) aware and avoidant enabling, (c) aware and disempowered enabling, and (d) aware and indulgent enabling. Uninformed and unaware enabling occurs, for the most part, during the initial stages of adolescent chemical use. The other three types of family enabling usually take place in the more advanced stages of adolescent chemical use when the drug-using behavior becomes known by family members.

Uninformed and unaware enabling can happen when parents are either unaware of or, at most, only mildly suspicious of their child's use of chemicals. This is usually due to the teenager's subterfuge in concealing the chemical use from parents.

Aware and avoidant enabling can take place when parents have concrete evidence of their child's chemical use but choose not to intervene. Among the reasons for the parents' nonintervention is their rationalizing the chemical use as an adolescent rite-of-passage that will be outgrown or their benign ignorance about possible problems that chemical use can pose for their child.

Aware and disempowered enabling can operate in families when parents attempt to intervene with their child's chemical use but their actions prove insufficient and ultimately unsuccessful. Some possible explanations for this type of enabling include "split" parental teamwork or inconsistent half-measures undertaken by parents to address their child's drug problem. Aware and disempowered parents often feel trapped on a treadmill of powerlessness with being unsuccessful at influencing the containment of their child's drug use.

Aware and indulgent enabling occurs when parents knowingly promote ongoing chemical use by their child. These parents may both supply their child with drugs as well as use drugs with their child.

Both this ongoing perpetuating environment for substance abuse and the original precipitating environment can be catalyzed through overwhelming family stress from different family factors. The sets of family factors that will be the focus here are: (a) family life factors, (b) family dynamics as a factor, (c) family crisis as a factor, and (d) the dysfunctional family—specifically families with substance-abusing parents—as a factor.

Before examining the four sets of family factors as they correlate with adolescent substance abuse, it is important to note the circular relationship between family functioning and adolescent substance abuse.

Adolescent substance abuse can indeed be an outgrowth of an inadequate family holding environment. At the same time a family's deteriorating holding environment can be the result of its capacity to cope with the teenager's drug problem becoming overwhelmed.

Family Life Factors and Adolescent Substance Abuse

Family life factors are those conditions of living that are a part of every family (Preto and Travis, 1985). Six family life factors are delineated here: (a) change in family structure, (b) family composition, (c) geography, (d) ethnicity, (e) socioeconomic status and (f) the family in the postmodern age.

What is significant about these family life factors in regard to adolescent substance abuse is the understanding that a family can experience debilitating stress resulting from many of these factors. Stress that cripples the family's holding environment, so vital to the teenager's emotional growth, can serve as a precipitant to an adolescent's substance abuse. In addition, a weakened family holding environment is at great risk of also becoming a perpetuating environment for this substance abuse.

Changes in Family Structure

Change is a fact of life throughout the life cycle of a family. There are the anticipated changes in family structure, such as the birth of a child or a child going away to college, and the new demands presented by these changes. There are also the unanticipated changes in structure, such as those that result from death, separation, divorce, or remarriage.

How well a family can grieve the losses and make the adjustments brought on by a changed family structure will go a long way toward it serving as a solid holding environment for the young person's emotional needs. Complication in the family's mourning and resolution processes can overwhelm the family's supportive capacity, rendering it a precipitating environment for substance abuse. The adolescent becoming a substance-abusing symptom bearer of the family grief represents how a family can become a perpetuating environment for substance abuse (Schiff & Cavaiola, 1989).

Family Composition

"The number of children in a family, their ages, and their rank are variables that influence the way in which families manage adolescence"

1985, p. 33). The overall management of these family
. ariables is one indication of a family's capacity to be an
⏤quate enough holding environment during the teenage years.
One way in which family composition might be a factor with an
adolescent's drug abuse is the role of siblings. In particular, older siblings
who use drugs seem to be a strong influence on younger siblings' chemical
use (Johnson & Pandina, 1991; Needle, McCubbin, Wilson, Reineck,
Lazar, & Mederer, 1986).

Geography

American families reside in rural, urban, and suburban communities.
A family's external boundary with its community is its lifeline for both
bringing in necessary nourishment for the family and keeping out unwanted contaminants to the family.

A family's congruence with its surrounding community depends in
part on a meshing of the needs of the family with the needs of the
community. This congruence varies for families throughout rural, urban, and suburban locales.

When a family's external boundary with its community is too rigid,
it runs the risk of being isolated from its community. This can prove
troublesome if the family's ability to deal with problems—such as a
child's drug problem—becomes incapacitated by the struggle and the
family is cut off from available help within the community.

If a family's external boundary is too diffuse it may become en-
meshed with its community. This can prove problematic when toxic
activity in the surrounding community—such as rampant drug use—ex-
erts a magnetic pull on young members from families with such diffuse
external boundaries.

Ethnicity

Ethnicity can exert an influence on adolescent drug involvement
through either contributing to a family being a precipitating environment or a perpetuating environment for the drug involvement. A family's ethnicity can contribute to overwhelming stress during adolescence in one of two ways: (a) through its rituals and customs being
undermined by the mainstream culture or (b) through ethnic minority
families experiencing rejection from the mainstream culture. Either
circumstance can lead to a family enduring extraordinary additional
pressure during the adolescent years, its holding environment weaken-

ing from this pressure, and conditions being present for precipitating a young person's involvement with chemicals.

Each ethnic group has its own values and attitudes about substance use and abuse, and this in turn affects family attitudes toward adolescent substance use and abuse (Kaufman & Borders, 1988). The extent to which these attitudes and values may play a part in enabling adolescent substance varies among different ethnic groups.

Socioeconomic Status

A family's socioeconomic status can influence its navigation of the adolescent passage. The absence of or abundance of financial and material resources in the family can have a part in how it copes with the teenage years.

Families in poverty are contending with the stresses of unemployment or underemployment, inadequate housing, limited or nonexistent health care, and other financial burdens. Dire living conditions can contribute to family members' sense of hopelessness, alienation, and powerlessness, and render them more vulnerable to substance abuse (Griswold-Ezekoye, 1986).

Families from higher socioeconomic groups may also experience a functional vulnerability due to their circumstances. Skagen and Fisher (1989) identify one way this might happen with some middle and upper middle class adolescents—the existential/boredom hypothesis. According to this hypothesis, "Life for young people growing up in affluent families is often barren in the sense that meaningful responsibilities and accomplishments are often lacking" (p. 137). Thus the young person's sense of identity becomes impinged upon, and chemical use becomes one desirable option of such "unstable identities." (Skagen & Fisher, 1989, p. 137).

Postmodern Age

The age in which we live dramatically affects families and the way they raise teenagers. The postmodern era has witnessed the deconstruction of the nuclear family, the age of the working mother, and the change from viewing adolescents as "immature" in favor of viewing them as "sophisticated" (Elkind, 1991).

The postmodern age presents greater challenges to families, especially during the adolescent years. Some families can cope with these challenges and thrive, while other families are not as fortunate and succumb to the pressures of the postmodern world.

By now, we are all too familiar with the vast social changes that followed World War II—the decline of the traditional family and rising rates of divorce, dual-career marriages, step families, increase in runaways, use of drugs and alcohol, confusion about male and female roles, about the meaning of family. But what we have yet to recognize is how these social changes have transformed the experience of growing up. (Hersch, 1990, pp. 22-23)

Family Dynamics and Adolescent Substance Abuse

Family dynamics interact to create the process that is a family's functioning. Fleck (1980) has offered a particularly orderly model for comprehending family dynamics. Adapted from Fleck's (1980) model, five major family dynamics are identified here. These dynamics are: (a) leadership, (b) family boundaries, (c) affectivity, (d) communication and (e) task/goal performance.

If a family experiences a breakdown in one or more of these dynamics then it is likely experiencing a weakening of its holding environment, which is essential to nurturing the emotional growth of the children. With families of adolescent substance abusers there is often a significant collapsing of family dynamics in such a way as to become organized around enabling the substance abuse.

Leadership

Parents demonstrate leadership in a family by delineating a clear hierarchy that models firmness and empathy. Leadership provides the family with a feeling of safety and stability.

Among the breakdowns in family leadership that correlates with adolescent substance abuse are when parents act either overauthoritative or too laissez-faire (Barnes, Farrell, & Cairns, 1986; Jurich, Polson, Jurich, & Bates, 1985) or when parents are "split," with one parent being overcontrolling and the other being undercontrolling. Ongoing, inconsistent limit setting and structuring by parents can be a factor in their child's ongoing drug problem (Reilly, 1978; Vicary & Lerner, 1986).

Boundaries

A family's boundaries are its emotional walls and doors. Boundary making establishes clear and appropriate differentiation between family members, between generations, and between the family and the outside world. When a family strikes a balance between the extremes of enmeshment and disengagement, its boundaries are optionally permeable and a cohesive holding environment exists for the children.

Breakdowns in family boundaries that can be particularly significant for adolescents include intergenerational boundaries, in which one parent is underinvolved with the child and draws a rigid boundary, while the other parent is overinvolved and has a diffuse boundary with the child. This dynamic results in a cross-generational split in the family, a pattern common when there is a substance-abusing adolescent.

> Whenever there is an acting-out adolescent, and especially where alcohol or drugs are involved, we may assume an exaggerated and unhealthy parent-child coalition, a divided marital relationship, resulting in secrets within the family as well as one or more siblings being "left out." (Huberty & Huberty, 1984, p. 133)

One way in which this cross-generational boundary split can perpetuate adolescent substance abuse is through the maintenance of a family triangle around the substance abuse. Steiner (1971) adapted the work of Karpman (1968) to explain how triangles can operate in a family with an alcoholic adult. Schaefer (1987) further adapted this model for application with adolescent substance abusers. In this model the dysfunctional yet operational triangle usually includes an underinvolved parent (the "Persecutor"), an overinvolved parent (the "Rescuer"), and the adolescent (the "Victim") (Karpman, 1968). This triangular dynamic is illustrated in the case of a drug-abusing male adolescent who was operating in the role of victim in his family. His father, who worked long hours and didn't have a close relationship with his son, was in the role of the persecutor as he unilaterally imposed excessive and reactive punishments for his son's drug-involved behavior (school suspension, arrest for disorderly conduct, and disregard for family rules). This adolescent's mother acted as the rescuer; she regularly intervened to "cushion" her husband's strong punishments on their son. By operating in these roles the parents experienced a breakdown in their family leadership. The parents were, in effect, enabling their son's substance use by not allowing him to experience consistent and appropriate consequences for his substance abuse behavior.

Other family members, the adolescents' peers, or extrafamilial professionals involved with the family (i.e., therapists, school personnel, police officers) can also end up functioning in one of these three roles in this family triangle. Roles within this triangle may change for family members. The adolescent may become a persecutor or rescuer, and one of the parents may become the victim. Unless the triangle (or sometimes multiple and overlapping triangles) is effectively interrupted, this triangulation will serve to further enable the teenager's drug abuse. Effectively interrupting a triangle involves parents relinquishing their respective roles within the triangle and assuming a more proactive position about intervening with their child's substance abuse problem.

Affectivity

A family's affectivity is optimal when a broad range of appropriate emotional expression—from affection and nurturance to anger, fear, and shame—is encouraged among family members. This overall sense of emotionality provides an affectively healthy holding environment for the children.

The affectivity in a family breaks down when this range of emotional expression becomes too constricted. This emotional constriction usually operates in one of two ways: (a) The family is consumed by anger, and interactions among family members are laced with hostility and fear; or (b) anger, and affective states associated with rage, are repressed and avoided at all costs in the family. In both cases the family experiences a lack of genuine intimacy, a characteristic common to families with adolescent substance abusers (Wight, 1990).

An emotionally constricted holding environment can contribute to a family's perpetuation of a child's substance abuse (Barnes & Windle, 1987). For example, one family with a 16-year-old, substance-abusing daughter was very avoidant of anger being openly expressed among family members. Conflict between the mother and father was shunned, and disagreements between the parents and children were, for the most part, avoided. The girl's steady acting-out behavior related to her substance abuse did, however, induce strong negative reactions from both her parents and her older sister. One way to look at this girl's substance abuse is that it served as a repository for family members' long-withheld angry feelings.

Communication

The communication within a family is indicative of its quality of expressiveness. Healthy communication habits of clarity, openness, and responsiveness correlate with a fluid holding environment.

A breakdown of communication within a family occurs when communication becomes more closed, unclear, and reactive. The three unspoken communication rules of alcoholic families (Black, 1981)— "don't talk, don't feel, don't trust"—are indicative of such a breakdown in family communication.

Ineffective family communication begets a suffocating holding environment that can precipitate a child's involvement with drugs. Ongoing dysfunctional communication patterns, such as blaming and shaming, can serve to perpetuate an adolescent's problem with drugs. In the case of one 14-year-old boy who was very rebellious and limit-testing towards his parents, his overall pattern of acting-out behavior (including chemical use) was an unconscious invitation for external structure in his life. This boy's parents, who were feeling scared for their son and uncertain how to respond to him, often vacillated between "being strict and being easy" on him. The wavering discipline by his parents resulted in this teenager's continuing to "push" behavioral limits as far as he could by greater defiant behavior, including deeper chemical involvement.

Task/Goal Performance

The task or goal performance in a family is exemplified by its general ability to deal with crises, solve problems, have fun, and plan for the future. This family dynamic illustrates the mutual interdependence of family members for the well-being of the family as a whole.

The family's breakdown in its task and goal performance results in a chaotic and unpredictable holding environment. Problems persist and remain unsolved. Essential ingredients in family life, such as the parents' discipline of children, are often ineffective. Ineffective discipline by parents has been linked to teenage drug problems (Piercy, Volk, Trepper, Sprenkle, & Lewis, 1991). Continued struggles by parents with intervening in their child's drug problem fuels the perpetuating environment for this drug problem.

Family Crisis and Adolescent Substance Abuse

Family crisis is a natural part of a family's growth. A family crisis in this context refers to "a breakdown of the rules that had previously governed family interactions satisfactorily" (Fishman, Stanton, & Rosman, 1982, p. 339). Depending on the overall family dynamics and coping capacity, a family crisis can weaken the family's holding environment and leave it vulnerable to being a precipitating environment for maladaptive behaviors by the children. Substance abuse is among possible maladaptive behaviors. Persistent unresolution of family crises can further weaken the holding environment, resulting in its becoming a perpetuating environment for substance abuse and other maladaptive behaviors by the children.

Three types of family crises and their possible relationships with adolescent substance abuse are considered in this book. These crises are: (a) developmental family crisis, (b) dramatic family crisis, and (c) structural family crisis.

Developmental Family Crisis

Just as adolescence is a period of life in which the adolescent is experiencing changes in and a reorganization of intrapsychic structure, it is also a time when the family is experiencing its own changes and the reorganization of its systemic structure. As Carter and McGoldrick (1980) succinctly point out, "Adolescence is something that happens to a family, not just an individual child" (p. 14).

This shifting of family dynamics, and the accompanying stress it brings to bear on the family, is the crisis of the adolescent phase of the family life cycle. Although this developmental crisis is a normal transition in family life, it can nonetheless create upheaval in the family's functioning. Klimek and Anderson (1988) have discussed developmental stresses of adolescence on parents and five kinds of problematic responses by parents:

- When parents' needs as individuals take precedence over the needs of their adolescent child
- Parents' own resistance to the change and flexibility that adolescence requires of a family
- Parents with unresolved separation issues being projected onto their child during adolescence
- Parents with unresolved issues from their own adolescence who have a shortsighted view of the fluidity of their own adolescent's development
- Parents who take on extremely shallow or narrow views of common everyday problems of adolescence

The weakening of the family's holding environment due to the stress from this developmental crisis can contribute to the family creating a symptom, such as substance abuse, which becomes embodied in one of the children (Fishman, Stanton, & Rosman, 1982). This family symptom of adolescent substance abuse can be further perpetuated by the family becoming mired in the tangles of unresolution with this family developmental crisis.

Dramatic Family Crisis

A dramatic family crisis is the sudden and often cataclysmic altering of family life that results from a significant change or loss. Death, separation, divorce, remarriage, moving to another community, a parent's job loss, and a change in the family's socioeconomic status are among the more common dramatic family crises.

If a family experiencing a family crisis becomes overtaxed in its ability to deal with the crisis, then a weakened holding environment might ensue and precipitate maladaptive behavior, such as substance abuse, by the children. Grieving and mourning are at the heart of a family working through a dramatic family crisis. Adolescent substance abuse can, however, serve to detour a family from its grief work by creating crises through drug-related problems and bringing life to an otherwise "dead" family (Kaufman & Kaufmann, 1979). For instance, one 15-year-old female with a history of marijuana use was also exhibiting signs of depression. The depression symptoms included, but were not limited to, suicidal gesturing. This teenager's parents had divorced 2 years earlier, and she lived with her mother. Both parents were experiencing much unresolved emotional pain from the divorce. One result of this adolescent's overall depressive and drug-influenced functioning was to have her parents remain "emotionally connected" to each other out of concern for their daughter.

Structural Family Crisis

Structural family crises are built-in and longstanding patterns of a family coping with an unresolved chapter in its history. The historical undertow of this structural family crisis may be a variety of troublesome behaviors including parental or grandparental substance abuse, a history of physical or sexual abuse, or a history of behavior that is a family "secret." Often such a structural family crisis becomes activated by new demands and pressures being placed on the family.

In a family where the holding environment seems to be teetering on the brink of decimation, the children are at high risk for problem behavior such as difficulties with drugs. In addition, full-blown problems by the children—such as developing a substance abuse disorder—can become interwoven with the continuing legacy of the dysfunctional family.

Family Dysfunction and Adolescent Substance Abuse

Family functioning can be thought of as falling along a continuum, with optimal family functioning at one end of the continuum and family dysfunction at the other end of the continuum. A dysfunctional family evolves out of some combination of family life stresses, breakdown in family dynamics, and unresolved family developmental crises. When a family is dysfunctional, it ceases to be a viable and growth-sustaining system for its members and is a particularly unsafe and unsupportive holding environment for the children in the family.

Dysfunctional families can be said to have a "chronically traumatizing environment" (Levoy, et al., 1991). This chronically traumatizing environment will eventually deplete the overall safety and support within the family. Such dysfunctional family environments are at high risk of precipitating and perpetuating substance abuse with adolescents. According to Rivinus (1991b),

> Many factors predictive of addiction are largely social and environmental. A traumatic, painful, or disorganized early environment can lead to higher rates of addiction. This does not refer so much to early "ego deficits," as suggested by the early analysts, as to traumatic conditions of various kinds, including the stress of growing up in an environment that itself was alcoholic. (p. 107)

Different Types of Dysfunctional Families

Family dysfunction can be organized around many different family behaviors and conditions. Among the more common family dysfunctions are: the physically abusive family, the sexually abusive family, the emotionally neglectful family, the family with a psychologically disordered parent, and the family with a substance-abusing parent. Sometimes a family can be organized around multiple dysfunctions.

> Many child abusing families are found also to be abusing alcohol. A family member, usually a parent, is frequently found to be suffering from the encroaching disease of alcoholism. In fact, the clinical profiles of the

alcohol abusing families and the child abusing families are remarkably similar. (Flanzer & Sturkie, 1987, p. 1)

Treatment considerations with families of adolescent substance abusers who are also physically or sexually abusive are discussed in Chapter 11. The remainder of this section focuses on families with substance-abusing parents and how this might be a factor in adolescent substance abuse.

Families With Substance-Abusing Parents

Families with substance-abusing parents are one type of dysfunctional family system. As mentioned earlier in this chapter, environmental vulnerability, such as a chemically dependent family, can indeed contribute to maladaptive developmental patterns in the children of the family. Substance abuse is one kind of maladaptive pattern. In short, substance abuse breeds substance abuse.

When a parent has a long-standing drug problem, perhaps dating back to her or his own adolescence, then the family dysfunction likely evolved from the inception of family life. In these early-onset, chemically dependent families there is great risk of an unstable holding environment for the children, especially during the critical early developmental years. When a parent's drug problem develops later into adulthood there is a greater likelihood that the family's holding environment might have provided some stability to the child during the early developmental years. However, this does not preclude the possibility of family stresses due to later-onset parental chemical dependency being experienced by the older child.

Five Types of Chemically Dependent Families. Drawing from Steinglass (1979, 1980) model of alcoholic families, five types of families with substance-abusing parents are identified here. They are: (a) the wet-covert family, (b) the wet-overt family, (c) the dry nonrecovering family, (d) the dry recovering family, and (e) the wet-dry fluctuating family.

Wet-covert families are families in which active parental substance abuse is hidden or is known but unspoken of within the family. Children growing up in this type of family often develop deep mistrust of other people due to an air of suspiciousness within the family.

Active parental substance abuse is openly acknowledged, yet not effectively dealt with, in *wet-overt families.* Children raised in this type of family will often internalize the hostile lifelessness that permeates the emotional climate of this type of family.

Dry nonrecovering families are families in which parental substance abuse is inactive, yet there is little or no resolution of the impact of the parent's substance abuse on the family. Due to the emotional ghosts that seem to lurk in this type of family, children growing up in this type of family often experience family life as a kind of "walking on eggshells."

Dry recovering families are families in which a parent's substance abuse is inactive, and family members are actively working at resolving issues related to the parent's substance abuse. There is often a spirit of openness and support in this type of family. This is essential for the child who needs to address emotional "unfinished business" for the years that his or her parent was drug-involved.

Usually the most chaotic type of chemically dependent family is the *wet-dry fluctuating family*. In these families the substance-abusing parent oscillates between periods of being actively drug-involved and periods of being abstinent. Children growing up in this type of family often experience much anxiety stemming from the overall unpredictability of the family's emotional foundation.

A family can shift from being one type of chemically dependent family to another throughout its developmental life as a family. These shifts may be due to the previously discussed stresses that occur during the family life span, such as family life stresses, breakdowns in family dynamics, and unresolved family crises. A family can also shift from being one type of chemically dependent family to another as the result of intervention and treatment with the substance-abusing parent.

Precipitating Adolescent Substance Abuse. Having a substance-abusing parent in a family presents a great risk of creating a chronically traumatic environment indicative of a dysfunctional family. This kind of environment can cultivate the seeds of substance abuse in children in a couple of ways. One way is by the child developing the children of substance-abusing parent (COSAP) syndrome, discussed in Chapter 4. The child who has this syndrome becomes developmentally vulnerable to maladaptive behaviors, including substance abuse. Another way in which a substance-abusing parent may influence a child to become involved with drugs is through exposing the young person to chemicals. This happens when a parent models chemical use for his or her child (Barnes, Farrell, & Cairns, 1986), when a child strongly identifies with the substance-abusing parent, or when the parent conveys a permissiveness about chemical use. (McDermott, 1984).

Perpetuating Adolescent Substance Abuse. A substance-abusing parent heading a family can also contribute to a family environment that enables and maintains a child's drug problem. Families rendered dysfunctional by parental substance abuse usually do not possess the internal capacity to interrupt a child's substance abuse without external intervention. As is often the case, the child's substance abuse can serve to distract the family from the parental substance abuse.

It is essential that the adolescent's family is a focus of treatment interventions. The young person needs a stable and safe primary holding environment as a foundation for his own recovery. Family life factors, family dynamics, family crises, and family dysfunction can each play a part in a young person's drug problem. Consequently, all of these need to be considered when attempting treatment interventions.

PEER RELATIONSHIP FACTORS
WITH ADOLESCENT SUBSTANCE ABUSE

Overview

The teenager's peer relationships are his "second family." Peers are a transitional or secondary holding environment to the primary holding environment of the family during adolescence. Emotionally fulfilling friendships help adolescents to coinfluence one another with healthy and adaptive psychological development. However, emotionally disruptive peer relationships during adolescence can thwart adaptive psychological development and leave the young person vulnerable to maladaptive coping means, such as drugs.

Peer crisis and substance-abusing peers, two factors that can be influential with an adolescent's substance abuse, are discussed here.

Peer Crisis and Adolescent Substance Abuse

Adolescent peer relationships can be divided into three categories: (a) same sex dyads, such as a "best friend" or "confidante"; (b) opposite sex dyads, such as "boyfriends" or "girlfriends"; and (c) the peer group, for example, one's "clique" or "gang." Within each of these three peer constellations an adolescent both seeks out friends as a resource and is a resource to friends in regard to the developmental tasks of this time of life.

All three categories of peer relationships make up the young person's secondary holding environment during the teenage years. However, certain categories of relationships exert a stronger influence during specific subphases of adolescent development.

Early Adolescent and Peer Relationships

Friendships with members of the same sex predominate during early adolescence. As Schave and Schave (1989) remark:

> Most early adolescents find peers who share certain similarities, including the same sex. Through this sense of similarity, in particular the oneness provided by twinship, peer groups provide the sense of safety from the rest of the world that parents provided earlier. (p. 79)

It is within this context that an adolescent's "best buddy" often emerges.

Middle Adolescence and Peer Relationships

By middle adolescence the teenager's need to fit into adolescent society and further psychologically separate from parents is strong.

> As adolescents move away from their parents, the adolescent peer group grows in importance. The peer group changes into a youth group that carries the youth culture, and differs from childhood peer groups in having somewhat of an anti-adult orientation and in becoming heterosexual. Thus it is not usually a "counterculture" but rather an age-appropriate subculture. (Lidz, 1983, p. 342)

Also during middle adolescence same sex friendships become more like "true friendships" rather than the symbiotic union of early adolescence. In addition, opposite sex relationships grow in importance. Dating, "first love" experiences, sexual experimenting, and establishing more mature and intimate attachments characterize opposite sex relationships during middle adolescence.

Late Adolescence and Peer Relationships

The couple is the predominant peer relationship of the late adolescent. Partnering corresponds with the late adolescent's psychological tasks of enhancing the capacity for intimacy and forming a fuller identity.

The peer group is the identity cohort of young adulthood. Interests, tastes, career plans, leisure activities, and political and religious convictions become more defined with the late adolescent's peer group. Same sex friends are comrades within this identity cohort.

Peer Crisis

Difficulties in any of these three constellations of adolescent peer relationships—same sex dyads, opposite sex dyads, or the peer group—can be emotionally painful experiences. These difficulties, or peer crises, interfere with a teenager's need to belong or make friends. Such peer crises can trigger any of the developmental crises (separation crisis, narcissistic crisis, or identity crisis) of adolescence.

Peer crisis, described as "peer shock" by Elkind (1984), can be broken down into three types of crisis. They are: (a) the shock of exclusion, (b) the shock of betrayal, and (c) the shock of disillusionment. The shock of exclusion—most commonly occurring within peer groups—happens when a group's cliquishness prevents a teenager from being a member of the group. A group may also display ostracizing and scapegoating behavior toward the teenager. The shock of betrayal usually takes place in a same sex dyad when a friendship is ruptured due to one adolescent exploiting another. The shock of disillusionment most often occurs in an opposite sex dyad through the breakup of a romantic relationship. Such breakups can be among the most painful emotional wounds of one's adolescent years.

Each of these three types of peer crisis can influence an adolescent's drug-involvement in at least two ways. One way is when the adolescent who has chemically using peers chooses to use chemicals in order to avoid experiencing any form of peer crisis. A second way is when an adolescent whose peers are not chemical users experiences peer shock and subsequently discovers a kind of emotional asylum among chemically involved teenagers. Peers can be a factor in a young person's drug use more from a standpoint of "peer acceptance" rather than from "peer pressure." This peer acceptance can be a very subtle process whereby the adolescent's need to belong makes the young person very vulnerable to cues to conform with peers.

Many adolescents, and this is particularly true of younger adolescents, will go to great lengths to avert the suffering that results from peer rejection.

This extreme sensitivity and vulnerability to shame and humiliation by peers is handled in a number of ways. Most early adolescents find peers who share certain similarities, including the same sex. Similarity between peers can also include the creation of a uniform or dress code as well as rules for greetings, what games can be played, or what topics can be discussed. A "language" is created by these peer groups with all the special idiosyncratic sayings that function to replace the protective umbrella previously provided by parents. (Schave & Schave, 1989, p. 79)

For some adolescents the price they pay for maintaining membership in their peer group and sustaining their peer relationships is participation in shared group activities, such as drug use. This "peer cluster" can be a strong influence in their initial and ongoing use of chemicals (Oetting & Beauvais, 1986). For example, one teenage girl with very strong ties to her peer group since junior high school was introduced to drinking, and eventually to marijuana and cocaine use, through her group of friends. Within this peer group there were unspoken rules for inclusion, and chemical use was one of the ties that bound this group together. Although she was experiencing much ambivalence about her progressive chemical use, this girl was fearful of dissenting from the group norm around chemical use. She was afraid of risking rejection, however real or imagined, by being different from her friends.

For other adolescents the pain of rejection by nonchemical-using peers can be devastating. In summarizing the work of Newcomb, Bentler, & Collins (1986), Walfish, Massey and Krone (1990) state that, "Adolescents may choose to belong to a crowd of other substance abusers in order to relieve feelings of rejection. Once involved with this 'deviant' peer group, feelings of alienation and isolation may decrease within this population" (p. 6).

One teenage boy who spent his younger childhood years on the periphery of groups of friends transcended this loneliness during adolescence by associating with some chemical-using peers. As this boy entered adolescence, he experienced much ostracism and scapegoating for being isolated from the mainstream teenage culture in his community. He felt considerable shame for being socially stigmatized. His need to "fit in" was fulfilled, although at a steep price, through his gradual attachment to a small group of similarly socially marginal peers. These peers were substance users and this teenager followed along. Although he was compromising his own development and ability to develop greater social competence, this adolescent felt a kind of protection from further social rejection in this insulated world of drug-abusing companions.

Substance-Abusing Peers and
Adolescent Substance Abuse

The substance-abusing peer group is a dysfunctional peer group that offers the adolescent a collection of mostly dysfunctional peer relationships. The substance-abusing peer group becomes the primary, although psychologically inadequate, holding environment for the adolescent substance abuser. The family's influence has been overrun by the influence of the adolescent's chemically dependent peers.

Instead of peers being coworkers in the tasks of adolescent psychological development, peers are co-enablers in the downward spiral of substance abuse and the ensuing developmental impairments. Due to their own developmental impairments, substance-abusing peers cannot share the sincere honesty, true emotional connection, necessary empathy, and sense of genuine fun that is essential for healthy adolescent psychological development.

Relationships among substance-abusing friends are generally emotionally empty. Sexual relationships among substance-abusing friends can be highly exploitive. These relationships make no growth-promoting emotional demands on the teenager. The adolescent's true hunger for external emotional resources of realness and support remains unsatiated, and this need becomes fed by the emptiness of drugs.

The substance-abusing peer group is a subculture of the larger adolescent subculture. It exists in the margins of adolescent society, and the alienation these teenagers experience as a group from this society mirrors the deep isolation from other people that the adolescent substance abuser experiences.

The substance-abusing peer group and all the relationships within this peer group serve as a perpetuating environment for the teenager's drug use. Friends reinforce one another's drug habit through encouraging each other's continued drug use, fostering each other's denial of a drug problem, and solidifying drug use as a primary social activity (Shilts, 1991).

Peer relationships need to be a focus of treatment interventions. The recovering adolescent needs the benefit of sober and supportive friends in order to continue on a healthy path of growth.

SUMMARY

Change is a natural state of affairs during adolescence. Just as the adolescent experiences myriad changes that impact on psychological development, so the interpersonal environment within which these changes occur is also undergoing a metamorphosis. One part of this interpersonal environment—the teenager's family— is not only the primary holding environment for the adolescent's psychological development but also experiences its own shift of dynamics during this phase of life. If this holding environment becomes overstressed and cannot adequately promote the adolescent's psychological growth, the adolescent may develop maladaptive means of coping—including substance abuse.

The other part of this interpersonal environment, the teenager's peer relationships, comprises the secondary holding environment for the young person's psychological development. Within these peer relationships the adolescent has friends who are also experiencing the transformation of the teenage years. Should peer relationships be more emotionally disruptive than emotionally fulfilling, the adolescent becomes more prone to activities that cultivate peer acceptance. Chemical use may be one such activity.

Adolescents in substance abuse recovery need to attend to reparative developmental work. Essential in their repertoire of recovery needs is that their interpersonal environment also be in recovery. This reparative environmental work, including both family recovery and peer relationships in recovery, is the subject of Chapter 10. If the adolescent's family and friends can be coparticipants in the creation of his or her drug problem, then they can also be coparticipants in the promotion of his or her recovery.

Part III

A BIOPSYCHOSOCIAL MODEL FOR TREATING ADOLESCENT SUBSTANCE ABUSE

Chapter 6

ESSENTIAL CONNECTIONS FOR TREATING ADOLESCENT SUBSTANCE ABUSE
A Biopsychosocial Approach

INTRODUCTION

The biopsychosocial model for understanding adolescent substance abuse discussed in this book (Chapter 3) involves multiple and interacting etiological factors. This book's biopsychosocial model for recovery-oriented treatment with adolescent substance abusers entails both multiple and interacting systems to be treated as well as multiple and interacting treatment interventions. In short, possible factors that contribute to this problem can become possible systems for the treatment solution.

The biopsychosocial model for understanding adolescent substance abuse encompasses five levels of causative factors. The biopsychosocial model of recovery-oriented treatment contains five levels of systems involved in the teenager's recovery. These systems are: the biological system and physical recovery, the psychological system of the adolescent's individual recovery, the recovery environment (both family and peer relationships), promoting recovery at the community level, and promoting recovery at the societal level (Figure 6.1). In addition, the treatment agents in this model—servicing interventions (assessment and treatment planning) and therapeutic interventions (therapists's use

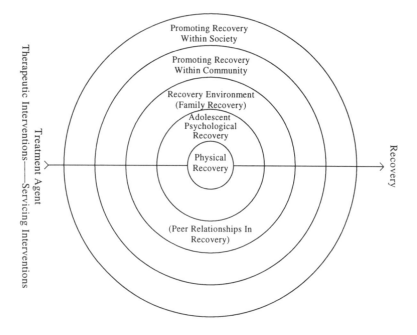

Figure 6.1. Biopsychosocial Model of Adolescent Substance Abuse Treatment

of self, therapeutic relationship, therapeutic modalities, and therapeutic elements of 12-step recovery)—ripple through all five levels of systems to influence the adolescent's recovery. The adolescent's recovery will, in turn, resonate through all five levels of systems involved in the teenager's recovery (Figure 6.1).

While this model of recovery-oriented treatment with adolescents presents a broad range of systems contributing to recovery, the emphasis in this model is on the triad of primary recovering systems—the adolescent's psychological recovery, family recovery, and peer relationships in recovery. Within this triad, adolescent psychological development in recovery is the preeminent recovering system. Biomedical interventions and physical recovery, while significant throughout the course of the adolescent's treatment, are most of the time more ancillary to this triad of primary recovering systems. The macrosocial systems in this model, the community and the larger society, influence the provisions of treatment services, rather than being systems for treatment intervention.

THE TREATMENT AGENTS:
SERVICING AND THERAPEUTIC INTERVENTIONS

As the biopsychosocial model for understanding adolescent substance abuse has a toxic agent, psychoactive substances, that activates drug abuse, so the biopsychosocial model of recovery-oriented treatment has treatment agents. The treatment agents are the combinations of servicing and therapeutic interventions that interrupt drug abuse and facilitate the young person's recovery. There is much overlap between these servicing and therapeutic interventions, but for the sake of clearer discussion they are addressed separately in this book.

Servicing Interventions

Helping adolescent substance abusers and their families flows out of the complementary processes of assessment and treatment planning along a continuum of care. These complementary processes are elaborated on in Chapter 7 (assessment) and Chapter 8 (treatment planning). As these two chapters are devoted to servicing interventions, the remainder of this section on the treatment agents concentrates on therapeutic interventions.

Therapeutic Interventions

Therapy is both an art and a science. The art of therapy with adolescent substance abusers is in both discerning the human rhythms of the therapeutic encounter, which includes the therapist, the adolescent (or family, or group), and the relational process between them, and cocreating—through these human rhythms—therapeutic encounters of healing and growth. The science of therapy with adolescent substance abusers includes building a therapeutic structure in which therapeutic encounters can flourish. Therapeutic structure-building in this context draws from the self of the therapist, the therapeutic relationship, the modality of therapy, and the therapeutic elements of 12-step recovery.

Before discussing the components of therapeutic structure, there are some general considerations about the art and science of therapeutic interventions with adolescent substance abusers that are important to mention. One consideration is that there are certain variables about the adolescent that should temper the tone of the intervention. These variables include: the developmental subphase of the teenager; the gender of the teenager; the overall level of psychological functioning of the adolescent, including cognitive capacities; and the stage of recovery that the young person is in.

A second consideration is that as teenagers are so action-oriented therapeutic interventions should reflect and respond to this activeness (Wexler, 1991). Direct and involved therapeutic approaches, as opposed to passive and detached approaches, are strongly indicated.

A third consideration is that therapy, and each modality of therapy, progresses according to its own cycle of beginning therapy, working in therapy, and ending therapy. Engaging the adolescent, facilitating active work with the adolescent, and terminating with the adolescent are separate genres in the art of therapy.

A final consideration needs to be given to the setting in which therapy is taking place. Different therapeutic settings are discussed at length in Chapter 8. However, the environmental factors, such as inpatient or outpatient, and temporal factors, such as short-term or long-term treatment, are significant ingredients in therapeutic interventions with adolescent substance abusers.

Therapeutic Use of Self

Therapists working with adolescent substance abusers need to summon their disciplined instincts to create the "therapeutic holding environment" in which healing and recovery can occur (Davis & Raffe, 1985). Being the chief architects of this holding environment, therapists must strike a delicate balance between communicating empathy for the emotional pain of the young person while also transmitting a compassionate firmness in helping the teenager to deal with his or her pain. The adolescent needs to feel a sense of safety and protection through the therapist's caring limit-setting, tolerance of the adolescent's intense challenge to both these limits and the therapist (with these challenges often representing the adolescent's projection of intolerable aspects of himself or herself onto the therapist), and sensitive strength with non-rejecting enforcement of therapeutic limits while helping the teenager to develop a more adaptive "internal structure" from the "external structure" created by the therapist.

Certain personal qualities of the therapist are important in creating this therapeutic holding environment. These personal qualities include:

Understanding and Liking Adolescents. In order to be helpful with teenagers, a therapist has to both like and "feel for" adolescents. Feeling for them means being genuinely attuned to their needs and their mercurial affects during this period of human development. Remembering—without reliving—one's own adolescence is an important resource for therapists.

Being Genuine. Teenagers value openness and honesty from adults. They are often vigilant in determining the trustworthiness of an adult, especially an adult seeking to help them.

Self-disclosure is one therapeutic tool that can demonstrate openness and honesty. However, as with any therapeutic tool, self-disclosure should be considered with the needs of the adolescent in mind, not the needs of the therapist.

The area of self-disclosure pertaining to a therapist's own chemical-use history can pose certain practice dilemmas. For therapists who are themselves recovering from substance abuse, sharing their history of substance abuse and recovery can be a tremendous asset in building trust with the teenager and being a role model of sobriety (Savage & Stickles, 1990). For therapists who do not have a history of substance abuse and recovery to bring to the therapeutic encounter, sharing about chemical use experiences, past or present, can be a bind. To reveal some history of chemical use experience, albeit non-problematic, can result in the therapist being perceived by the adolescent as "in denial" or "unrecovered" and unhelpful to the young person. For the therapist not to reveal any information about his chemical use experiences can be perceived by the adolescent as the therapist's not being truly able to understand his plight with drugs because the therapist has not "been there." Often judiciously redirecting the therapeutic focus off the therapist and back onto the adolescent can resolve this bind.

Sense of Confidence. Adolescents need to feel their therapist's emotional strength as a person. What this strength implies is that therapists "have resolved, for the most part, the developmental issues of adolescence" (Jaynes & Rugg, 1988, p. 137). Adolescents do not need their therapist to be their "friend." They need their therapist to be a parent-like model of disciplined empathy and firmness.

Sense of Humor. With adolescents a little bit of laughter can go a long way toward communicating understanding and building trust. Therapeutic use of humor means "laughing with" the human side of a young person's experience, not "laughing at" or ridiculing his or her vulnerabilities.

Knowledge About and Clear Values About Chemical Use. Therapists who treat adolescent substance abusers are going to be called upon to dispense information and ideas about drugs. Sometimes drug-abusing teenagers know more about chemicals than their therapists do. So therapists should be informed about and be current with the factual side of adolescent chemical use.

In addition, therapists will need to be clear about their own attitudes and values about teenagers and chemical use. Going beyond simplistic "drugs-are-bad-for-you" stances means therapists need to develop values based on "up-to-date information and thoughtful synthesis of the 'advantages' and disadvantages of drug-taking behavior" (Rachman & Raubolt, 1985, p. 364). For a therapist even to consider the advantages of drug-taking is not an endorsement of chemical use. Rather it demonstrates genuineness to the adolescent for having a dialogue about drugs, including some thoughtful challenging of chemical-using attitudes by the therapist. As Rachman and Raubolt (1985) remark, "Youth can only be influenced by honest, direct, vulnerable dialogue. They will not listen to, or be influenced by, defensive, hypercritical, uneducated, or dishonest interaction" (p. 365).

The Therapeutic Relationship

In many ways the therapist working with an adolescent substance abuser is a parent figure to the teenager (Williams, 1986). In assuming a parent-like position with the adolescent, the therapist is cultivating a particular kind of relationship. Wexler (1991) succinctly characterizes this relationship as the adolescent having a respectful adversarial relationship with an authority figure.

Within this therapist-adolescent relationship functions the relational dynamics of transference and countertransference. Transference and countertransference in this context will be discussed in the broader sense of these terms rather that the classic psychodynamic definition of these concepts.

Transference. Transference shall be defined as the feelings and reactions, both positive and negative, that the teenager experiences toward the therapist. Strong negative transference reactions are usually the more difficult for therapists to manage. Intense feelings of depression and rage—commonly experienced by teenagers in early recovery—are translated into challenging and devaluing messages directed at the therapist. Such waves of "negative affect" can provoke the therapist's own "negative feelings" toward the adolescent.

Strong positive transference, however, can also prove to be troublesome for therapists. Teenagers who develop deep, idealizing dependencies on their therapist can remain cut-off from the "normal" rage and sadness that is part of growing in recovery. Both positive and negative transference reactions are a natural part of the therapeutic relationship with teenagers and need to be worked with as such.

Countertransference. Countertransference shall be defined as the feelings and reactions, both positive and negative, that the therapist experiences towards the adolescent. Both positive and negative countertransference feelings are a natural part of the therapist's experience, but in the extreme they can interfere with the therapeutic process with adolescents. Extreme negative countertransference reactions by the therapist can be the result of: (a) the adolescent attempting to induce the therapist to act-out "negative impulses" experienced by the teenager or (b) unresolved issues of the therapist that become enacted in a rejecting and punitive stance towards the adolescent.

Some positive transference reactions are a necessary ingredient of the therapeutic process. As mentioned previously, the therapist must possess an appropriate parental/caretaker liking of a teenager in order to be truly helpful.

Transference/Countertransference and Therapist's Enabling. Mixtures of strong positive and negative transference reactions by the adolescent and intense positive and negative countertransference feelings by the therapist can combine to create an enabling dynamic from the therapist toward the adolescent. Among the possible interactions is that the positive transference of the adolescent can fuel the positive counter-transference of the therapist, resulting in the therapist's being reluctant to be appropriately confrontational with the substance-abusing teenager. This reluctance stems from the therapist's not wanting to "upset" the younger person, from whom he enjoys a positive regard.

Another possible interaction is that the negative transference of the adolescent and the negative countertransference of the therapist are mutually exacerbating. In such a negative clinch the therapist might act out hostilities toward the teenager by either: (a) excessive and unproductive confrontation or (b) detaching from the adolescent and, in essence, compromising treatment. Either behavior by the therapist is setting up the adolescent to fail in treatment and subsequently risk returning to drug abuse.

There are a number of other ways in which transference and countertransference dynamics can unfold into an enabling pattern by the therapist. The point is that the therapeutic relationship can evoke strong feelings in both the adolescent and the therapist. Careful self-monitoring of the therapist's own feelings and reactions towards the teenager can help to avert the pitfalls of the therapist's enabling.

Therapeutic Modalities

The three major therapeutic tools available to those who treat adolescent substance abusers are individual psychotherapy, family therapy, and group therapy. These therapeutic modalities combine with the therapeutic elements of 12-step recovery to create the hybrid treatment model—recovery-oriented treatment.

Individual Psychotherapy. Among those who have comprehensively discussed individual psychotherapy with adolescents are Weiner (1992) and Mishne (1986). Individual psychotherapy with adolescents can be useful conducted according to a developmental approach, similar to the model suggested by Esman (1985).

Applying a developmental approach to individual psychotherapy with adolescent substance abusers poses certain considerations to the therapist. These considerations include: (a) being aware of the particular developmental subphase of the adolescent (early, middle or late adolescence), (b) being aware of psychological implications of the adolescent's gender, (c) being aware of which stage of adolescent substance abuse recovery the young person is dealing with (Chapter 9), and (d) the overall psychological functioning of the adolescent, including his or her level of cognitive abilities.

Woody and colleagues (Woody, McLellan, Lubursky, & O'Brien, 1986) discuss individual psychotherapy techniques with substance abusers as potentially including techniques from drug counseling, as well as two common forms of individual psychotherapy—supportive-expressive therapy and cognitive-behavioral therapy. In this context drug counseling means therapeutic work with the substance abuser that focuses on coping with external forces that relate to addiction, supportive-expressive therapy pertains to the substance abuser's working on relational themes as experienced intrapsychically and enacted in interactions with others, and cognitive-behavioral therapy centers on "uncovering and understanding the influence of automatic thoughts and underlying assumptions on problematic feelings and behaviors" (Woody, et. al, 1986, p. 553).

The model of individual therapy with substance abusers—encompassing drug counseling, supportive-expressive therapy, and cognitive-behavioral therapy—has implications for individual therapy techniques with adolescent substance abusers. During the early stages of adolescent recovery, when management of feelings and coping are primary goals, drug counseling and cognitive-behavioral techniques are more strongly indicated. This combination of drug counseling and cognitive-behavioral techniques is indicated regardless of which subphase of adolescence the teenager is in. Supportive-expressive techniques are more indicated, particularly with middle to later adolescents, during the advanced stages of adolescent recovery. Supportive-expressive therapy can be useful in helping the young person to work through developmental crises and intrapsychic conflicts by making unconscious experiences conscious, remembering, and abreacting. An illustration of this is the case of a substance abusing female adolescent who was treated initially in individual therapy as an outpatient for problems of depressive symptoms and sexual acting-out behavior. The treatment plan also called for periodic parental consults. The therapist was able to quickly establish rapport with this teenager, who disclosed her substance use early in the course of treatment. Although revealing her substance use, the adolescent asserted that it was not a problem in her life. Her therapist responded by introducing the behavioral strategy of an abstinence contract, whereby the girl would "prove" that her substance use was not a problem by making a commitment to remain drug free. The teenager agreed to the plan, did not maintain abstinence, and followed her therapist's recommendation to enter a partial hospital program (PHP) for adolescent substance abusers. While in the PHP she participated in a number of different group therapies, including a gender group. It was within the supportive environment of this group that she first disclosed experiences of being sexually abused by an uncle when she was younger. This adolescent progressed satisfactorily in the PHP, was able to remain chemically free, and was discharged and referred back to her original therapist for aftercare individual therapy. Along with using cognitive-behavioral strategies to assist the teenager with her early recovery, this therapist also introduced a supportive-expressive approach to facilitate healing related to her sexual abuse.

Family Therapy. Fishman (1988), and Mirkin and Koman (1985) are among those who have comprehensively discussed family therapy with adolescents. Effective family therapy with adolescent substance abusers includes, in part, the integration of the adolescent's recovery goals with the family's recovery goals (Chapter 10).

Friedman (1990) identifies 12 types of family therapy that are applicable with adolescent substance abusers. These 12 types are: psychodynamic, experiential, behavioral, structural, strategic, communication, family systems approach, problem-centered systems family therapy, contextual family therapy, functional family therapy, integrative family therapy, and intergenerational family therapy. It is beyond the scope of this book to discuss each type as it relates to adolescent substance abusers and their families. What is important to be aware of is the diversity of family therapy approaches that can be used in treating these families.

Fishman, Stanton, and Rosman (1982) suggest several family therapy techniques that are particularly useful with families with a drug-abusing adolescent. These techniques are: working with resistance, reframing, enactment, boundary making, intensity, unbalancing, search for strength, and complimentarity. Some of these family therapy techniques are elaborated on in the discussion of family recovery in Chapter 10.

What is key in applying a particular type of family therapy with the family of an adolescent drug abusers is to match the therapy with the level of family functioning as well as with the stage of family recovery. One therapeutic rule of thumb is that a combination of structural and strategic family therapy (Stanton and Todd, 1982) seems more indicated during early family recovery, particularly with more disorganized families. This blend of structural and strategic therapy can help the family in early recovery to deal with the homeostatic imbalancing of working to not be an enabling system for the teenager.

Another therapeutic rule of thumb is that during later stages of family recovery, and primarily with more functional families, experiential and communication types of family therapy appear more indicated. Experiential and communication therapy can help guide a family in working to resolve some historical family issues that might be underpinning the adolescent's drug problem. For example, in family therapy with one family with a chemically involved male adolescent, the initial therapeutic focus was on the family's enabling of the boy's drug use. The therapist employed a blend of structural and strategic family therapy approaches to intervene with the parents' "split" around their son's drug use and to work at reinforcing the hierarchial position of the parents being "in charge" in this family. As this teenager progressed in substance abuse recovery, other family themes emerged in family therapy. In particular, some marital issues that were affecting the parents' functioning as a team came to the surface. The therapist did some intermittent couples therapy, along with the family therapy, using a communications approach to address their marital issues. Effective treatment of a family with a substance-abusing adolescent often involves a blending of different types of family therapy and various techniques of family therapy throughout the course of a family's recovery.

Group Therapy. Group psychotherapy with adolescents has been comprehensively discussed by Azima and Richmond (1989) and Sugar (1975). What is important in group therapy with adolescent substance abusers is the fit between the respective individual goals of each adolescent in the group and the overall group goals. Individual adolescent goals are determined by a young person's subphase of adolescent development, overall psychological functioning, and stage of substance abuse recovery.

The overall group goal with teenage drug abusers is to create a group—to work through the process of forming an emotionally safe and supportive peer environment for the therapeutic needs of the young person. Some of the benefits of the group environment for recovering adolescents are as follows:

> The group setting offers increased opportunity to bring into operation such curative factors as positive peer pressure, identification with the experiences of other group members, an opportunity to see that one is not alone in one's problems, and reduced dependency on the therapist. Within the group the adolescent also has the opportunity to observe positive emotional growth and behavioral change in other members. This offers the skeptical adolescent a sense of hope and reinforces both the importance and usefulness of therapy. Moreover, the interpersonal relationship among group members may offer an important opportunity for developing a mutual support system within the group. (Fischer, 1985, p. 304)

Group therapy techniques with adolescent substance abusers include "direct encountering" and "indirect encountering" techniques for facilitating "here and now" insight and action with each group member (Raubolt, 1983). One example of an essential direct encounter technique in group therapy with adolescent drug abusers is group confrontation. Bratter (1989) has summarized seven guiding principles of group confrontation with adolescent substance abusers.

1. Point out the maladaptive and dysfunctional behavior.
2. Challenge the teenager's justification of the behavior.
3. Direct the teenager toward assuming responsibility for the behavior.
4. Help the teenager to evaluate his or her behavior.
5. Facilitate the teenager's awareness of, and anticipation of, payoffs and consequences with certain behaviors.

6. Encourage the teenager to access and make use of more of his or her internal resources.

7. Provide a behavioral map for the teenager to continue growing and developing.

Indirect encountering techniques for facilitating the group members' "here and now" insight and action include activity therapies and creative therapies within the group context. Such indirect techniques may be experienced as less psychologically threatening to the adolescent than the more confrontational direct encountering techniques.

Direct encountering techniques and indirect encountering techniques can be applied in a complementary manner by clinicians conducting group therapy with adolescent substance abusers. Direct encountering techniques can enhance the structure building of the group, while indirect encountering techniques can help to create support and intimacy within the group.

Therapeutic Elements and 12-Step Recovery.

Twelve-step recovery programs, such as Alcoholics Anonymous (AA) and Narcotics Anonymous (NA), contain certain therapeutic elements that can be responsive to the needs of the recovering adolescent. These therapeutic elements include group meetings, the 12-step structure, the folk psychotherapy slogans for recovery, and a sponsor in recovery. The therapeutic elements mix with the previously discussed therapeutic modalities to form the foundation of recovery-oriented treatment with adolescent substance abusers.

Before reviewing the four therapeutic elements of 12-step recovery, it is worth noting the observations of some professionals in endorsing NA as the 12-step recovery program of choice for adolescents. The following is a summary of Gifford's (1989) rationale for advocating NA instead of AA for teenagers.

- NA encourages emotional insight rather than the intellectual approaches of AA.
- NA takes into consideration the cognitive concreteness of many adolescent substance abusers.
- NA's program—promoted as a "family"—fits with the developmental needs of many adolescents.
- The relatively younger age of NA members is more appropriate for adolescents.
- The NA program's differentiation from the "parent" 12-step program of AA mirrors the adolescent experience of differentiation from parents.

- NA is a program for abusers of any chemicals, not just alcohol, which is consonant with the experience of many adolescent substance abusers.

Although there may appear to be some advantages of NA for adolescents, AA can indeed be an acceptable 12-step program for a good number of recovering teenagers.

Group Meetings. Twelve-step self-help meetings are a supportive environment in which the recovering teenager can feel a sense of belonging while addressing recovery issues. "Attendance at 12-step meetings allows the adolescent to examine his or her own struggles in a framework that provides a vocabulary and system for self-exploration" (Ungerleider & Siegel, 1990, p. 441).

Program meetings are a culture of recovery, contrasting with the young substance abuser's peer group, which is a culture of addiction. As the NA "Big Book" states (Narcotics Anonymous, 1982), "Whatever the type or format a group uses for its meetings, the function of a group is always the same: to provide a suitable and reliable environment for personal recovery and to promote such recovery" (p. 91).

The 12 Steps. The respective 12 steps of AA and NA (see Appendix) provide a structure for the stages of a teenager's recovery from drug abuse. The stages of adolescent recovery (Chapter 9) and these 12 steps mirror each other in being a roadmap for the young person's journey into sobriety.

The 12 steps are replete with pro-recovery messages and values. Such a pro-recovery system of values is essential for adolescents, who are in a period of psychological development in which values formation is in flux (Ungerleider & Siegel, 1990).

Folk Psychotherapy. The slogans of AA and other self-help programs—including such homespun wisdom as "Do first things first" and "Live and let live"—represent a type of "folk psychotherapy" (Alibrandi, 1985). These cognitive-behavioral-like proverbs are used by program members to advise and counsel one another in recovery.

These adages can be particularly useful with simplifying and apportioning the demands of recovery for teenagers. For example, as Evans and Sullivan (1990) remark, "For the adolescent overwhelmed with the idea of never drinking again, focusing on 'one day at a time' and abstaining 'just for today' is useful" (p. 124).

Sponsors. A sponsor is a mentor for the recovering adolescent. The choice of a sponsor is a very personal decision for the teenager, as this program member may become privy to intimate aspects of the young person's experiences in addiction and struggles in recovery.

In addition, sponsors can be both parent-like or therapist-like to the young person. Consequently, transference and countertransference dynamics, in the broader sense of these terms, are indeed operating between the adolescent and his or her sponsor. As teenagers progress in recovery and are "working a twelfth step," in which they reciprocate by giving back to the self-help program they have benefited from, they may become sponsors to other recovering teenagers.

LEVELS OF BIOPSYCHOSOCIAL SYSTEMS INVOLVED IN ADOLESCENT RECOVERY FROM SUBSTANCE ABUSE

There are five levels of systems that can be involved in an adolescent's recovery from substance abuse. These levels are: the biological system and the physical recovery of the adolescent, the adolescent's recovery with his or her psychological functioning, the recovery environment (family recovery and peer relationships in recovery), promoting adolescent recovery at the community level, and promoting adolescent recovery at the societal level.

Biological System and Biomedical Interventions

Teenagers in substance abuse treatment may require a variety of biomedical interventions to enhance physical recovery. These interventions may include emergency medical attention for conditions related to acute intoxication, ongoing medical treatment throughout the course of recovery for some chronic physical condition or disorder, and overall promotion of physical health as part of recovery.

Emergency Medical Treatment

Acute episodes of intoxication can bring about the need for medical care with the direct physical or psychological effects of intoxication, the secondary physical effects from intoxication (such as from an accident or injury), or both.

Adolescents in withdrawal are sometimes in need of detoxification. Although the signs of withdrawal in adolescents are not usually as severe as those presented by adults, teenagers in withdrawal nevertheless may need medical monitoring and attention (Cohen, 1989). Overdoses and toxicity related to poisonous diluent material are other physical conditions necessitating immediate medical attention.

Some acute psychological reactions to chemical use may also need medical management. As listed in the Adolescent Chemical Use Problem (ACUP) Index in Chapter 1, these acute psychological reactions include chemically-induced psychosis, flashbacks, and panic reactions.

The ACUP Index also lists other acute physical, psychological, or behavioral consequences secondary to chemical use that may require emergency medical care. Conditions that might require prompt medical attention include injuries sustained from accidents, impulsive behaviors, or violent behaviors.

Ongoing Medical Treatment

A complete physical examination early in treatment is mandatory for evaluating the adolescent's overall physical health as well as for diagnosing any biomedical problems that may need continuous medical care. Such biomedical problems can include: (a) conditions unrelated to chemical use, such as diabetes or asthma; (b) conditions that may be related to chemical use (or at least have been aggravated by chemical use), such as gastrointestinal problems or migraine headaches; or (c) conditions possibly related to behavioral consequences from chemical use, for example the potential effects from unprotected sexual intercourse (Human Immunodeficiency Virus [HIV] infection, contracting a sexually transmitted disease, or an unwanted pregnancy).

The issue of the pregnant adolescent who is also a substance abuser raises particular medical concerns, not only for the health of the teenager, but also for the health of the newborn. The health of the teenager as well as the newborn need to be considered. According to Schiff and Cavaiola (1990), "Pregnant teenagers may still drink and use drugs. Consequently, these adolescent girls are at a high risk for producing fetal alcohol and drug syndrome offspring" (p. 41).

Promoting Physical Health

The physical recovery of the adolescent involves care for acute and ongoing biomedical conditions. It also means the teenager needs to acquire habits that encourage a physically healthy lifestyle. Regular exercise, proper sleep, adequate nutrition, and good hygiene—habits often absent in a drug-abusing lifestyle—should be instilled in the recovering teenager. One context for promoting such physically healthy habits is the recovery skills curriculum discussed in Chapter 9.

The Triad of Primary Recovering Systems:
Adolescent Recovery, Family Recovery,
and Peer Relationships in Recovery

The three primary systems involved in the young person's recovery are the psychological recovery of the adolescent, the recovery of the adolescent's family, and growth with peer relationships in recovery. These different systems of recovery interact, and so, consequently, the different treatment interventions with these systems interact. This bio-psychosocial model of adolescent substance abuse treatment underscores the confluence of treatment interventions, particularly with the triad of primary recovery systems. For example, as the individual teenager begins to change and grow in sobriety, this can have an imbalancing effect on her family. At the same time, the eventual rebalancing by her family will have an impact on her progress in sobriety. Additionally, as peer relationships undergo changes in recovery these changes will circularly interact with both the adolescent's and the family's recovery.

Adolescent Recovery

The adolescent's reparative psychological development is the pre-eminent system of the triad of primary recovering systems. This reparative psychological development is a process by which the teenager moves from a chemically entrenched self to a chemically free self. During this process the young person gains a foothold on a path of more adaptive psychological functioning and healthier psychological development. The four stages of recovery presented in this book are: (a) the shifting stage, (b) the sampling stage, (c) the conversion stage, and (d) the coalescing stage.

Recovery skills, intended to support the teenager's heightened self-awareness and need for new coping techniques, can further enhance the young person's growth in sobriety. Teaching recovery skills can be adjunctive to direct therapeutic interventions throughout the four stages of recovery. Four categories of recovery skills are: (a) addiction awareness, (b) developmental awareness, (c) managing internal changes in recovery, and (d) managing external changes in recovery.

Relapse treatment, strategies for intervening when the adolescent backslides in recovery, is an additional area for concern in adolescent recovery. There are three possible levels of relapse treatment that can be provided to recovering teenagers: (a) Level 1, relapse prevention; (b) Level 2, relapse management; and (c) Level 3, relapse intervention.

The treatment paradigm of the four stages of adolescent recovery, as well as adolescent recovery skills and adolescent relapse treatment, are further discussed in Chapter 9.

Recovery Environment

The recovery environment is composed of the other two systems from this triad of primary recovering systems. Both the adolescent's family recovery and his peer relationships in recovery are systems that need to undergo their own changes in recovery along with supporting the adolescent's changes in recovery.

Just as with the adolescent's psychological recovery, family recovery can also be understood as happening along four stages, with a therapeutic framework for treatment within these stages and recovery skills specific to families for augmenting this family recovery work. The four stages of family recovery presented in this book are: (a) the disengagement stage, (b) the empowering stage, (c) the integration stage, and (d) the individuation stage.

The adolescent's peer relationships in recovery are another system of change in sobriety. The changes with peer relationships that a teenager experiences during the four stages of individual recovery are often both a change of actual friends and a transformation of perception in how to view friendships. An important part of peer relationships in recovery is how the sober sexual self of the adolescent, who is in a period of developmental sexual emergence, is expressed in healthy ways.

Chapter 10 is devoted to the treatment paradigm of family recovery and family recovery skills and the adolescent's peer relationships in recovery.

Promoting Recovery at the Community Level

Biomedical interventions and physical recovery, the adolescent's psychological recovery, and the recovery environment can all be supported at the community level. As discussed in Chapter 3, the community can contribute to adolescent substance abuse by not having implemented successful primary, secondary, and tertiary programs for teenage drug problems. The community can help to prevent substance abuse and promote recovery with teenagers who develop drug problems by successfully implementing such programs.

Secondary prevention programs, which can facilitate earlier interventions with adolescents having difficulties with drugs, and tertiary prevention programs, which can help support the recovery of those young people who develop more advanced problems with drugs, are the more applicable prevention programs for adolescents. Junior high schools and high schools increasingly have become outpatient settings for providing interventions and assessments with students experiencing a drug problem (Wight, 1990; Anderson, 1987). In addition, schools—along with community organizations, neighborhood groups, churches, and local government services and institutions—have become more involved with offering services associated with tertiary prevention programs. Services have included sponsoring AA and NA meetings, developing support and recovery groups for adolescents, hosting Families Anonymous meetings, and creating support groups for parents.

Communities can be a part of the problem with adolescent substance abuse, and they can also be part of the solution. Communities can be both advocates for treatment for adolescent substance abusers and their families, and providers of some pieces of this treatment.

Promoting Recovery at the Societal Level

All other levels of systems involved in the adolescent's biopsychosocial recovery from substance abuse are encircled at the societal level. Among the ways that the larger society can promote recovery with young people is by continuing to make treatment both acceptable and accessible.

The *zeitgeist* of pro-recovery that has spread in the American culture in recent years has gone a long way toward removing the stigma of chemical addictions for adults, adolescents, and families. Media portrayals of successful recovering people and government public service campaigns endorsing the benefits of treatment have contributed to an overall increased acceptance of substance abuse as a health problem, not a moral one. Continued media and government advocacy of addiction treatment in general, and specifically for adolescents, will further enlighten the public and make treatment even more acceptable.

Creating greater access to treatment is another way of supporting the recovery of adolescent substance abusers at the societal level. Treatment availability and accessibility, for both public and private treatment programs, can be improved.

Treatment in publicly funded programs can be made more available through the federal government's reordering of its priorities in the war on drugs (Chapter 3). One way the government can fulfill its promise and responsibility with the national drug problem is to shift its emphasis from the "supply side" of the problem—the criminal justice approach—to the "demand side" of the problem—the education and treatment approach.

Treatment in privately run programs can be made more accessible through continued efforts by both the treatment providers and the health care reimbursement systems to work at more collaborative relationships. Treatment providers need to accept the reality that treatment is a limited resource. Creative and resourceful treatment planning, along with greater congruency between the level of treatment needed and the level of treatment provided, is in order. Striving to work effectively with reimbursement systems is in the best interest of the young people that treatment providers are serving.

On the other hand, health care reimbursement systems need to practice responsible managed care, not just management of cost. Working effectively with treatment providers means recognizing that treatment may seem costly in the short run, but ultimately may prove to be cost-saving over the long haul.

SUMMARY

This chapter offers a biopsychosocial model of recovery-oriented treatment for adolescent substance abusers. The model highlights five levels of systems—biological, adolescent psychological, interpersonal (family and peer), community, and societal—that can have a part in the teenager's recovery. At the same time, this model stresses a triad of primary recovery systems—the adolescent's psychological recovery, family recovery, and peer relationships in recovery—that are the core of treatment interventions.

The following is a continuation of the metaphor presented in the summary of Chapter 3. The original metaphor symbolizes the biopsychosocial model of understanding adolescent substance abuse, and this elaboration represents the biopsychosocial model of treating adolescent substance abuse.

In the initial metaphor the growing adolescent is symbolized by a young apple tree in springtime on the threshold of fruition. A fire that ravages the tree represents drugs destroying the development of the teenager. Surrounding trees in the orchard, which can spread the fire to other trees, are like the young person's family and friends who may be involved in dynamics of enabling the substance abuse. Larger environmental elements—climate and weather conditions—that can affect the burning of the fire upon the young tree are similar to community and societal enabling of adolescent substance abuse.

In further embellishing this metaphor, the focus is on blending efforts to stop the fire, repairing the damage to the tree, and stimulating renewed growth of the tree. This blending of efforts symbolizes the combining of treatments to interrupt the adolescent's substance abuse and to promote his reparative developmental work and growth in sobriety. Fighting the fire in the blazing tree is analogous to therapeutic intervention to influence abstinence; the destruction has to cease before healing can take place. The integration of technological tools, such as tree surgery and horticultural care, with the natural elements of sun, rain, and air, represents the recovery-oriented hybrid model of blending mental health treatment with the therapeutic elements of 12-step recovery. Just as both science and nature are needed to restore the growth of the young apple tree, the combination of mental health interventions and self-help care are necessary ingredients for supporting the recovery of the adolescent. Surrounding trees in the orchard—like the recovery environment of the teenager—may also have been damaged by the fire and be in need of treatment. Finally, overall restorative measures for the young apple tree can be aided by favorable conditions in the larger environment, the climate and weather conditions. Similarly, the adolescent's recovery from substance abuse can be promoted by forces supportive of treatment in the macrosocial system, the community and society.

Chapter 7

SERVICING ADOLESCENT SUBSTANCE ABUSERS
Part I: The Assessment

INTRODUCTION

Providing effective substance abuse services to adolescents and their families flows from the complementary processes of assessing and planning treatment. Assessing is the process of collecting, synthesizing, and interpreting data concerning the young person and his chemical use. Treatment planning is the process of acting on this data by mapping out a course of treatment and placing the adolescent along the continuum of care. Assessment and treatment planning continue in juxtaposition throughout the course of the young person's recovery in order to responsibly service his treatment needs. This chapter discusses the assessment, and treatment planning is the subject of the next chapter.

Assessment by a therapist should focus on adolescent substance abuse as a biopsychosocial process. Approaching the assessment of a teenager from a biopsychosocial perspective permits weighing a fuller range of systems of the young person's functioning as well as considering the interactions among these systems (Donovan, 1988).

Assessing an adolescent's substance abuse is both an event that occurs at the onset of treatment and a process that is ongoing for the duration of treatment. As an event, the assessment entails two stages. First, a brief screen is completed to give a broad sense of the adolescent's drug use problem. Second, and if indicated by the brief screen, a more thorough assessment is undertaken with the teenager.

In this chapter the assessment is discussed according to some state-of-the-art assessment models, the Drug Use Screening Inventory (DUSI) and the Adolescent Assessment/Referral System (AARS). In addition, an assessment model based on the Adolescent Chemical Use Problem (ACUP) Index, which was introduced in Chapter 1, is presented.

MODELS OF ASSESSMENT

Assessment models for adolescent substance abuses have become highly comprehensive in recent years. The Drug Use Screening Inventory (DUSI) and the Adolescent Assessment/Referral System (AARS) are examples of such comprehensive models. The DUSI employs a decision-tree approach to gather and weigh assessment data with a drug involved teenager (Tarter, 1990). Ten domains of the adolescent's functioning that might be affected by drug use are assessed. The 10 domains are substance use, behavior patterns, health status, psychiatric disorder, social skills, family system, school adjustment, work, peer relationships, and leisure or recreation. The assessment with the DUSI involves three phases: (a) the screening assessment, (b) the diagnostic evaluation, and (c) formulating the treatment plan. It utilizes assessment data from the 10 domains.

The AARS is an assessment and referral system developed by the National Institute of Drug Abuse (NIDA, 1989). The AARS focuses on 10 problematic functional areas for chemical-using adolescents. The 10 areas are substance use (abuse), physical health status, mental health status, family relations, peer relations, educational status, vocational status, social skills, leisure and recreation, and aggressive behavior and delinquency. The AARS system breaks down an assessment according to three steps that are used to make decisions about the 10 problematic functional areas of the teenager: (a) screening (Problem-Oriented Screening Instrument for Teenagers [POSIT]), (b) the comprehensive assessment (Comprehensive Assessment Battery [CAB]), and (c) the referral (Directory of Adolescent Services).

Both the DUSI and the AARS are state-of-the-art assessment models with widespread application for drug-involved teenagers. In addition, the Adolescent Chemical Use Problem (ACUP) Index, introduced in Chapter 1, can be adapted as a format for assessing adolescent chemical use. The ACUP Index is derived from the problem identification categories of both the DUSI and the AARS.

ASSESSMENT USING THE ACUP INDEX

The ACUP Index can be used as the organizing axis for the assessment process with adolescent substance abusers. The Index lists various acute and cumulative effects for adolescents who use chemicals. These acute and cumulative effects, divided according to six problem domains, can serve as the focus of assessment as well as the focus of treatment planning and placement. In this sense, using the ACUP Index as a format for assessment directs a biopsychosocial approach to servicing adolescents with drug problems.

The six problem domains of the ACUP Index are: chemical use effects, physical health, psychological health, behavioral functioning, social functioning, and interpersonal environment. They can be assessed according to some major methods of assessment, such as: (a) laboratory tests, (b) the physical exam, (c) the adolescent interview, (d) the family interview, (e) instrumentation, and (f) gathering collateral data. There is need for clinical judgement in applying this model of six domains and six methods with assessing adolescent substance abusers. Not every domain needs to be assessed with every adolescent. In addition, the clinician doing the assessment will need to exercise flexibility in determining which methods to apply for assessing any given problem domain. In applying Skinner's (1981) assessment model with adult alcoholics to adolescent substance abusers Blum (1987) states, "There are three intersecting questions fundamental to drug abuse assessment: 1. What are the important variables to assess? 2. How can they best be measured? 3. How can the assessment information be used best to make treatment decisions?" (p. 528). The following assessment model, using the ACUP Index, is an example of how each of the six problem domains can be assessed using different tools of the six major assessment methods.

Domain 1: Chemical Use Effect

The goal in assessing the chemical use effect domain is to determine the intensity of the adolescent's chemical use. This intensity involves the teenager's pattern of and progression with chemical use. The intensity

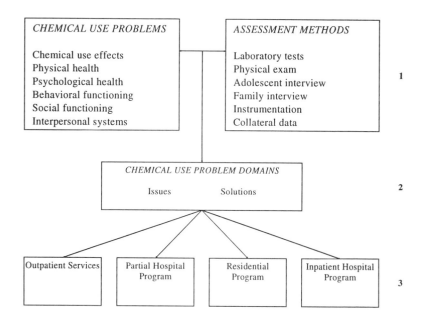

Figure 7.1. Assessment, Planning, and Levels of Treatment
1. Assessment. 2. Treatment planning. 3. Levels of substance abuse treatment.

of use for each chemical used by the teenager can be delineated as follows:

- The length of time used: Date when use began and date last used?
- The frequency of use: How often used during a day/week/month? Used during what part of day/week/month?
- The amount of use: Amount initially used? Amount most recently used? Development of any tolerance to amount of use?
- The control of use: Episodes of using more than planned? Any attempts to reduce or discontinue use? Results of attempts to reduce or discontinue use?

Laboratory tests, the adolescent interview, the family interview, instrumentation, and collecting collateral data are the primary methods for gathering chemical use effect information. Information from a physical exam can also be helpful.

Laboratory Tests. The medical laboratory can be used for urinalysis tests, which can indicate the presence of particular drugs in an adolescent. Several urine screening techniques have been developed and used over the past decade. However, no one technique is perfect (Gold & Dackis, 1986). According to MacKenzie, Cheng, and Haftel, "Each technique has its advantages and limitations, and no single technique is capable of detecting every drug in all types of specimens" (MacKenzie, Cheng & Haftel, 1987, p. 420). As urinalysis results might be challenged by the adolescent, it is important for therapists to be familiar with the different techniques and their strengths and limitations (MacKenzie, et al., 1987).

It is also important for therapists to be aware of the factors that may contribute to inaccurate urinalysis results, referred to as false-positives (erroneously indicating the presence of chemicals when the person has not been using them) or false-negatives (erroneously indicating no drugs when the person has been using them). Among the factors that can contribute to inaccurate urinalysis results are diluting or eliminating traces of drug in the urine and contaminating, or substituting urine samples to be tested.

Along with being a useful assessment tool, urine screening techniques can be a helpful therapeutic tool for monitoring the teenager's abstinence from chemicals. A drug test, or the possibility of a drug test, is an external structure that a therapist can use to influence continued abstinence.

Another laboratory method, the breatholizer, can also be useful for specific monitoring of abstinence from alcohol during recovery. This method has its limitations, however, as only alcohol that has been consumed a few hours prior to taking the breatholizer test can be detected.

Adolescent Interview. Interviewing the adolescent is another means of gathering information on his chemical use history. The format for conducting this interview can range from a formal structured interview, such as the Adolescent Diagnostic Interview (Winters & Henly, 1992), to a routine questioning of the adolescent's chemical use experiences.

Regardless of which format or technique is used to interview the teenager, the accuracy of his self-report is critical to the usefulness of the interview. Two factors that affect the accuracy of this self report are his ability to recall and his willingness to be honest.

Both psychological and physical factors can affect memory of drug use. Psychological functioning can repress recall for long periods of time, but fuller memories of experiences with drugs may occur along the course of treatment. Physical impairments to memory may have to do with neurological deficits or the effects of intoxication. For the latter reason, a minimum of 12 hours since the last episode of drug use is suggested before interviewing the teenager (Washton, Stone, & Hendrickson, 1988). The adolescent's openness about his chemical use history is another matter. Distortion and denial of the reality of his chemical use experiences can take the form of him "faking good or faking bad" (Winters, 1990). Faking good is when the teenager selectively recalls aspects of his drug use so as to make his drug use seem like less of a problem. Faking bad is when he exaggerates his drug use so as to appear more drug involved than he truly is. Establishing rapport during the interview and sequencing questions during the interview by asking less threatening questions first and building up to the more provocative questions, might be ways of keeping the adolescent's distortion and denial to a minimum (Anglin, 1987).

Family Interview. The family interview can be helpful for rounding out the chemical use history presented by the teenager. Separate interviews with parents about their awareness of their child's drug use experiences or questioning with all family members present are two formats for getting a family perspective on the adolescent's use.

Through either format it is possible that another family member's active substance abuse might be revealed. If that occurs, it is important to take note of it for future treatment purposes without shifting the focus away from the current assessment of the adolescent (Schroeder, 1989).

Instrumentation. Instruments to measure an adolescent's chemical use experience have become more available in recent years. These instruments include quick screen devices, questionnaires, and clinically tested inventories.

Quick screen instruments can be administered in several minutes, and offer a general indication of an adolescent's drug use. The Personal Experience Screen Questionnaire (Winters 1992) is an example of a standardized quick screen for drug-involved adolescents. In addition, the Perceived-Benefit-of-Drinking and Drug Use Scales (Petchers & Singer, 1990) and the CAGE Questionnaire (Bush, Shaw, Cleary, Delbanco, & Aronson, 1987) can also be used for a swift grasp of the young person's use.

Questionnaires are more detailed instruments for ascertaining a teenager's chemical use experience. The Adolescent Drug Involvement Scale is an example of one questionnaire for evaluating drug use

(Moberg & Hahn, 1991). The Rutgers Alcohol Problem Index (White & Labouvie, 1989) and the Adolescent Alcohol Involvement Scale (Moberg, 1983) are among the available questionnaires for evaluating teenage drinking.

There are also inventories available for a more extensive assessment of an adolescent's chemical use and related problem areas. The Personal Experience Inventory (Winters & Henly, 1989) and the Adolescent Drug Abuse Diagnosis Instrument (Friedman & Utada, 1989) are two major assessment inventories that have become available in the past few years.

These instruments can be useful tools in assessing an adolescent's chemical use intensity, but a therapist needs to incorporate data from such instruments with his own clinical sense of the teenager. In short, "There is no substitute for clinical judgement in any setting in which the adolescent is seen" (Ungerleider & Siegel, 1990, p. 439).

Collateral Data. Gathering data about the adolescent's chemical use history from a number of sources can help in developing an accurate history. Schools, probation departments, and previous treatment providers are among other resources that can help shed light on understanding the teenager's drug use intensity. "Treatment decisions require consideration of several lines of assessment evidence. Relevant information about the client needs to be collected from multiple sources (client, parent, school officials, etc.) and with multiple methods (questionnaire, interview, laboratory, school and legal records, etc.)" (Winters, 1990, p. 47)

Domain 2: Physical Health

The goal in assessing the adolescent's physical health is to determine if there are any acute or cumulative biomedical effects from his drug use. In addition, the teenager's overall physical health, as well as any nondrug related biomedical concerns, needs to be considered in comprehensive treatment planning.

A physical examination by a physician is the primary method for assessing the adolescent's physical health. During the examination the physician may see indications for a neuropsychological evaluation or a neuropsychiatric examination. In cases indicating a neuropsychological evaluation, a test battery would assess neuropsychological functioning. If a neuropsychiatric examination is indicated, considerations for an electroencephalogram and CI scan should be made (Friedman, 1985).

Laboratory tests, medical history interviews with the teenager and his parents, and health records from other sources can supplement the assessment of the adolescent's physical health.

Domain 3: Psychological Health

One goal in assessing the adolescent's psychological health is to explore the relationship between the teenager's chemical use and his psychological functioning. Acute psychological symptoms—including flashbacks, panic attacks, psychosis, and dysphoria—need to be assessed as either drug involved, or indicative of a possible coexisting psychological disorder. In addition, patterns of cumulative psychological symptoms need to be identified and further evaluated for the existence of a possible psychological disorder. Often an ongoing assessment of a sober adolescent is necessary to diagnose a coexisting psychological disorder with some degree of accuracy (Bukstein, Brent, & Kaminer, 1989).

A second goal in assessing the adolescent's psychological health is to identify his psychological resources. Identifying strengths, as well as limitations, is fundamental for effective treatment planning. These strengths and resources will be valuable tools as the adolescent negotiates coping with a sober lifestyle.

An interview with the adolescent, a family interview, certain instrumentation, and the use of collateral data are the primary methods for assessing the adolescent's psychological health. A physical examination and some laboratory tests may be helpful in the process of assessing for a coexisting psychological disorder. One example of this is a blood test, the dexamethasone suppression test, which can be helpful in diagnosing depression (Oster & Caro, 1990).

Adolescent Interview. An interview with the adolescent, in the format of a mental status exam, can delineate dimensions of his psychological functioning. In such an interview, the teenager would be queried regarding his attitudes and general behavior, speech and thought processes, perceptions, emotional reactions, orientation, memory, attention and concentration, intelligence, and insight.

Family Interview. A family interview can allow for questioning parents about their child's developmental history. In addition, any history of psychological problems with either parent or any history of psychological disorders in each parent's family of origin should be explored.

Instrumentation. Different psychological tests can help evaluate the teenager's psychological health. If a clinician chooses to do psychological testing during the assessment process it is crucial that the adolescent is free of psychoactive substances. Friedman suggests some guidelines for psychological testing with adolescent substance abusers:

> A battery of standardized psychological tests administered and interpreted by a qualified clinical psychologist (if the program has the resources to provide this service) can answer difficult diagnostic questions, elucidate emotional and mental states, and provide psychodynamic understanding of the individual's behavior. To facilitate accurate results on this kind of test, a period of approximately 1 week should elapse between the last drug toxicity and time of testing. (Friedman, 1985, p. 76)

The exact amount of time between an adolescent's last episode of drug use and any psychological testing is a contentious issue. Some advocate that an adolescent be "clean" several weeks before psychological testing, while others insist that the adolescent be chemically free for up to 6 months before such testing is undertaken.

Collateral Data. Assessing a substance abusing adolescent's psychological health, and evaluating for the possibility of a concurrent psychological disorder, can be extremely complicated. Consequently, additional sources of information, including school reports on academic performance and overall behavior and any prior psychological treatment records, can assist in this difficult task.

Domain 4: Behavioral Functioning

The goal in assessing the adolescent's behavioral functioning is to delineate any possible connection between the adolescent's chemical use and any presenting behavioral concerns. Possible behavioral concerns include violent and assaultive behavior, sexual acting out, and antisocial activity. Much of the assessment of this domain overlaps with the assessment of the domain of the adolescent's psychological health.

Interviewing the adolescent, interviewing his family, use of some instrumentation, and gathering collateral data are the primary methods for assessing his behavioral functioning. A physical examination, which can help in identifying possible physical or sexual abuse of the teenager, might also be indicated.

Adolescent Interview. An interview with the adolescent should include questions about any behaviors, drug-related or not, that are a problem for him. Exploring related concerns, such as any history of physical or sexual abuse, needs to be done. Uncovering evidence of such abuse, or other significant concerns, might necessitate focusing away from the adolescent's substance abuse as the immediate concern.

> To shift the focus early in treatment from adolescent drug abuse to another problem such as one of these is not usually recommended. However, another problem may emerge that also threatens an individual's health. Some possibilities include: the threat of physical or sexual abuse, severe parental drug or alcohol abuse, running away, pregnancy of an adolescent, or a suicide attempt. Any one of these possibilities may require immediate attention in construction of an initial treatment plan. (Quinn, Keuhl, Thomas, & Joanning, 1988, p. 68)

Family Interview. Family members often have valuable information and insight regarding the adolescent's behavior. However, a word of caution is in order if the adolescent has revealed himself to be a victim of physical or sexual abuse and the offender is a family member. Cover up and denial are common in abusive families. Efforts must be made to protect the safety and well-being of the adolescent (which includes involving the local child protection services), prior to making any inquiries or interventions with the family. This is discussed in detail in Chapter 11.

Instrumentation. As with assessing psychological health, psychological testing can assist with evaluating behavioral concerns with the adolescent. In addition, Tarter recommends the use of the Child Behavioral Checklist for an "expeditious and comprehensive measure of the behavioral disposition," of the adolescent chemical user (Tarter, 1990, p. 24).

Specific concerns about possible physical or sexual abuse of the adolescent can be initially probed through using specific questionnaires. An example of a questionnaire that can be used to inquire about possible physical abuse is the Violence Needs Assessment (Barnhill, Squires, & Gibson, 1982). The Adolescent Sexual Concern Questionnaire can elucidate any particular sexual concerns of the adolescent and be a means to perhaps begin exploring any possibility of sexual abuse of the young person. (Hussey & Singer, 1989).

Collateral Data. Assessing a drug-involved adolescent's behavioral problems, especially as may relate to a possible coexisting psychological disorder or physical or sexual victimization, requires considerable information gathering. Other systems involved in the teenager's life,

such as his school, as well as specific systems invol٧
teenager who has behavioral problems, such as the juven
system or the child protection system, are necessary allies in this data
collection process.

Domain 5: Social Functioning

The goal in assessing the adolescent's social functioning is twofold:
(a) to determine his school and work performance and the quality of his
leisure or recreational pursuits and (b) to look for the linkage between
his chemical use and his school and work performances and his leisure
and recreational pursuits.

Interviewing the teenager and his family as well as obtaining information from other sources, such as the school system, are the major
methods for assessing the adolescent's social functioning. In addition,
use of instrumentation is indicated, especially with assessing the young
person's school performance.

Whereas there is a greater percentage of learning-disabled students
in the adolescent substance-abusing population than in the general
adolescent population (Obermeier & Henry, 1989), this merits particular attention. Administering a battery of intelligence and education
testing may be necessary if a learning disability is strongly suspected.
For teenagers who have previously been diagnosed with a learning
disability, updated testing may be indicated, especially in light of the
possible impact of chemical use on their cognitive functioning.

An undiagnosed or underdiagnosed learning disability can interfere
with school performance, and can affect the adolescent's overall self-
esteem. The school performance part of assessing this social functioning domain should receive necessary attention during the assessment
process.

Domain 6: Interpersonal Environment

The goal in assessing the adolescent's interpersonal environment is
to explore any relationship between his chemical use and his family
functioning and peer relationships. In assessing family functioning, it
is necessary to determine the family's level of functioning across five
major family dynamics (leadership within the family, boundary maintenance, communication patterns, range of emotional sharing, and family problem-solving abilities). In addition, other essential data include
the role of the adolescent's chemical use within his family, any enabling

patterns within the family, and any history of parental or grandparental substance abuse.

In assessing the teenager's peer relationships it is useful to find out as much as possible about his peer group, his role with his group of friends, chemical use among friends, and enabling patterns among friends. Interviewing the adolescent, interviewing his family, and the possible use of instrumentation to assess his family's functioning, are the primary assessment methods for the interpersonal environment domain.

Adolescent Interview. Questions about the teenager's family and friends can be interspersed throughout a diagnostic interview with him. Inquiries about family dynamics, family reactions to his chemical use, and any chemical use by other family members, can complement information gathered from interviewing the adolescent's family directly.

Data about peer relationships can be probed for by asking about the quality of the young person's peer relationships (including questions about trust and closeness among friends, as well as experiences of hurt and rejection by friends), and the role of chemical use among his group of friends.

Family Interview. The primary focus of the family interview should be on gathering information about family dynamics, the function of the teenager's chemical use within this system, and being alert to substance abuse by other family members, particularly parents.

It is highly recommended to include the adolescent substance abuser's entire family in the family assessment interview (Schroeder, 1989). By having the whole family present, the therapist has a greater opportunity to fully observe the family dynamics and organization being played out. Also, every family member is a source of information about family history and dynamics and the adolescent's chemical use. In addition, since family recovery is an integral part of the adolescent's overall recovery, it is advantageous to engage into the therapeutic process as many family members as possible, as early as possible.

Instrumentation. There are various family assessment instruments that can be used to assess the adolescent's family functioning. One example is the Family Adaptability and Cohesion Evaluation Scales (FACES-II) (Olson, Portner & Bell, 1982).

Instruments for assessing peer relationships are not as widespread as family assessment instruments. "Standardized tests measuring peer relationships have not been developed. Self-report instruments have, however, been devised for use in research. Bearing in mind their experimental status, they can nonetheless help the clinician characterize the adolescent's peer network if used prudently" (Tarter, 1990, p. 33).

Illustrating how to conduct an assessment is the case of a 15-year-old female adolescent. This girl had been an occasional user of alcohol over the past year, and was found intoxicated at an after-school function. The school administration required that the girl receive a preliminary substance abuse assessment by the school psychologist. The psychologist met with the girl 2 days after the incident and did a brief substance abuse screening, which included interviewing the girl and having her complete a quick screen instrument. The psychologist determined that chemical use was a concern, that a more comprehensive assessment was indicated, and discussed with the girl and her parents a referral to an outpatient clinic that specializes in adolescent substance abuse. The outpatient clinic routinely conducts adolescent substance abuse assessments by scheduling two assessment sessions a few days apart. The clinician conducted an assessment of this girl by gathering collateral data from the school concerning this teenager and her chemical use, by requiring a urinalysis (which detected marijuana use by this adolescent), by interviewing the teenager to assess her mental status as well as her chemical use history and pattern, and by interviewing the girl's family, including her parents and older brother, to observe family dynamics and to get further data related to her chemical use. At the time of the assessment there were no indications that a physical exam was required. The clinician organized all the assessment data into categories, similar to the six problem domains of the ACUP Index, as a way of both offering a thorough recommendation to the girl and her parents and as a way of beginning initial treatment planning.

SUMMARY

Assessment and treatment planning with adolescent substance abusers and their families rely on doing the most responsible information gathering and making the most responsible treatment decisions with this information. There are, of course, limitations with how comprehensive and accurate the data is.

As always in the face of uncertainty we still must act. We must still make diagnoses using imperfect instruments and refer to treatment programs of which we know little. The hope is that perhaps we can improve our

diagnostic questioning and investigation of the treatment programs to
which we may refer patients. (Blum, 1987, p. 535)

This chapter suggested that the complementary processes of assessing and planning treatment need to work in conjunction with each other
throughout the course of the adolescent's treatment. The assessment of
the adolescent was the focus of this chapter. The next chapter concentrates on treatment planning.

Along with reviewing some assessment models, a model based primarily on the Adolescent Chemical Use Problem (ACUP) Index was
presented. This model involves flexibly applying six possible assessment
methodologies—laboratory tests, physical exam, adolescent interview,
family interview, instrumentation, and gathering collateral data—to the
six problem domains being assessed. The ACUP Index assessment
model is suggested as a guide, recognizing that a brief screen will
suffice for some adolescents, and that a more thorough assessment
across most or all of the problem domains is in order for others.

Chapter 8

SERVICING ADOLESCENT SUBSTANCE ABUSERS
Part II: Treatment Planning

INTRODUCTION

Treatment planning is the process whereby data from the assessment is acted on to service the substance-abusing adolescent and her family. This process entails the clinician both creating a map through a systematic identification of treatment needs and services and following this map by placing the adolescent along a continuum of care. It is within the context of the clinician's creating and following a treatment map that the adolescent is directed in her recovery.

Treatment planning involves approaching adolescent substance abuse as a biopsychosocial problem. The impact of chemical use on the adolescent's biological, psychological, and social functioning necessitates identifying needs and appropriate services to address the problems within these levels of functioning.

Just as with the assessment, treatment planning is both an event and a process. Beyond the initial assessing and treatment planning, ongoing treatment yields further assessment data that perpetuates further treatment planning. As Friedman (1985) remarks in discussing assessment and treatment planning with adolescent substance abusers,

The many sources of information that comprise the diagnostic evaluation procedure must now be integrated into a meaningful picture somewhat like a jigsaw puzzle. Unlike a puzzle, these pieces form a dynamic reality that changes over time and may require repeated assessments. (p. 77)

In this chapter the larger treatment planning process is broken into two subprocesses: (a) developing the actual treatment plan, the map making; and (b) placing the adolescent along the continuum of care, following this treatment map. Developing the treatment plan for the substance-abusing adolescent is illustrated by applying a model based on the Adolescent Chemical Use Problem (ACUP) Index. The placement of the adolescent is described through a model that delineates four levels along a continuum of care.

DEVELOPING THE TREATMENT PLAN

In order to create a useful treatment for the substance-abusing adolescent, his treatment needs have to be identified. This can be accomplished by organizing a list of specific concerns with which the adolescent presents himself and by generating solutions to the those concerns.

As with conducting an assessment, developing a treatment plan can be done by also utilizing the Adolescent Chemical Use Problem (ACUP) Index. This index can serve as both a data base for developing an initial treatment plan and as a mechanism for revising the treatment plan. The ACUP Index presents six problem areas in which to identify specific concerns, both acute and cumulative. With any of these concerns in each problem area specific solutions can be devised.

For example, an initial treatment plan using the ACUP Index was developed for a 13-year-old adolescent male who was hospitalized following an overdose of alcohol while drinking with friends. Interviews with the boy and his mother revealed that he began smoking cigarettes a year ago and began drinking alcohol 6 months ago. Last month he was detained by police for possession of alcohol by a minor. The teenager lives with his mother and younger sister. His parents are divorced and his father, who has sporadic contact with the boy, is an active alcoholic. This adolescent's academic performance at school has been below average during his first year of junior high school. He has stopped participating in sports, which he previously enjoyed. His physical health has been satisfactory, with the exception of a minor asthmatic condition. A sample of this adolescent's initial treatment plan, using the ACUP Index as a model, is presented in Table 8.1.

The treatment plan serves as the map for the direction of treatment. How specific solutions to identified concerns become fulfilled grows out of the work in individual psychotherapy, family therapy, group therapy, and collaboration with other services and systems in the young person's life. Addressing concerns in all relevant areas of the substance-abusing adolescent's life is key, as overlooking any important areas of concern can compromise the success of treatment.

PLACEMENT ALONG THE
CONTINUUM OF CARE MODEL

In addition to developing the actual treatment plan, responsible treatment planning with the substance-abusing adolescent also includes placing her along the continuum of care. Determining a treatment placement involves utilizing the assessment information, as well as the concerns and solutions identified in the treatment plan, to answer the following questions:

- What services are indicated for treating the adolescent's specific chemical use problems?
- What level of substance abuse treatment can optimally provide these services at this time?
- What services and level of care might continue to be needed to treat the adolescent's chemical use problems?

The levels of treatment comprise the continuum of care for chemically involved adolescents. Kusnetz (1986) and Nowinski (1990) have discussed the continuum of care as including types of treatment services and programs. The services and programs include outpatient services, partial hospital programs, residential programs, and inpatient hospital programs. As treatment professionals devise more relevant ways of serving the treatment needs of adolescents, new styles and designs of services and programs will evolve.

As they currently exist, most programs for adolescent substance abusers share some common characteristics. Among the major characteristics of an adolescent program are the following:

Table 8.1
Sample Treatment Plan

Domain #1—Chemical Use Effects

Acute	*Cumulative*
Issue: Risks from being intoxicated	Issue: Progressive misuse of
Solution: Receive education about	psychoactive chemicals
harmful acute effects of psychoactive	Solutions: (a) Receive education about pro-
chemicals	gression of chemical use and addiction
	(b) Work to maintain abstinence from
	chemical

Domain #2—Physical Health

Acute	*Cumulative*
Issue: Physical complications from	Issue: Cigarette smoking aggravating
overdose episode	preexisting asthmatic condition
Solution: Follow through with medical	Solutions: (a) Follow through with
recommendations	ongoing treatment for asthma
	(b) Work to discontinue cigarette use

Domain #3—Psychological Health

Acute	*Cumulative*
Issue: Overdose episode as possible	Issue: Inadequate coping skills for
suicide attempt	managing feelings
Solution: Explore and address suicide risk	Solution: Learn more effective coping
Issue: Prevalent depressed mood	strategies with feelings
Solution: Assess further for possible	
symptoms of depression	

Domain #4—Behavioral Functioning

Acute	*Cumulative*
Issue: Violating community standards	None
pertaining to possession of alcohol	
Solution: Complete community service	
program as supervised by local police	

Domain #5—Social Functioning

Acute	*Cumulative*
None	Issue #1: Decline in school performance
	Solution: Develop contract with guidance
	counselor for:
	(a) Promoting regular attendance at all classes
	(b) Completion of homework assignments
	Issue #2: Decreased involvement in
	prosocial leisure activities
	Solution: Identify and participate in
	leisure activities not organized around
	chemical use

---

continued

Table 8.1
Continued

Domain #6—Interpersonal Environment	
Acute	*Cumulative*
None	Issue #1: Chemical use in violation of family rules
	Solution: Develop abstinence contract with parent
	Issue #2: Effects of being child of a substance abusing parent
	Solution: Receive education about COSAP issues
	Issue #3: Relationships with chemical using peers
	Solutions: (a) Discontinue relationships with chemical using peers
	(b) build relationships with abstaining peers

- A clear position on the necessity of abstinence during treatment
- Services that are developmentally appropriate for the needs of adolescents
- Inclusion of family members in treatment
- Education about substance abuse
- Therapeutic interventions to both interrupt the pattern of substance abuse and address underlying issues
- Emphasis on educational and vocational goals
- Attention to relapse concerns

The issue of whether or not chemical-using adolescents should be required to maintain total abstinence is a contentious one with many treatment professionals. Therapists working with adolescents line up on both sides of this issue.

Some treatment professionals contend that promoting controlled use of chemicals by adolescents is an acceptable therapeutic stance (Peele & Brodsky, 1991; Smith, 1984). One argument is that chemical use is an adolescent rite-of-passage and a developmentally appropriate testing of limits. Another argument is that many teenagers who use chemicals are not addicted and likely will not become addicted. Consequently, promoting controlled use instead of abstinence is a more relevant therapeutic goal.

There are also treatment professionals who strongly argue on behalf of total abstinence for all adolescents, regardless of their experience with chemicals (Jaynes & Rugg, 1988; Muldoon & Crowley, 1986). The argument for abstinence for all adolescents hinges on two primary beliefs: (a) that all adolescents are at risk, to varying degrees, to chemical addiction due to their developmental vulnerability; and (b) consuming chemicals is illegal for adolescents and to not require strict abstinence is to collude with an illicit activity.

The position of this book is to endorse a pro-abstinence position with adolescents. At the same time it is recognized that there are some adolescents who can and do practice controlled use of chemicals without developing significant chemical use problems. As discussed in Chapter 1, adolescents at Stage 1 or 2 of the Adolescent Chemical Use Experience (ACUE) continuum are not necessarily headed toward addiction. These teenagers may indeed be using chemicals in a manner that is relatively appropriate for their adolescent years. What cannot be easily, or absolutely, determined, is which users will progress into deeper substance abuse problems. "Controlled use may be a viable option for the true social user, but the habitual abuser and the addict are not candidates for controlled use" (Nowinski, 1990, p. 136). Requiring abstinence for as long as the adolescent is in treatment for substance abuse is a sound therapeutic stance.

The American Society of Addictive Medicine's (ASAM) "Patient Placement Criteria for the Treatment of Psychoactive Substance Use Disorders" (ASAM, 1991) is one widely accepted model for a continuum of care for adolescent substance abuse. The ASAM model delineates four levels of care, from the less structured to the more structured, for treating adolescent substance abusers. The services previously mentioned for adolescent substance abusers (outpatient services, partial hospital program, residential program, and inpatient hospital program) correspond in general with the four levels of care of the ASAM continuum of care model: Level I (outpatient treatment), Level II (intensive outpatient/partial hospitalization program), Level III (medically monitored intensive inpatient treatment), and Level IV (medically managed intensive inpatient treatment).

The continuum of care model presented in this chapter discusses four levels of care for adolescent substance abusers according to criteria for placement at the treatment level, benefits and drawbacks to placement at the level of care, therapeutic elements available at the level of care, and types of programs generally offered at the treatment level. The criteria for placement discussed in this model are adapted in part from the placement criteria for adolescents as established by the American Society of Addictive Medicine (ASAM, 1991).

Although they are not specifically discussed in this continuum of care model, dual diagnosis services and programs are becoming increasingly available at all four levels of care. Dual diagnosis programs are a more recent development in the matrix of treatment services for adolescent drug abusers. They are designed for those adolescents who present both a substance abuse disorder and a psychological disorder. Because such psychological disorders can be masked by the teenager's drug abuse, the presence of the existing psychological disorder might not be diagnosed until later in the course of treatment.

Outpatient Services

Placement Criteria for Outpatient Services

Outpatient treatment is the least structured level of care for adolescent substance abusers. In the absence of any acute or chronic medical, mental health, or behavioral concerns, placement in outpatient treatment should be based on at least one of the following:

- No previous treatment for substance abuse and an interpersonal environment that is sufficiently supportive of sobriety
- Previously successful outpatient substance abuse treatment and an interpersonal environment that is sufficiently supportive of sobriety
- Maximum benefit from a more structured level of substance abuse treatment and an interpersonal environment sufficiently supportive of sobriety

Benefits and Drawbacks to Outpatient Services

The primary benefit of outpatient care is that the teenager receives treatment in the "natural environment" of his family, school, and community. Progress in treatment can be gauged according to how well the adolescent is handling, in a drug-free manner, the day-to-day demands of adolescence, family life, friendships, and other responsibilities.

The primary drawback to this level of care is that it is not appropriate ongoing treatment for a teenager in the more advanced stages of substance abuse. Therapists who attempt to treat severe and active drug abusing adolescents on an outpatient basis are running the risk of enabling the teenager's continued and progressive use of drugs. Due to the extent of drug involvement by these teenagers, a more intensive treatment structure is most often indicated.

Therapeutic Elements With Outpatient Services

Individual psychotherapy, family therapy, and group therapy can all be appropriately provided to chemical-using teenagers on an outpatient basis. In addition, self-help groups, such as AA and NA, can be useful adjuncts to outpatient treatment.

Types of Outpatient Services

Outpatient services for adolescent substance abusers can be offered in a variety of settings, including the offices of private therapists, outpatient clinics, and the outpatient departments of hospital-based or residential programs. In addition, schools are becoming more actively involved as outpatient treatment resources. Often designed according to a Student Assistance Model (Anderson, 1987), outpatient service systems for adolescents who use chemicals are being created in junior high schools, high schools, and even colleges (Suchman & Broughton, 1988).

> The American school faces a new challenge: to confront, and actively strike back at, the substance-abuse problems of its students. This effort must reach far beyond the establishment of alcohol and drug education programs, and the referral services provided by the substance-abuse counselor. The strategy must include a knowledge of systems theory, and a thorough understanding of the family system of the chemically-dependent adolescent. Only then can the school fully recognize the nature and importance of its own position within the adolescent's family system. (Wight, 1990, p. 74)

There are, however, limitations on the extent to which school systems can be outpatient treatment resources. Among the considerations that impact the school system's providing such services are liability issues, confidentiality concerns, and boundaries with including family members. Consequently, school systems' treatment role is usually confined to contributing to the assessment process and providing support groups for adolescents.

The four types of outpatient services discussed here are: crisis intervention, an extended screening, an intervention, and aftercare treatment. The first three usually precede placement in a more intensive level of treatment and, within this context, can be considered as models of brief treatment for adolescent substance abusers. Brief treatment as defined here refers to either a limited number of treatment sessions occurring over a short period of time, or an apportioned number of treatment sessions occurring over a longer period of time.

Brief Treatment—Crisis Intervention. Crisis intervention is the therapeutic response to an immediate sense of distress, experienced by the adolescent or his family, resulting from a problem related to an episode of chemical involvement by the adolescent. Crises that often trigger this sense of distress include:

- The adolescent's possessing, or being found under the influence of chemicals at school
- The adolescent's being arrested for possession of alcohol by a minor or for possession of an illicit substance
- Parents' discovering their child to be in possession of chemicals or intoxicated
- The adolescent's being arrested for chemically induced behavior, such as disorderly conduct or assault.
- The adolescent's experiencing some medical or psychiatric emergency due to a chemical use episode.

Ewing (1978) discusses crisis intervention as being specific psychotherapeutic techniques applied to individuals or families who are experiencing severe emotional maladjustment to a precipitating event. The goal of crisis intervention is to assist the young person, or the young person and his family, in making an adaptive reaction.

Crisis intervention in these instances is often a single session encounter with an adolescent or his parents. The therapist's initial response is to elicit individuals' feelings about the adolescent's crisis and to be empathic toward those feelings. Following this initial laying of an empathic foundation, the therapist can, based on the stability of the individuals, either move to begin gathering more data for assessing the adolescent's chemical use, or facilitate a prompt referral to complete the assessment process.

Brief Treatment—Extended Screening. An extended screening is one outpatient strategy that a therapist can employ when she is unable to determine whether or not a teenager has a substance use disorder. The rationale behind this strategy is to use the treatment process as a diagnostic tool to determine whether it is substance abuse or occasional use.

Using the treatment process itself as a diagnostic tool enables one to avoid the typical "cops and robbers" game, in which the parents make accusations about their kids' drug use that they cannot prove and thus set up endless rounds of recriminations and denial. (Treadway, 1989, p. 140)

The bolt that holds the extended screening strategy together is the abstinence contract. Written behavioral contracts can be powerful therapeutic tools between adolescents and their parents (Fatis and Konewko, 1983). The abstinence contract is one such tool for laying a solid therapeutic foundation from the outset of working with adolescent chemical users and their parents.

The primary goal in using an abstinence contract in an extended screening is to keep the responsibility squarely on the teenager for determining whether or not he has a drug problem. In short, it is not the job of his parents or his therapist to "prove" that he has a drug problem—it is the job of the adolescent to demonstrate that he does not have a drug problem by abiding by his abstinence contract.

A secondary goal is that the abstinence contract allows the therapist and adolescent an opportunity to explore the role of chemicals in the young person's life. Zweben sums up this reasoning in stating,

This "experiment" allows patient and therapist to examine the attachment to alcohol and drugs; by subtracting it out, one gains a clearer perspective of the role it plays in the patient's life, whether or not the criteria for addiction can be met in each individual case. (Zweben, 1989, p. 124)

There are some guidelines that are important for therapists to keep in mind when using an abstinence contract during extended screenings. It is important for the therapist to adjust her therapeutic perspective to a time-limited intermittent therapeutic approach when doing extended screenings. Also, therapists need to consider parents' responsibility and the benefit of adjunctive services, such as support groups, when employing this extended screening strategy.

Guidelines for Abstinence Contract. The abstinence contract should explicitly state: (a) that it is not permissible for the adolescent to use any mood altering chemical, (b) that the adolescent is to remain above suspicion of using chemicals by upholding his responsibilities within his family and in other areas of his life, and (c) that there are specific consequences if the adolescent is discovered to have used a chemical or is creating strong suspicion of chemical use by irresponsible behavior.

It is also important to clearly state under what conditions the teenager would be expected to enter treatment.

The willingness of the adolescent to go along with the abstinence contract will, in part, be determined by how the therapist presents the plan. A couple of different reframing approaches might make the adolescent more receptive to the abstinence contract. One reframe might be to discuss the contract as an opportunity or challenge to prove that substance abuse is not a problem in his life. Another reframe might be to offer the contract as a "research task" (Zweben, 1989, p. 125) to ascertain the teenager's ability to stay away from using chemicals.

The duration of the abstinence contract needs to be negotiated between the adolescent and his parents. One approach is to ask the adolescent to commit to abstinence for a designated period of time. A guideline for the actual length of expected abstinence is for the teenager to be chemically free for the same amount of time that he has used drugs (Singer & White, 1991). In other words, if the young person has been using chemicals for a year, then he would be expected to commit to total abstinence from chemical use for a minimum of one year.

Time-Limited Intermittent Treatment. Another issue to be dealt with is how the therapist can work with the adolescent and his parents over an extended period of time and, essentially, monitor the parents' monitoring of the abstinence contract. Treatment is a limited resource. In the current health care reimbursement climate, therapists often have a limited number of sessions with which to treat an adolescent. Consequently, therapists are being called upon to be more resourceful in their use of these limited number of outpatient sessions. One way is for therapists to use a time-limited intermittent therapeutic (TLIT) approach (Kreilkamp, 1989).

In utilizing TLIT, the therapist starts off by meeting with the adolescent and his family for an initial session or two. An abstinence contract would be drafted during these initial sessions. For the next 2 to 3 months, the therapist could schedule twice-monthly sessions with the adolescent and his parents to monitor progress with the abstinence contract. Monitoring progress could be done within the framework of a "solution-focused therapy" approach (de Shazer, 1985). The focus is on changes the adolescent is making to remain drug-free—changes in activities, friends, attitudes, and goals. Simultaneously, parents can work on steps they are taking to successfully implement the abstinence contract.

If the adolescent is not complying with the abstinence contract or if parents are unable to effectively monitor the contract then a modification of the extended screening is indicated. This can include a more intensive outpatient treatment approach (2 or 3 sessions per week) for 3 to 4 weeks. If this more intensive approach proves successful, and the adolescent abstains from all chemical use, then the therapist can gradually shift to monitoring progress and meeting less frequently. If this intensive outpatient approach with the abstinence contract is not successful, then a referral to a more structured level of treatment should be considered.

If both the adolescent and his parents are working with the abstinence contract, then continuing this course of treatment is indicated. The therapist can schedule longer periods of time between sessions, perhaps moving to one session per month for a few months, before terminating with the teenager and his parents.

Time-limited intermittent therapy allows for a minimum number of therapy sessions over an extended period of time. Such a therapeutic approach is indicated in many cases with adolescent substance abusers.

> If this is the first time an adolescent has become aware of the severity of the problem, and has not tried to quit, a less intrusive recommendation than inpatient or residential treatment should be tried. A no-use contract along with supportive outpatient counseling or treatment may avert the need for inpatient. (Nakken, 1989, p. 86)

Parents' Responsibilities with Extended Screenings. Teenagers who use substances need their parents. They need their parents to send a clear message about the unacceptability of chemical use during this time in their development. They also need their parents to back up this message with action—creating and monitoring an abstinence contract.

For parents to be a resource to their child during an extended screening, they need to be open to examining any enabling pattern they have fallen into and be willing to work on changing this pattern. In addition, parents need to examine their own chemical use and their own values and attitudes about teenage chemical use.

There are some rules of thumb that therapists might consider in working with parents about developing rules and consequences for an abstinence contract with their child:

- The teenager should have input into the creation of limits and consequences.
- Limits and consequences should be consistent with the norms for teenagers in the community.

- Limits and consequences should be relevant to the developmental sub-phase of the adolescent (i.e., different considerations go into creating limits and consequences with a 14-year-old and with a 17-year-old).
- Limits and consequences are designed to place expectations on the adolescent's behavior, that are measurable, and not on his attitude, which is not measurable.
- Both limits and consequences need to be realistic and enforceable.
- Limits and consequences need to be reviewed and modified as the adolescent manifests greater responsibility and the parents' expectations change.

Monitoring an abstinence contract also necessitates some guidelines for parents. Keeping in mind that the rationale for an abstinence contract is for the adolescent to prove that he does not have a drug problem, not for his parents to prove that he does. Parents need to practice vigilance without surveillance. The parents' responsibility is to see to it that their child is honoring the terms of the contract, not to act like detectives with their teenager.

Group Treatment and the Extended Screening. The adolescent's participation in group treatment can be a valuable adjunct to the extended screening process. Group treatment is congruent with the goals of TLIT and can be an alternative to individual therapy. Raubolt's (1983) model of brief, problem-focused group psychotherapy with adolescents is an excellent therapeutic framework for such group treatment. Applying this model, therapists can facilitate a time-limited group experience that might be both supportive and problem-solving for the teenage chemical user.

Two types of time-limited group treatment that can be made available to adolescent chemical users during an extended screening are the chemical awareness group and the abstinence support group.

The *chemical awareness group* is intended for teenagers who are ambivalent about discontinuing their drug use. The purpose of this group is to use "persuasive education" (Smith, 1985) as a means of influencing the adolescent to examine his chemical use pattern seriously, and to lead to decision making about continued chemical use. Through discussion and exercises group members can learn about aspects of chemical use and addiction, self-assess their stage of use according to the ACUE continuum (Chapter 1), and identify likely consequences of continued chemical use. Confrontation from the group leader or fellow group members can be a useful strategy with some adolescents in this type of group. However, confrontation should be attempted with the underlying messages of nurturance and support for the adolescent.

The *abstinence support group* is intended for adolescents who have become aware of some problems related to their substance use and who are self-motivated to abstain from substance use. The purpose of this group is to use peer support to assist the teenager in dealing with the developmental challenges of adolescence without resorting to using chemicals.

In doing time-limited group treatment with teenage substance users, it is important to conduct pregroup interviews with prospective group members. This pregroup interview can serve the dual purpose of: (a) determining if an adolescent has the psychological stability and capacity to genuinely benefit from time-limited group treatment and (b) to prepare the young person for the group and to contract with him about his responsibilities as a group member.

Extended Screening Outcomes. There are three possible treatment outcomes from an extended screening with an adolescent chemical user and his family. One is that the teenager's chemical use is indicative of Stage 1 or Stage 2 chemical use, that his chemical use is not a significant issue for him, and that no further treatment is indicated.

Another possible outcome is that the adolescent's substance use is indicative of Stage 1 or Stage 2 use (or even possibly early Stage 3 use), that the substance use itself is not a primary problem, but that treatment not focused on substance abuse is indicated. In such cases, the adolescent's chemical use might be more reflective of a developmental difficulty or psychological disorder and treatment specific to those concerns should be pursued. It is also possible that the young person's substance use might be more symptomatic of some masked family problem and that family treatment would be the most appropriate course of treatment. As Kaufman (1985) remarks, "Some adolescents may use substances in a peer-appropriate way without any impairment of function. In these families, the major problem may be the parents' overreaction or scapegoating" (p. 249).

Still another possible outcome of the extended screening is that the adolescent's chemical use is well into Stage 3 or Stage 4 of the chemical use experience continuum and is an active and primary problem. In such cases, recovery-oriented treatment is indicated. Recovery-oriented treatment for adolescents and their families is discussed in Chapters 9 and 10.

Brief Treatment—The Intervention. Another outpatient strategy that a therapist can use is the intervention. The intervention is a specific therapeutic strategy whereby a family, and sometimes other concerned persons, attempt to: (a) make the adolescent aware of how his substance use has adversely affected him and areas of his life and (b) influence the adolescent to comply with plans for treatment. In essence, by facilitating an intervention a therapist is creating a crisis for the adolescent to compel him to enter substance abuse treatment.

The original model for an intervention was developed by Vernon Johnson in his pioneering treatment approaches with adult alcoholics (Johnson, 1973). Schaefer has since adopted this adult alcoholic intervention model for application with adolescent substance abusers (Schaefer, 1987).

An intervention is strongly indicated for adolescents demonstrating signs of being in Stages 3 or 4 of the ACUE continuum. This is even more the case for those teenagers who have participated in an extended screening without successfully responding to their abstinence contract.

There are three basic steps in an intervention with an adolescent. The first step is for family members and other concerned persons to gather data about the adolescent's chemical use behavior. Such data can include behaviors while under the influence of substances, overall behavioral changes, and the young person's noncompliance with his abstinence contract. The second step is for these family members and others to prepare for a caring confrontation of the teenager (for a detailed explanation of a caring confrontation see Chapter 9). Prior to the actual intervention, the therapist can help coach the intervention participants in how to present the chemical use data to the adolescent, how to share feelings about how his chemical use has personally affected each of them, and how to state in an unyielding manner their supportive expectation that the adolescent enter substance abuse treatment. The third and final step of the intervention is the actual caring confrontation with the adolescent. The therapist's primary job during the caring confrontation is to create an environment that is as supportive as possible, in which family members and concerned others can share their concerns with the teenager, and in which the teenager can hear these concerns. The intervention confronts the delusion and denial of the adolescent. At the conclusion of the intervention, the family informs the adolescent about the plans for treatment, and the adolescent's assent to those plans, however grudging, is viewed as success (Wheeler & Malmquist, 1987, p. 441).

The intervention is viewed as unsuccessful when, in spite of a skillfully orchestrated caring confrontation, the adolescent steadfastly refuses to enter substance abuse treatment. In such cases the adolescent has opted for his likely alternative choice—not to be allowed to live at home until substance abuse treatment is successfully completed. In cases when the drug-involved adolescent has, in effect, chosen not to continue living at home, parents may still have some responsibilities for the well-being of their child. Depending on the age of the child, parents may need to be both involved with facilitating an alternative living arrangement for their child as well as aware of their legal responsibilities with any alternative living arrangement. It is exactly for this reason that therapists should not force the strategy of an intervention upon parents. Some parents just are not ready to confront their drug-involved teenager and risk their son or daughter living on the streets.

> Parents are not simply pathological, resistant, or stupid when they cannot confront their children. They're scared and they know that it is a matter of life and death. I don't want to be the one who aggressively pushes the parents in this crisis-of-change stage, because they ultimately have to be prepared to hold the line and take the consequences of what might happen. (Treadway, 1989, p. 153)

When the intervention is not successful in influencing the teenager to enter treatment and the teenager chooses the option of leaving home, it is hoped that subsequent opportunities will arise to direct him to treatment. Perhaps adverse living conditions away from home or some crisis might eventually make the adolescent more amenable to treatment.

Aftercare Treatment. If the three brief treatment strategies are outpatient approaches at one end of the recovery process, prior to the adolescent entering recovery-oriented treatment, then aftercare treatments are outpatient approaches applied at the other end of the recovery process, when the adolescent is well along his recovery journey. The conventional understanding is that aftercare is the individual, family, and/or group therapy that a teenager receives following substance abuse treatment in a partial hospital program, an inpatient hospital, or a residential program.

Upon leaving a structured therapeutic milieu, returning home, and continuing in recovery, the adolescent is faced with ongoing challenges. There are two primary issues to be dealt with by the adolescent in aftercare treatment: (a) his reentry into his family, his school, and his community and (b) his continuing on a reparative developmental path in his psychological functioning.

During the period of reentry, the changes that the adolescent experienced while in treatment are put to the test. Each recovering adolescent's test is unique.

> No two adolescents will face identical lifestyle circumstances once they leave a treatment program. Some may need to return to families and make new adjustments, while others have no families. Some have evolved more constructive coping skills and some are more educated or intelligent. Most of these young people have not been taught how to cope with the problems that they face once they reenter society. (Freudenberger & Carbone, 1984, p. 97)

Continuing in recovery also means continuing to progress in psychological development, enhanced by repair of those parts of his development that have been impaired by substance abuse. Learning coping skills and abilities in sobriety can be the reparative tools that help the adolescent reach his developmental potential.

Partial Hospital Programs (PHP)

Placement Criteria for PHP

A partial hospital program is the "middle ground" (Feigelman, 1987) between the home-based structure of outpatient treatment and the intensely structured milieu of inpatient or residential treatment. Placement into an adolescent PHP for substance abuse should be based on the existence of at least one of the following criteria:

- An unsuccessful trial of outpatient treatment and no acute or chronic medical, mental health, or behavioral concerns that would prevent participation in a PHP
- A relapse during outpatient aftercare following a successful period of inpatient or residential treatment
- A continuity of treatment to a less structured treatment level following a successful period of inpatient or residential treatment.

Benefits and Drawbacks to PHP

One of the benefits of a PHP for a teenage substance abuser is that he receives treatment while remaining in the natural recovery environment of his family and community. For some adolescents a PHP affords the advantage of being an alternative to hospitalization—the adolescent is steered onto the path of recovery without having to enter an inpatient program. For other adolescent substance abusers who needed and successfully completed inpatient hospital or residential programs, a PHP can be extremely supportive during that critical period of reentry.

Among the drawbacks of a PHP with adolescents at more advanced stages of substance abuse is that they will more likely undermine initial treatment efforts. Such teenagers often need to get some distance from their families, peer groups, schools, or communities for a period of time in order to have an optimal chance for initial sobriety.

Therapeutic Elements in a PHP

Most adolescent PHPs for substance abuse include a full range of therapeutic modalities including individual, family, and group therapy, as well as exposure to AA and NA meetings. In addition, the structure of the milieu provides the teenager with a pro-recovery environment for a significant portion of his day.

Types of PHPs

Adolescent PHPs for substance abuse can be designed exclusively for adolescent substance abusers or may be set up to respond to the needs of adolescents with a concurrent substance use disorder and psychological disorder. The length of stay in most PHPs runs from several weeks to a few months.

Daytime PHP. The daytime PHP engages the mornings and afternoons of the recovering adolescent; he returns to his family during evenings and weekends. A therapeutic school is the foundation of the program, with different group therapies offered both during and after school. Individual and family therapy are integrated into the adolescent's treatment plan as needed.

After-School PHP. The after-school PHP provides an ongoing recovery program following the teenager's school day. The advantage of this type of PHP is that the adolescent can work on his recovery while remaining in his home school. An adolescent may be placed in an after-school PHP following a period of success in a daytime PHP.

Residential Programs

Placement Criteria for Residential Programs

Residential level of care is intended for adolescents whose drug use is posing a significant problem. Placement in a residential program should be based on the existence of at least one of the following criteria:

- The adolescent was unsuccessful in a less-structured level of substance abuse treatment, outpatient treatment, or PHP.
- The adolescent was responsive to a less-structured level of substance abuse treatment yet is at high risk for relapse due to an inadequate recovery environment.
- The adolescent presents acute medical, mental health, or behavioral problems related to substance abuse; the acute presenting problem(s) necessitates being in a safe environment with medical and psychiatric services immediately available to monitor acute needs.
- The adolescent presents ongoing medical, mental health, or behavioral problems related to substance abuse; the ongoing presenting problem(s) necessitates being in a safe environment with medical and psychiatric services immediately available to monitor ongoing problems.

Benefits and Drawbacks to Residential Programs

One advantage of a residential program is that acute and chronic chemical use problems can be dealt with in the safe and structured confines of the residential milieu. Another advantage is that if the adolescent's family or peer environment has been a prominent factor in his substance abuse, then the adolescent can be removed from this environment as he seeks to stabilize in recovery. An additional benefit of a residential program is that ongoing medical and psychiatric management is available, not only for problems that are present during the time of admission, but also for latent problems that may surface during the course of the young person's recovery.

There are also some drawbacks to a residential program. Removing the adolescent from his family and community, although often necessary with highly drug-involved teenagers, can create the eventual stresses of the adolescent's having to reenter and rejoin his family and community following residential care. Another drawback to residential treatment is that there is the risk of "overtreating" the teenager. There have been instances of adolescent chemical users being inappropriately treated in a residential program when a less-structured level of treatment was indicated (Nakken, 1989). Such misdiagnosing and overtreating is not only unresponsive to the needs of the young person and his family, but might result in their becoming closed to the appropriate level of care needed.

Therapeutic Elements With Residential Programs

The therapeutic elements of a residential program usually include a full range of therapies—individual, family, and group—as well as access to AA and NA meetings. In addition, a major therapeutic element is the residential milieu itself. The recovery environment of the milieu offers a community of round-the-clock support and structure, which is so important to the emerging sober identity of the teenager.

Another feature of many residential programs is non-verbal therapies such as art therapy (Singer and White, 1991) and activity therapies such as recreational therapy (Singer and White, 1991) and outward bound programs (McPeake, Kennedy, Grossman, & Beaulieu, 1991). Substance-abusing adolescents who are highly resistant to treatment are often quite responsive to such nontraditional therapies, which take a more indirect route tapping into the teenager's inner experience.

Types of Residential Programs

Residential programs for teenage drug abusers range from short-term programs to long-term programs. The Minnesota Model is an example of a short-term residential program, and therapeutic communities and group homes are examples of long-term residential programs.

The Minnesota Model. For a number of years the Minnesota Model has set the standard for residential treatment with adolescent substance abusers (Wheeler & Malmquist, 1987). Adopted from the 28-day adult alcoholism residential model, adolescent programs based on this model have been designed for residential stays for up to 45 to 60 days. However, in the current health care reimbursement climate these pro-grams are having to modify their treatment regimen to considerably lessened lengths of stay. The impact of this is that people are transferred to less-structured levels of treatment more quickly than before.

Therapeutic Community (TC). Therapeutic communities for adoles-cent substance abusers are intended for teenagers who need the structure and support of a residential milieu for an extended period of time. According to Schinke, Botvin, and Orlandi (1991, p. 47), "The objective of most residential communities is not only to change substance-use behavior, but also to develop social skills, assist in education and vocational skills, and build self-esteem and confidence."

Group Home. Group homes are smaller residential programs of usually a dozen or fewer teenagers. While residing in the group home, the recovering adolescent might have considerable interaction with the outside community, including attending a local school or holding a job at a nearby location.

Inpatient Hospital Programs (IHP)

Placement Criteria for IHP

Inpatient hospitalization is intended for adolescents whose drug use is posing a significant problem. Placement criteria for inpatient hospitalization programs and residential programs have much overlap. However, a primary difference between the two levels of care is that inpatient programs are organized to medically manage acute or ongoing physical, mental health, or behavioral programs, whereby residential programs are organized to medically monitor such problems (American Society of Addiction Medicine, 1991). Placement in an inpatient hospital program should be based on the existence of at least one of the following criteria:

- The adolescent was unsuccessful in a less-structured level of substance abuse treatment, outpatient treatment, or PHP.
- The adolescent presents acute medical, mental health, or behavioral problems related to substance abuse; the acute presenting problem(s) necessitates being in a safe environment with medical and psychiatric services immediately available to medically manage acute needs.
- The adolescent presents ongoing medical, mental health, or behavioral problems related to substance abuse; the ongoing presenting problem(s) necessitates being in a safe environment with medical and psychiatric services immediately available to medically manage ongoing problems.

Benefits and Drawbacks to IHP

The benefits of IHP are similar to those of residential programs. These advantages include the teenager's being in a safe and structured therapeutic environment and removed from the enabling environment of family and peers. However, in those cases in which separation from family and community is more problematic than advantageous, inpatient hospital programs, with their emphasis on short-term stabilization of the adolescent, offer a strong benefit.

There are also some drawbacks to an inpatient hospital program. One drawback is that an admission to an inpatient hospital program can be stressful and crisis-inducing for the adolescent and family and needs to be carefully considered by a referring clinician. Another drawback is that inpatient hospital programs, with their emphasis on short-term stabilization, may run the risk of "undertreating" the teenager and not adequately coordinating a continuity of treatment once the adolescent has stablized.

Therapeutic Elements with IHP

Most inpatient hospital programs offer individual, family, and group therapies, as well as making AA and NA meetings available. Because the emphasis with inpatient programs is on short-term stabilization, most therapies are offered according to a brief treatment approach. The therapeutic focus is intensified to rapidly mobilize the inner resources of the young person and the coping skills of the family in order to bring about this stabilization.

Types of IHP

Detoxification Unit. A detoxification unit provides medical management to the substance abusing adolescent experiencing withdrawal symptoms or related biomedical complications. Becoming physically chemically free can be a necessary beginning in recovery for some persons.

Brief Treatment Unit. One outcome of decreased lengths of inpatient stays due to the changed health care reimbursement climate is the emergence of brief hospitalization programs for adolescent substance abusers. In these programs the goal is for short-term stabilization of the adolescent, whereby the teenager gets a foothold on sobriety without prolonged separation from his family, his school, or his community. Van Meter and Rioux (Van Meter & Rioux, 1990) discuss the effectiveness of a 21-day inpatient program for adolescent substance abusers. It is likely that in the current health care reimbursement climate programs designed for even shorter lengths of hospitalization will be developed.

As the adolescent's needs change during the course of treatment, decisions about placing the adolescent along the continuum of care have to be ongoing. Further decisions with the teenager will need to be made about continuing at a level of treatment, being moved from a level of treatment, and being admitted to another level of treatment.

SUMMARY

Treatment planning with adolescent substance abusers and their families entails the action—developing a treatment plan and placing the adolescent along the continuum of care—that is generated from the data of the assessment. The circumstances of each young person who uses chemicals are unique. Developing a useful treatment plan and facilitating an appropriate placement along the continuum of care requires the clinician to respect this uniqueness.

This chapter discussed developing a treatment plan by both identifying specific concerns about the chemical-using adolescent and identifying solutions to these concerns. The ACUP Index, which can be adapted as a model for organizing assessment data, can also be used as a model for mapping out a treatment plan addressing acute and cumulative concerns with the chemically involved teenager.

This chapter also discussed continuum of care models and the common characteristics of treatment programs at different levels of care. A four-level continuum of care model was presented according to: (a) placement criteria for each level of care, (b) benefits and drawbacks for each level of care, and (c) therapeutic elements at each level of care, and (d) types of programs operating at each level of care.

Outpatient services are at the least structured treatment level of the continuum of care. Brief treatment—including crisis intervention, an extended screening, and an intervention—as well as aftercare treatment for recovering adolescents are among the types of outpatient services available at this level of care.

Partial hospital programs (PHPs) are the next least structured level of treatment along the continuum of care. PHPs provide an adolescent with a milieu for addressing her chemical use issues, while allowing her to remain in the natural recovery environment of her family.

Residential programs are a more structured level of treatment along the continuum of care. For many recovering adolescents the residential setting offers necessary structure and support as they progress along the path of sobriety.

Inpatient hospital programs (IHPs) are a structured level of treatment designed for the short-term stabilization of the adolescent. This initial stabilization can be the catalyst for continued recovery by the adolescent.

Chapter 9

ADOLESCENT RECOVERY

INTRODUCTION

The adolescent's recovery from substance abuse is a process of evolving from a chemically imprisoned pseudo-self to a chemically free real self. By participating in this process the teenager takes on the rigors of repairing the developmental destruction from his drug habit.

This recovery process is an individual journey for the teenager, yet it intersects with the recovery process with his family and with his peer relationships. The adolescent's individual recovery and his family's recovery are not necessarily parallel processes. There are four possible treatment outcomes with the recovery process for an adolescent and his family:

1. Both the adolescent and his family improve in treatment. This offers a positive prognosis for continued recovery for the teenager and his family.
2. The adolescent progresses in treatment, yet his family remains at a problematic level of functioning. This outcome offers a questionable prognosis for the teenager's further successful recovery (Robinson & Greene, 1988). However, sometimes teenagers receive enough extra-familial support to maintain their sobriety or discontinue living with their families.
3. The teenager remains mired in a pattern of substance abuse and denial, yet his family moves away from its part in enabling this pattern. Although this presents a poor prognosis for the young person, there is the hope that the family's new found strength might promote the teenager's openness to receiving treatment when the next drug-related crisis occurs.

4. The adolescent and his family experience no change as a result of treatment interventions or possibly each or both deteriorate in functioning. This outcome offers the worst prognosis, and usually a further adolescent or family crisis is needed to provoke some mobilization for recovery.

This chapter presents a model of adolescent recovery involving four stages, as well as a discussion of recovery skills and relapse treatment, which support the recovery process. As young persons evolve in recovery, the challenge for the therapist is to change how the therapist is being helpful with the teenager's shifting therapeutic needs.

STAGES OF ADOLESCENT RECOVERY

The teenager's progression in recovery can be construed as unfolding through different stages. Cohen (1989) and Nowinski (1990) have presented models for stages of individual adolescent recovery. The model for adolescent recovery presented in this book encompasses four stages of recovery, with each stage involving eight components composing the therapeutic framework.

Overview of Stages

The four stages of adolescent recovery entail the teenager's progress from terminating a relationship with chemicals to developing a chemically free self. This transformation happens as the adolescent develops emotionally safe, supportive and challenging relationships (a combination of other sober teenagers, family members, a therapist, a treatment team, a program sponsor, and others) that he or she internalizes.

The stages of recovery are general guidelines representing the realities of recovery. As such, there is much overlap among the stages and much variability with how any given adolescent progresses through the stages.

One way of viewing these four stages is to look at them as rungs on a ladder, symbolizing the adolescent's climb out of the abyss of addiction. As the four stages of adolescent chemical use experience (discussed in Chapter 1) can be viewed as a chute the teenager descends when chemical use becomes more of a problem, so these four stages of recovery can be seen as the reverse of this process. As the young person grows through each stage of recovery, he climbs another rung away from chemical use problems and toward sober adolescent development.

Overview of Therapeutic Framework

The eight components of the therapeutic framework for each stage of this model are:

1. The adolescent's intrapsychic process
2. The adolescent's recovery crisis
3. Therapeutic goals for working to resolve the recovery crisis
4. The adolescent's resistance to working on these goals
5. Therapeutic strategy for treating the adolescent's resistance
6. AA/NA step(s) that corresponds with stage of recovery
7. The adolescent's resistance to working the AA/NA step(s)
8. Therapeutic strategy for treating the adolescent's resistance to working the step(s)

These eight therapeutic components are organized around two concepts of psychological development: crisis and resistance. The nature of recovery is change, and change is both an antecedent to and a result of crisis. Crises in recovery are opportunities for further growth for the adolescent. At the same time, crises are psychologically threatening, and it is natural for individuals to resist psychological danger.

Resistance is based on the adolescent's "psychological need for protection" (McHolland, 1985, p. 349). It is a therapeutic pitfall to perceive the chemically dependent adolescent's resistance in treatment as mere willful opposition. In her discussion of resistance and recovery, Zweben describes resistance as "all those forces within that resist change, and it is the subject of therapeutic work, not an obstacle to it" (Zweben, 1989, p. 125). In discussing how to treat resistance constructively during the course of recovery, Zweben goes on to say, "A therapist who views resistance as a given, not a sign of anyone's failure, creates the conditions for approaching it productively" (p. 126).

Therapeutic strategy in this eight-component model involves working with the teenager's resistances to help him work through his recovery crises and grow onward in recovery. There are a couple of assumptions for therapists to keep in mind as they choose a therapeutic strategy. One assumption is that each adolescent is different, and therapeutic strategies often need modifications to respond to the unique needs of each recovering teenager. A second assumption is that creativity and versatility are the art of therapy. Although some samples of therapeutic prescriptions are discussed in this chapter, there is much room for variety in therapeutic approach. The recovering adolescent might respond to an array of strategies within each modality of therapy.

A Model for Adolescent Recovery

Stage 1: The Shifting Stage

Process. This initial stage of adolescent recovery consists of the teenager beginning the process of terminating his relationship with chemicals. The young person rarely lets go of this relationship without a fight. Drugs have played an important part in holding together his sense of self. Giving up drugs is giving up an experience that has become a vital component of his psychological organization.

Recovery Crisis. The first crisis of recovery, the abstinence crisis, characterizes this stage. As the teenager separates from his relationship with chemicals, his chemically bound psychic structure becomes loosened and disorganized. Addiction defenses—including denial, projection, rationalization and splitting (Chapter 3)—intensify to protect this fragile internal state. Often these addiction defenses are manifest by the adolescent's acting out toward authority figures, such as treatment staff or parents, whom the teenager perceives as thwarting his drug use.

With this loosening and disorganization of psychic structure, strong affective states are experienced by the young person. Rage is often quite pronounced (Wurmser, 1987), and this rage fuels his defensive acting-out behavior.

Because the adolescent is vulnerable to explosive bursts, such as violent behavior, and impulsive bursts, such as suicidal behavior and other impulsive acts, this abstinence crisis may require inpatient treatment. The initially recovering teenager often needs this safety and structure to contain his overwhelming feelings and to give himself a foothold on sobriety.

Goals. The primary goals for the adolescent in this first stage of recovery are:

- To become aware of the impact of his drug use on himself, his family, and his life
- To make a commitment to abstinence
- To learn about the process of addiction

Resistance to Goals. A common resistance by the adolescent to these therapeutic goals are the addiction defenses of denial, projection, rationalization, and splitting. These addiction defenses serve to protect the young person from an awareness of the severity of his drug problem and the need to stop using drugs.

Strategy With Goal Resistance. One therapeutic strategy that can be used to approach the adolescent's denial of a drug problem and to promote his awareness of this problem is the "caring confrontation" (Rachman & Raubolt, 1985, p. 368). This strategy has two main parts. The first part involves the therapist's creating an emotionally safe environment within which the adolescent will likely be more receptive to receiving feedback on his substance-abusing behavior. The second part involves presenting this feedback to the teenager and processing the teenager's reaction. This feedback might include adverse consequences from using drugs, family members and peer reactions to the adolescent's drug behavior, or the consequences of breaking an abstinence contract.

A caring confrontation can usually be orchestrated most effectively in the context of family therapy or group therapy, where the adolescent can receive feedback from multiple sources. However, depending on the quality of the therapeutic relationship and the timing of this feedback, the caring confrontation might also be used effectively within the context of individual therapy. (Ungerleider & Siegel, 1990).

Step Work. The first step of AA and NA most closely complements the adolescent's therapeutic work in Stage 1 of recovery. The messages of powerlessness and unmanageability stated in this step need to be accepted by the adolescent. The teenager needs to gain the awareness that he has lost control of his drug use and that abstinence is necessary in his life. In discussing adolescent recovery, Ungerleider and Siegel (1990) note, "The methods of the 12-step programs provide an environment in which the denial can be addressed while containing the anxiety that results from the gradual relinquishment of the defense" (p. 441).

Resistance to Step Work. The first step message of powerlessness will likely fan the flames of resistance for most adolescents. As Ehrlich (1987) states, "Young people who are trying to stand on their own are learning to develop and apply personal power. Admitting powerlessness is antithetical to who they are" (p. 313).

Strategy With Step Work Resistance. As discussed in Chapter 2, doing modified 12-step work (Evans and Sullivan, 1990) according to the developmental needs of teenagers is a way of making step work adolescent-friendly. One strategy for facilitating this modified step work is to use reframing with adolescents. Reframing with teenagers is a technique to help them form an alternative, or more useful, mental construct of an issue or concept (Wexler, 1991). In this way the young person can more comfortably engage the mental construct.

One way that a therapist might work with the young person around the theme of powerlessness would be to process a redefinition of personal power. This reframe might include exploring how the adolescent has relinquished personal power through the negative effects of his drug use, how he has the power to take back control of his life, and how abstinence can be a manifestation of personal power.

Stage 2: The Sampling Stage

Process. The second stage of adolescent recovery involves the teenager's progressing from detaching from chemicals to attaching to external resources for recovery. These external resources for recovery are persons—sober peers, his parents, his therapist, and others—the adolescent will need to rely on and internalize. Much as drugs served as a transitional object during the teenager's development, a recovery network serves as a transitional object for the teenager's recovery. Internalizing these external resources will support the young person's psychic restructuring and reorganizing that began with abstinence.

Crisis. The process of attaching to external resources in recovery constitutes the second recovery crisis, the trust crisis. As the adolescent further breaks away from his relationship with chemicals, his chemically bound psychic structure becomes further loosened and disorganized. Painful affective states may be experienced, and the pull to return to the established pattern of drug use or act out in some maladaptive way is strong.

The adolescent in this stage of recovery is at a crossroads. Substance use and related behaviors have previously been a known resource for managing painful feelings and overwhelming impulses. The teenager struggles with whether or not to trade a known, albeit maladaptive, resource for the unknown resource of genuinely relying on others.

Goals. The primary goals for the adolescent in this second stage of recovery are:

- To make a commitment to a plan of recovery as necessary for continued sobriety
- To become more actively involved in different therapies and the therapeutic process
- To become more actively involved in AA or NA

Resistance to Goals. A common resistance to these therapeutic goals is the teenager's admitting to the adverse impact of drugs on his life yet denying the need to engage in treatment. The adolescent's addiction defenses delude the teenager into believing that abstinence is enough.

Treatment is a supportive process. However, it does place intrapsychic and interpersonal demands on the adolescent. Substance-abusing teenagers are accustomed to avoiding such demands through their drug use. Many continue such avoidance in early recovery.

Strategy With Goal Resistance. One therapeutic strategy that can be used to respond to the young person's denial of a need to work in recovery is to work with the adolescent's "preferred defense structure" (Wallace, 1985, p. 23). Wallace offers this as a strategy for working with adult alcoholics' resistance, and the principles of this strategy are applicable to teenage substance abusers.

The strategy is predicated on three assumptions:

1. The adolescent's addiction defenses are an outcome of his addiction and do not precede the addiction.
2. By aligning with the adolescent's addiction defenses, the therapist is paradoxically supporting the very defenses that are key to initial recovery.
3. The addiction defenses will become transformed during the course of recovery, as the intrapsychic structure and chemically free self of the teenager evolves.

Working with the adolescent's preferred defense structure can be applied in individual, family, and group therapy. The therapeutic elements and themes of AA and NA are even geared toward joining with, rather than challenging head-on, the teenager's preferred defense structure. An example of a therapist working with a recovering adolescent's preferred defense structure involved the case of a 16-year-old male who was in a long-term residential program for adolescent substance abusers. While this teenager came to an awareness through treatment of how his denial and defensive style restricted his consciousness of his substance-abuse problem, he was not as aware of how his externalizing and avoidant defensive style blunted his consciousness of his feelings of anxiety and sadness. His therapist worked with him around recognizing his tendency to externalize and avoid feelings and also accepting these defenses as self-regulating behaviors that protected him when he felt overwhelmed. In this way the adolescent came to realize how his defensive style, which made him unaware of the seriousness of his drug problem, could also help him to cope in early recovery.

Step Work. The second and third steps of AA and NA most closely correspond with the adolescent's Stage 2 of recovery. The central message of these two steps calls for the addicted individual to trust and commit to a power outside himself. This reliance on and relationship with an external power is expected to bring stability and structure to the nascent, sober self of the person in early recovery.

Resistance to Step Work. With the themes of higher power, believing, and God, Steps 2 and 3 are often considered to be the spiritual steps. The spirituality suggested in these steps is a broad concept. The spirituality of AA and NA, as experienced by any given recovering person, may include religious worship, relationships, or other manifestations.

It is in this area of spirituality and relationships, that recovering adolescents may reject the message of Steps 2 and 3. Chatlos (1989) sums up this dynamic by observing,

> Step 2 often deals with the deepest levels of mistrust and alienation, as addicted teenagers feel betrayed by their family, by the world, and by God. There is a re-experiencing of disappointments in the ideal model of parents, or the real disappointments of losses and abandonments, both physically and emotionally. (p. 198)

Strategy With Step Work Resistance. One strategy for working with the teenager's resistance to the spirituality themes of Steps 2 and 3 is to combine reframing techniques with mental imagery and visualization techniques. Beginning with reframing, the therapist can help the adolescent to define higher power, or God, in a relationship sense. This can be done by helping the teenager to identify persons, such as friends, family members, teachers, or others who have been a source of comfort, inspiration, and encouragement in his life. Next, imagery and visualization techniques can be applied. Wexler (1991, p. 83) discusses a particular imagery and visualization technique, " the ally," which could be particularly applicable to adolescents at this point.

The ally technique has three parts:

1. The therapist presents the concept of an internal ally. This internal ally can be construed as internalized experiences of persons (ally figures) identified in the aforementioned reframing.
2. The therapist helps the adolescent to process imagining and remembering feelings of ally figures during his life.

3. The therapist encourages the adolescent to practice accessing his internal ally as a strategy for managing feelings and sensations.

By using reframing, and imagery and visualization techniques, a therapist can help make the concepts of higher power and God more relevant for the teenager. In experiencing these concepts as more relevant, the young person will be aided in bridging his resistance to Steps 2 and 3.

Stage 3: The Conversion Stage

Process. By this third stage of recovery, the adolescent has experienced some initial stability with being sober. However, this stability becomes challenged through the emergence of unresolved feelings related to his adolescent developmental crisis experiences. The extent of the challenge is related to the intensity of the developmental crisis. The teenager's continued growth in recovery occurs through meeting this challenge head-on by resisting the regressive pull to resume a relationship with chemicals; recommitting to recovery and forming a stronger attachment to the external resources, or relationships, of recovery; and through a stronger reliance on his relational resources in recovery, developing a more internalized and firm chemically free self.

Recovery Crisis. The third crisis of recovery, the catharsis crisis, characterizes this stage. As the adolescent becomes more open to incorporating his external resources of recovery into his sober self, his addiction defenses are gradually shed. This relaxing of his addiction defenses allows contained and repressed inner experiences to break through to the adolescent's awareness. Often these contained and repressed inner experiences are feelings and memories, related to any or all of the adolescent developmental crises—narcissistic crisis, separation crisis, or identity crisis. (As mentioned in Chapter 4, any of these crises may have been a factor with propelling the adolescent into substance abuse.) The emergence of these repressed affective states and associated memories can threaten to overwhelm the tenuous, chemically free self of the adolescent.

Among the experiences that can precipitate this cathartic crisis is the adolescent's reintegration with his family and peers (following inpatient or residential treatment). Returning home, being reunited with his family, and resuming involvement with peers in his community can pose new demands and struggles. Feelings of shame, anxiety, and confusion that had been defended against through drug use might reemerge and seem overwhelming for the recovering teenager. It is at this critical juncture in recovery that the adolescent needs to hold firm to his commitment to sobriety and to treatment. Through staying firm in this recovery commitment he can work at more adaptive coping skills for dealing with his feelings and these crises. Without a sufficiently strong commitment to recovery, the adolescent risks intensified psychological vulnerability from these powerful inner experiences, and relapse becomes a higher risk.

Goals. The primary goals for the adolescent in this third stage of recovery are:

- To become more aware of his feelings
- To develop more adaptive skills for coping with and expressing his feelings
- To make a continued commitment to his recovery, his treatment, and his 12-step program

Resistance to Goals. A common resistance to these therapeutic goals by teenagers is being more avoidant of the therapeutic processes, 12-step meetings, and other demands of ongoing recovery. This is commonly manifested by the adolescent who goes through the motions of being in recovery while actually becoming increasingly less invested in his recovery. Such a diminished commitment to recovery serves to protect the young person from being aware of, and striving to work though, the often highly charged feelings that can reemerge when confronting developmental crises.

Strategy with Goal Resistance. One therapeutic strategy that can be used to approach the adolescent's avoidance of further recovery work, while at the same time encouraging this further recovery work, is encompassed in Flores' (1988) adaptation of supportive psychotherapy. Flores' (1988) application of supportive psychotherapy focuses on chemically dependent adults yet is relevant with recovering teenagers.

This approach has two basic parts:

1. Support the recovering person's affective and emotional experiences through empathy, praise, and encouragement.
2. Support the recovering person's cognitive experiences through information sharing, clarification, and interpretation of emotional-behavioral aspects of his emerging awareness.

This adaptation of supportive psychotherapy can be used within the contexts of individual, family, and group therapy. In addition, empathic and reality-based therapeutic ingredients, similar to those of supportive psychotherapy, can be found in AA and NA meetings and within a relationship with a program sponsor.

Step Work. Steps 4 and 5 of AA and NA parallel the recovery themes of this third stage. The themes of these two steps pertain to developing a greater emotional honesty with oneself and to risk sharing this greater emotional honesty with another person.

Resistance to Step Work. The resistance often exhibited by adolescents to working Steps 4 and 5 is the avoidance of confronting the shame they experience. This experience of shame is both a feeling and a response to feelings for many recovering adolescents. Avoiding such experiences of shame may have been a contributing factor in developing a substance abuse problem, and, conversely, substance abuse can lead to feelings of shame. In discussing adolescents' experience of their shame during recovery, Nowinski (1990) states:

> Substance abuse leads its victims to commit many acts that hurt themselves and others. Lying, stealing, and cheating, prostitution and burglary; these are but a few of the wrongs commonly committed by addicts. The shame associated with these moral failings helps maintain denial, and it can undermine recovery after denial has broken down. (p. 153)

Strategy With Step Work Resistance. Reframing can be useful with resistance to the messages of Steps 4 and 5. Reframing shame can help an adolescent to confront his shame. Wexler (1991, p. 94) presents a reframe, the "Your Behavior Makes Sense" reframe, that can help lay the groundwork for an adolescent to come to terms with his shame. The message of this reframe is that all behavior is in the service of self-protection. In having a therapist apply this reframe with a substance-abusing adolescent, he remarks:

> It's shocking and disorienting for teenagers to hear a respected adult say that taking drugs "makes sense." They perk up and listen. This doesn't mean that it make sense for health reasons, moral reasons, social reasons, or legal reasons—but that there have been important psychological conditions leading to this powerful urge. (Wexler, 1991, p. 96)

What this kind of reframing seeks to do is to offer empathy and respect to the adolescent's experience with chemicals without absolving him of responsibility for his chemical use. Where there is empathy and respect, openness and self-esteem may grow. In one instance with a teenage girl who was struggling with the fourth step in her recovery, reframing her prior sexual promiscuity, for which she felt considerable shame, proved to be a useful strategy. This girl was first sexually active when she became involved with a drug-abusing peer group. She felt uncared for by her family and equated having sex with someone with being cared for by that person. She was sexually exploited by peers, and a profound sense of shame began taking hold of her. She was caught in a vicious cycle of chemically anesthetizing her feelings of self-deprecation, while at the same time being rendered more vulnerable to sexual exploitation when under the influence of chemicals. With her therapist helping her to reframe her prior sexual promiscuity as taking care of her need to be cared for and to reframe her substance abuse as a form of self-protection during a period of extreme emotional vulnerability, this adolescent became more able to deal with her shame and openly work her fourth step.

Stage 4: The Coalescing Stage

Process. The fourth and final stage of adolescent recovery occurs when the teenager becomes increasingly reliant on his own internal resources, developed during recovery, for hanBLing the demands of continued sobriety. At the same time, the adolescent becomes less reliant on, but not completely divorced from, the external resources or relationships with which he has connected in recovery. In short, his chemically free self grows from surviving in recovery to thriving in recovery.

Crisis. During this final stage of recovery, the recovery crisis is the crisis of continuous change. Resembling the adolescent developmental process discussed in Chapter 5, this crisis of continuous change is the natural process of further losses and attachments that are part of growing up.

Goals. The primary goals for the teenager in the fourth stage of recovery are:

- To continue supporting the development of his chemically free self
- To make a commitment to a developmental path reflective of "normal" adolescence (this includes the six developmental tasks discussed in Chapter 5)

Resistance to Goals. Adolescents manifesting resistance to these therapeutic goals are, for the most part, exhibiting the more adaptive defense and coping mechanisms of adolescence. Complacency is common as teenagers might avoid the deeper therapeutic work involved in more fuller intrapsychic integration.

Strategy With Goal Resistance. Supportive psychotherapy, recommended for Stage 3 of recovery, can also be useful in this stage. One difference between utilizing supportive psychotherapy in this stage and in the previous stage is that, based on the teenager's level of cognitive development and overall capacity for insight, this approach can be undertaken with a more psychodynamic orientation. In discussing psychotherapy and chemically dependent adolescents, Meeks (1988) remarks, "After treatment of the chemical dependency, basic psychotherapy is still often required to ameliorate basic personality deficiencies" (p. 520).

Step Work. Steps 6 through 12 of AA and NA reflect the recovery themes for adolescents in this final recovery stage. Steps 6 and 7 pertain to the character impairments of the teenager, Steps 8 and 9 deal with repairing relationships and resolving guilt, and Steps 10 and 11 are primarily reinforcements of earlier steps. Step 12 relates to the adolescent's need in recovery to share and give back to the program. Often young persons working a twelfth step will become sponsors to other young people in early recovery.

Resistance to Step Work. One possible resistance to working Steps 6 through 12 of AA and NA relates to the aforementioned avoidance by the adolescent in this recovery stage. He may choose to distance himself from the more intensive developmental demands implied in these steps.

However, another possible resistance to working with these steps may pertain to the teenager's overall differentiation from his 12-step program. This is a contentious issue among treatment professionals who work with chemically dependent adolescents.

Some therapists hold that adolescents can develop a lifelong dependency on AA and NA, much like a dependency on drugs. They believe 12-step programs can become a refuge from life rather than a bridge into life. Furthermore, they advocate for adolescents to be weaned from their reliance on 12-step programs. In doing so, they claim to support the normal individuation striving of the teenagers. Summing up this position, Peele proposes that, "It may be possible to convince young people they are lifetime addicts who cannot hope to control their behavior, drinking, or otherwise, without the constant presence of AA or therapy in their lives. What remains to be seen is whether as many people will mature out of AA reliance as do so from drug and alcohol dependence" (Peele, 1989, p. 195).

But other therapists assert that an adolescent's healthy dependency on AA or NA should be encouraged for as long as possible. They claim that supporting detachment from AA or NA would cut off the adolescent from a necessary lifeline for sobriety, enable relapse, and be developmentally disastrous. Flores (1988) argues on behalf of nurturing this healthy dependency by claiming, "It is preferable to have a dependence on an organization that promotes health, sobriety, and helping others to a drug that promotes sickness, death, and unmeasurable suffering to oneself, family, and society" (p. 216).

There is no simple answer to this dilemma for a therapist. A therapist dealing with this clinical gray area truly has to rely on his knowledge about his adolescent client.

Strategy With Step Work Resistance. Conventional psychotherapy can help the adolescent to integrate the messages of Steps 6 through 12 with the specific recovery issues and processes relevant to him. Psychotherapy can also be useful in assisting the adolescent with any reevaluation of the role of 12-step work in his recovery.

RECOVERY SKILLS

Overview of Recovery Skills

During the course of the adolescent's recovery process, the teenager's acquisition of recovery skills can help him solidify his hold on sobriety. Recovery skills result from increased awareness of new coping techniques and behavioral tasks that can enhance the adolescent's competency with progressing through the four stages of recovery.

If the four stages of adolescent recovery can be compared to four rungs on a ladder used to climb out of addiction, then recovery skills are exercises that strengthen the teenager during this climbing experience.

Recovery Skills Training

There are four categories of recovery skills, from which an adolescent can derive guidance and support in sobriety:

1. Addiction awareness
2. Developmental awareness
3. Managing internal changes in recovery

4. Managing external changes in recovery

Therapists and treatment programs can use these four categories of recovery skills to aid in treatment planning. The range of recovery skills encompassed by these four categories addresses the six domains of chemical use problems—chemical use effects, physical health, psychological health, behavioral functioning, interpersonal functioning, and social functioning—that compose the Adolescent Chemical Use Problem (ACUP) Index (Chapter 1). The first category of recovery skills can address the teenager's chemical use effect problems. The second category is geared toward the young person's physical health and psychological health problems. The third category of skills can be useful with the adolescent's psychological health and behavioral functioning problems. The fourth category is aimed at the behavioral pattern, interpersonal functioning, and social functioning problems of the adolescent. Depending on a particular adolescent's needs, recovery skills in a specific category can be emphasized to respond to that teenager's needs within a specific problem domain.

Therapists and programs can help to facilitate the adolescent's accommodation of recovery skills by integrating recovery skills training into the process of individual therapy or group therapy or through a variety of psychoeducational methods, including psychoeducational groups. In addition, the therapeutic elements of AA and NA provide a form of recovery skills training.

Addiction Awareness

This category addresses the adolescent's need for understanding addiction in general, the specifics of chemical dependency, and the unique aspects of adolescent chemical dependency. Psychoeducational themes can focus on addiction as: a biopsychosocial process; the disease model of addiction; recovery and relapse; and the role of multiple therapeutic elements in recovery, including different therapeutic modalities and 12-step programs.

Developmental Awareness

This category of recovery skills educates adolescents about normal teenage development. The five factors influencing adolescent psychological development—physical development, sexual emerging, cognitive development, moral development, and developmental factors from early childhood—are the focus of this category of recovery skills.

Adolescents can learn that their changing bodies and corresponding body images need not be perceived as enemies. They can discover the benefits of healthy nutrition, exercise, and self-care habits. The physical problems that can result from substance abuse can also be explored.

The difference between developmentally adaptive sexuality and sexual behavior and more maladaptive tendencies is another area the recovering teenager needs to consider. A possible relationship between their sexual development and their chemical use might become clear to some adolescents as they are educated about sexual issues.

Awareness of their own cognitive abilities, how these abilities evolve during adolescence, and how learning disabilities can compromise cognitive functioning is also valuable for teenagers to understand. How drug use can contribute to cognitive impairment can be infused into education about their cognitive capacities.

Adolescents can be guided in their moral development as part of their developmental awareness. While understanding that a relationship exists between their evolving cognitive abilities and their moral reasoning, adolescents can be assisted with exploring their values and identifying a moral code that is in line with a sober lifestyle.

Finally, the importance of early developmental experiences and the impact of these experiences on overall psychological development are an additional focus of developmental awareness. Information can be presented on how impaired development during early childhood might have created a developmental vulnerability for an emotional disorder, substance abuse, or both. Discussions about what physical abuse and sexual abuse are and how they impact psychological development can be presented. In addition, the impact of growing up in a dysfunctional family, and how this experience can affect psychological development, can be valuable information for the recovering teenager.

Managing Internal Changes in Recovery

The internal metamorphosis of growing from a chemically dependent self to a chemically free self necessitates the teenager taking on the job of his own self-development. He needs tools to do this job. A variety of techniques that can be learned through a range of therapies can help the adolescent to acquire these tools. Relaxation training skills, stress management techniques, values clarification exercises, affect awareness training, decision making skills, problem-solving skills, and goal development skills are among the self-building tools that can be useful for the recovering adolescent.

Managing External Changes in Recovery

As the teenager's sober self is growing, he needs to deal not only with the feelings, moods, impulses, and urges of his internal world but also with the relationships and responsibilities of his external world.

Skills for functioning in relationships, including communication skills, social skills training, and assertiveness training can help the recovering adolescent who may have the desire but not the know-how to function in relationships in sobriety (Walfish, Massey & Krone, 1990). The adolescent needs to continue developing his relationship tools for his changing relational needs throughout his recovery.

Recovering adolescents also need to learn how to handle responsibilities of daily living. They are often relearning, or learning for the first time, the benefits of educational and vocational pursuits. Study skills and work habits are areas for training.

In addition, recreation and leisure skills for adolescents, whose leisure time had previously revolved around drug use, are vital to continued recovery. While learning how to have fun without drugs, the recovering adolescent also has the chance to discover dormant creative, mechanical, artistic, or athletic talents and abilities. Such discovery of long hidden or forgotten talents can bolster self-esteem.

RELAPSE TREATMENT

Overview of Relapse Treatment

Just as an adolescent can experience confidence with climbing up the ladder of recovery, an adolescent might also experience vulnerability, possibly resulting in a relapse and a slide back down the ladder. Teenagers, like all recovering people, are vulnerable to relapses throughout the four stages of recovery.

Adolescent relapsing during the course of recovery is quite common. What is important for therapists to remember is that a relapse is not necessarily devastating for the teenager's recovery. Relapses can even be tremendous opportunities for promoting further growth during recovery. With this understanding, a therapist needs to approach an adolescent's relapse within the overall context of the young person's recovery. In discussing adolescents and relapse, Brown, Vik and Creamer (1989) assert that, "While a single relapse does not necessarily imply treatment failure, multiple relapses within the first 3 months clearly merit additional intervention" (p. 298).

As discussed in Chapter 4, relapse is a biopsychosocial process that involves four stages: (a) immediate determinants stage, (b) crossroads stage, (c) breaking of abstinence stage, and (d) abstinence violation coping stage. This biopsychosocial relapse process also encompasses the six domains of chemical use problems (ACUP Index). Chemical use problems in any or all of these six domains can serve as antecedents to relapse. Consequently, these six problem domains need to be the focus of adolescent relapse treatment.

Three Levels of Adolescent Relapse Treatment

There are three levels of relapse treatment that can be provided to an adolescent during the course of recovery:

Level 1: Relapse prevention
Level 2: Relapse management
Level 3: Relapse intervention

Relapse Prevention

Relapse prevention is a collection of skills and strategies that an adolescent can learn during recovery for anticipating and responding to the internal and external stresses that may lead to relapse. The sources for these stressors are the six domains of the Adolescent Chemical Use Problem (ACUP Index).

Teenagers can assimilate the skills and strategies of relapse prevention through recovery skills training or through specific relapse prevention skills training.

Recovery Skills Training. The four categories of recovery skills discussed earlier in this chapter address the six chemical use problems domains, the antecedents to relapse. Being engaged in learning recovery skills is one way for adolescents to be learning about relapse prevention.

Relapse Prevention Training. Relapse prevention skills are strategies for focusing on and dealing with specific internal and external stressors that may lead to relapse. Marlatt and Gordon (1985) and Gorski and

Miller (1982) are pioneers in relapse prevention for adult chemical abuses. The essence of the relapse prevention models proposed by these pioneers is for the addict to learn and apply specific cognitive and behavioral coping strategies to potential relapse situations.

What is key in relapse prevention training, especially with adolescents, is that relapse skills be developed for the individual addict's unique experience in recovery. As Brown, Vik, and Creamer (1989) state:

> Individualized evaluation of high-risk relapse situations may direct coping skill training efforts, heighten adolescent awareness of relapse risk, and facilitate the development of new strategies for adolescents to cope with direct or indirect social pressures to use drugs or drink alcohol. (p. 299)

A key relapse prevention strategy for an adolescent is the development of refusal skills (Goldstein, 1989). These refusal skills involve learning how to disengage from social situations with peers who are using drugs. Assertiveness training and role playing are two common techniques that help the teenager to develop such refusal skills.

Adolescents who participate in relapse prevention training might not completely avoid relapse during recovery. But the skills they acquire through this training may give them a better chance of containing any relapses they do experience.

Relapse Management

Relapse management is a preemptive intervention with an adolescent who is exhibiting some of the signs of being in the relapse process. These signs can range from presenting early signs of relapse, such as demonstrating difficulty in any of the six chemical use problem domains, to showing later stages of relapse, such as strong indications of resumed chemical use.

One relapse management strategy might be for the therapist to use a caring confrontation to challenge the adolescent's complacency in recovery or relapse behavior. The spirit of such a caring confrontation, within the context of relapse management, is summed up in the Narcotics Anonymous "Big Book" (1983): "Relapse is never an accident. Relapse is a sign that we have a reservation in our program. We begin to slight our program and leave loopholes in our daily lives" (p. 72).

In instances when the adolescent's relapse results in actual chemical use, the therapist's relapse management approach needs to include a processing of the adolescent's abstinence violation effect (Marlatt & Gordon, 1985). The teenager's abstinence violation effect is a combination of his feelings and self-perception over having given up his sobriety. Issues of shame and powerlessness are common with teenagers in this state. This can be illustrated by the case of a 16-year-old male with a 3-year history of alcohol, marijuana, and hallucinogen abuse. This adolescent began his first period of appreciable sobriety following a short-term treatment in an inpatient hospital program for adolescent substance abusers. After he returned to his community, he continued his sobriety and earned his NA key chain for 90 days of being chemically free. Shortly thereafter, however, he began demonstrating noticeable signs of relapsing. These signs included denying the need to continue working in recovery, discontinuing his outpatient aftercare treatment, and beginning to associate again with his former drug-abusing friends. This teenager eventually succumbed to the urge to drink again. His father, noticing some distinct mood and attitudinal changes with his son, confronted him about his suspicions of resumed drug use. The adolescent acknowledged his relapse, and his father facilitated his return to aftercare treatment. He resumed group therapy where he discussed his disappointment with himself for "throwing away" his sobriety. At the same time, group members helped him to identify personal strengths that he discovered and used to maintain his initial sobriety and how he might apply these strengths again in continued recovery.

If an adolescent has resumed a pattern of significant substance abuse and is in denial again, then the relapse-containing strategies of relapse management might not have sufficient impact to mobilize him back into recovery. In such cases, a relapse intervention might be necessary.

Relapse Intervention

When the teenager is showing all the signs of having returned to a pattern of substance abuse, then a relapse intervention is indicated. A relapse intervention is similar to an intervention that is initially undertaken to mobilize an adolescent to enter treatment. Reality-based feedback is used to confront the young person in a supportive manner about his return to chemical use and to help him break through his denial. Often the result of this relapse intervention is that the adolescent moves to a more structured level of care.

SUMMARY

An adolescent's recovery from substance abuse is a process. This process can be viewed as occurring across different stages of recovery, can be supported by the adolescent's learning and applying recovery skills, and can go through periods of relapse.

This chapter offers a four-stage model of adolescent recovery. A therapeutic framework consisting of eight components for therapeutic focus is presented for treating the teenager during each of these four stages. The paradigm of stages and components can be used by clinicians to measure the adolescent's growth in recovery, as well as to suggest areas requiring continued intervention.

Recovery skills, which are a combination of awareness, coping techniques, and behavioral tools, can be learned by the recovering adolescent. These skills can strengthen the teenager's strivings for continued growth in sobriety.

Most adolescents experience relapses during the course of their recovery. Relapse treatment throughout recovery can help the young person to derive benefit from, rather than deteriorate from, relapse episodes.

Chapter 10

THE RECOVERY ENVIRONMENT
Family Recovery and Peer Relationships in Recovery

INTRODUCTION

The young person's family and peer relationships together form his recovery environment. If the adolescent's climb through the stages of recovery can be compared to ascending the rungs on a ladder, then his recovery environment can be compared to the wall that this ladder leans on, supporting his climbing effort.

Just as the adolescent's family and peers can interact in four possible ways to influence his chemical use (as discussed in Chapter 5), so his family and peers can interact in four possible ways to influence his recovery. Family and peers might combine to support him in recovery. His family and peers could be opposing influences, with his family supporting recovery and his peers encouraging continued substance use, or his family enabling continued drug involvement and his peers supporting recovery. A final possibility is that both family and peers combine to undermine recovery and influence continued substance abuse.

Comprehensive adolescent substance abuse treatment includes the teenager's recovery environment being a focus of treatment. Family recovery is in the service of adolescent recovery. The adolescent's family accompanies him into treatment in order to develop into a stable enough recovery environment to support him in his recovery quest. At the same time, recovery-supportive peer relationships are also in the service of the teenager's recovery. The recovering adolescent needs to develop a network of sober peers and to deal with issues with peers as they occur in recovery.

This chapter presents a model of family recovery. Similar to the model for adolescent recovery in the previous chapter, this model encompasses four stages. In addition, family recovery skills, which aid the family in their own recovery process, are also discussed.

This chapter also identifies peer relationship concerns as they arise as treatment issues throughout the four stages of adolescent recovery. Because sexual issues during a teenager's recovery are so often inter-related with peer concerns, sexual issues and peer relationships are addressed as well.

This book's biopsychosocial model of adolescent substance abuse treatment focuses on a triad of primary recovering systems. The previous chapter addresses one of these systems, the adolescent's psychological recovery. This chapter discusses the remaining two systems of this triad, family recovery and peer relationships in recovery.

FAMILY RECOVERY

Overview of Family Recovery

Much as the adolescent's own recovery process is growing from a chemically dependent self toward a chemically free self, so the family undergoes a transformation through their recovery process. The family recovery process entails the family progressing from functioning as a chemically dependent system toward functioning as a chemically free system.

Also, just as each teenager is different and his recovery path is a distinct journey, each family is different and has its own esoteric course of recovery. The treatment implication of families' uniqueness is summed up by Heaslip, Van Dyke, Hogenson, and Vedders (1989):

> Addressing the needs of families of young people in treatment has just begun. Much remains to be discovered and applied to family situations and interventions. What is known, though, is that just as each young person is unique, so each family is a unique unit. Patients and families

change and grow at different rates. Given this, each family requires an individual response from the treatment community. (p. 117)

Family Life Factors and Treatment

Family life factors, discussed in Chapter 5, exist in different ways for families. Some of these family life factors—particularly change in family structure, family composition, ethnicity, and socioeconomic factors—can represent a family's unique treatment needs.

Separated or divorced families have different treatment needs from intact families. For example, the single parent of an adolescent substance abuser presents special needs in treatment (Kaufmann, 1979). Often, but not always, the single parent is a mother. The single parent is without the supportive resources of a partner in dealing with the challenges posed by the adolescent in substance abuse treatment. For this reason single parents often require additional supportive resources. Inclusion of extended family members such as grandparents, aunts, and uncles, and extrafamilial adults such as family friends, can be useful resources to the single parent of an adolescent substance abuser. In addition, parents' support groups are particularly indicated for single parents.

Recovering families with younger children also represent a distinct treatment need. As discussed in Chapter 5, substance abuse can be contagious from older siblings to younger ones. Consequently the needs of these younger children should not be overlooked. Support groups for siblings of substance abusers are among the strategies that can be useful in attempting to stop the spread of drug problems among the children in the family (Coleman, 1979).

A family's ethnicity may also present treatment needs that require sensitivity and focus by therapists and programs.

We are living in an open, dynamic, and continuously changing society. Identifying the relevant risk factors for drug use and abuse should be a continuous process, while models, programs, and treatments should be revised accordingly based on the mixture of society and pattern of risk elements for different cultural and social groups. (Maddahian, Newcomb, & Bentler, 1988, p. 22)

A family's socioeconomic circumstances may present yet other distinct needs during substance abuse treatment. Poor families in need of material resources, including food and clothing, may need concrete services in order to be engaged in and stabilized in treatment (Flanzer & Sturkie, 1987). Therapists may need to initially act as advocates and brokers of such concrete services as a "requisite first step in treatment" (Flanzer & Sturkie, 1987, p. 72). Family life factors, such as change of family structure, family composition, ethnicity, and socioeconomic concerns, represent a family's unique needs. These unique needs should be considered by clinicians when planning interventions with families.

Family Abstinence in Treatment

Before discussing this chapter's model of family recovery, the role of family members' abstinence during family recovery deserves some attention. Parents and siblings of chemically dependent teenagers may be appropriate and responsible in their chemical use. One example of this might be the occasional and moderate drinking of alcohol at a social gathering or with a meal. However, family members may also have a problem with their own chemical use. While in treatment, however, there are strong indicators for all family members to abstain from all chemical use.

Advocating on behalf of family abstinence, Huberty and colleagues (Huberty, Huberty, Flanagan-Hobday, & Blackmore, 1987) state, "It is always advisable to require (although not always possible to implement) total and complete abstinence from all drugs and alcohol by all family members during therapy, particularly both parents and the identified adolescent patient" (p. 517).

The benefits of recommending family abstinence are twofold. As Huberty and colleagues further state, "In addition to detecting otherwise hidden parental and sibling drug or alcohol abuse, an 'abstinence contract' also removes the 'double standard' usually implied to the adolescent drug abuser in therapy" (Huberty et al., 1987, p. 517). Family abstinence should be an identified goal in treatment. The presence of family abstinence reinforces the message of sobriety for the teenager, and the absence of family abstinence raises relevant family issues for the recovering teen.

A Model for Family Recovery

Family recovery with families of substance-abusing adolescents has previously been discussed by Cohen (1991) and Treadway (1989). The model presented in this chapter depicts four stages of family recovery, with five components composing the therapeutic framework for each stage. As with the model of adolescent recovery (discussed in Chapter 9), these four stages overlap, and, because each family is unique, there is much variance with how families progress through these stages.

The five components of the therapeutic framework for each stage of this model are:

1. The family's dynamic process
2. The family's recovery crisis
3. Therapeutic goals for working to resolve the family crisis
4. The family's resistance to working on these goals
5. Therapeutic strategies for treating the family's resistance

These five components are organized around crisis and resistance, similar to the model of adolescent recovery. However, family recovery crisis and family resistance are the foci in this model.

Family resistance in this context has been discussed by Anderson and Stewart (1983). They write, "There are many factors that contribute to the resistance exhibited by a family. However, the major sources seem to be a family's natural striving for stability and a family's equally natural, if sometimes irrational, fear of change" (p. 38).

In using this five-part therapeutic framework, a therapist needs to connect with a family at its level of family functioning. As discussed in Chapter 5, family dynamics of leadership, boundaries, affectivity, communication, and problem solving are organized differently in each family.

The family's recovery work across these four stages can occur from the interventions of different family treatment modalities. Family therapy is usually the primary family treatment modality. However, multifamily group therapy and parent training, as well as parent support groups like Families Anonymous, can also greatly assist families in their recovery.

The following is the four-stage family recovery model, and the five-component therapeutic framework for each stage.

Stage 1: The Disengagement Stage

Family Process. In the first stage of family recovery, the family process is the progression from being entrenched in a pattern of enabling drug use, toward initial attempts to change this enabling pattern. The four patterns of parental enabling discussed in Chapter 5 are:

1. Uninformed and unaware parents
2. Aware and avoidant parents
3. Aware and disempowered parents
4. Aware and indulgent parents.

A family's particular enabling pattern is a primary treatment focus in this first stage of family recovery.

Family Recovery Crisis. The family crisis in this stage is the crisis of unbalancing. By beginning to interrupt or stop a family pattern, such as enabling, the family's homeostasis becomes unbalanced. This homeostasis in family functioning has been organized around the adolescent's drug abuse problems, and the resultant reorganization with its focus on abstinence creates the recovery crisis.

Family Goals. The primary goals for the family in the first stage of family recovery are:

- To transform family denial of the adolescent's drug problem by becoming aware of their pattern of enabling, and how this enabling has related to the teenager's substance use
- To learn about the process of addiction and the factors that influence the process of adolescent chemical dependency.

Resistance to Family Goals. The resistance that many parents show in this stage is related to how their enabling pattern provides some self-protection. This self-protection can serve as a distraction from the parents' own issues (such as midlife concerns, issues from their own families-of-origin, marital concerns, or unresolved separation and divorce issues) and offer insulation from the pain of unsuccessful parenting or an avoidance of the fear of changing. It can be very threatening for parents to consider giving up this self-protection.

Strategy with Family Goal Resistance. Therapists need to find a way to join (Minuchin, 1974) with parents in this stage. This joining includes a therapeutic attitude of acceptance of parents' own struggles and pain with raising a child who is addicted to chemicals. Parents at this point feel tremendous guilt, and they need help in coming to terms with their guilt in order to effect change in their family's life (Robinson, 1990).

Weidman (1985, pp. 100-101) suggests a few general principles for engaging in treatment for the families, particularly parents, of substance-abusing adolescents:

- The therapist, not the family, should decide who to include in treatment.
- The therapist should approach the family with a "rationale for treatment that is non-judgmental and non-pejorative."
- The therapist should try to reframe in positive terms a family member's resistance to participate in treatment.
- The therapist should adopt the parents' goals for the adolescent in treatment.
- The therapist should show interest in the family by demonstrating flexibility in attempts to include the family in treatment.
- The therapist must strongly believe in the treatment being provided and convey this sense of conviction to the family.

Parents need to feel supported as they begin the difficult task of examining their enabling pattern and considering effective ways of influencing their child to cease using drugs. These several guidelines can be useful in helping parents and families overcome their first hurdle in treatment.

Stage 2: The Empowering Stage

Family Process. The family process in this second stage of family recovery entails family members actively working to avoid enabling the adolescent's drug use. Family members actively pursue strategies and enact patterns for having the teenager be accountable for his chemical use and his chemical use behavior.

Family Recovery Crisis. The family recovery crisis in this second stage is the crisis of risking change. By doing something other than enabling, family members are continuing the unbalancing of homeostasis from Stage 1 of family recovery. This alternative pattern to enabling occurs despite the teenager's pull to return the family to the homeostasis of family enabling.

Family Goals. The primary family goals of this stage are:

- For parents to take greater control of the family environment through the use of effective limit-setting and consequences using such tools as abstinence contracts
- For parents to be more in control of their own reactions toward the adolescent's behaviors
- For parents to relate to the adolescent as a recovering adolescent by becoming aware of their child's needs in recovery.

Resistance to Family Goals. A common resistance that many parents display is their fear of change. They feel alone and guilty about putting different demands on their child and often carry much doubt about their ability to become a more effective parent. Thus their fear interferes with making the necessary changes.

Strategy With Family Goal Resistance. Helping parents to feel empowered requires a fair amount of empathy and guidance on the part of the therapist. Treadway (1989) sums up this therapeutic attitude toward parents as follows:

> The two key elements for empowering parents are for the therapist (1) to communicate to the parents that they represent the core of the solution rather than the cause of the problem and (2) to help them learn how to pick their battles carefully. Parents cannot truly control adolescents, but they can learn how not to be controlled by them. (p. 149)

One strategy for assisting parents to bridge their sense of aloneness, doubt, and ineffectiveness is for therapists to direct parents to become involved with a parents' support group. In one situation involving the parents of a 14-year-old female chemical user, a parent support group was a crucial early intervention. In the summer before entering high school, this girl became out of control with her chemical involvement and related behavior (including staying out past curfews, sneaking out of the house in the middle of the night, and ignoring her parents' disciplinary actions). These parents felt lost, believed that they had no way of "controlling" their daughter, felt scared for their daughter, and felt resentment that their family life was being "held hostage" by this girl. A family therapist referred these parents to a parent support group, where they immediately felt less alone in their plight. They were supported in taking initial steps, which included involving the juvenile probation system, to intervene with their daughter and reclaim their authority as parents.

Families Anonymous is one parental support group based on a 12-step self-help model (LaFountain, 1987). One advantage of a 12-step support group is that parents get to learn about the culture and language of such a group. This experience can build understanding and communication with the teenager, who is also engaged in a 12-step recovery process (Ungerleider & Siegel, 1990).

Stage 3: The Integration Stage

Family Process. During this third stage of family recovery, the family progresses from a period of stable sobriety, through the daily practice and work of family recovery, to addressing unresolved family crises. These family crises, as discussed in Chapter 6, are family legacies that have impacted on family functioning.

In discussing family treatment with substance-abusing adolescents, King and Meeks (1988) note, "We have found most families quite dysfunctional and in need of substantial treatment above and beyond assistance in diminishing their enabling behavior" (p. 533). Just as abstinence with the recovering adolescent is a start but not enough to maintain long-term sobriety, so with recovering families stopping enabling is a beginning but not always enough to support the adolescent's long-term recovery.

Family Recovery Crisis. The family recovery crisis in this third stage is the crisis of revelation. With a gradual shift from exclusively focusing on substance abuse and recovery issues to including longer-standing family problems or family secrets in the treatment focus, intense grief, rage, shame, and guilt may be experienced by family members. In essence, the family experiences another unbalancing in coming face-to-face with aspects of its family legacy. Next follows a period of rebalancing by becoming stabilized in sobriety.

Family Goals. The primary family goals of this stage are:

• For parents to continue their family recovery work while gradually turning attention toward unresolved family crises
• For family members to begin to come to terms with, and heal from, the legacy of unresolved family crises

Resistance to Family Goals. It can be terrifying for family members to attempt to discuss openly with one another their shared and often pain-filled history. Many family members may feel unsafe and unready for such a bold step.

Dramatic family changes, perhaps related to death or divorce, or family secrets, possibly related to parental substance abuse, or physical or sexual abuse, are among the unresolved legacies in families. An adolescent relapsing during this stage is often one way of the family signaling to the therapist that they are not yet ready to deal with a dormant, but alive, family crisis. Often a therapist might need to align with the family resistance and help the family to restrain from change (Treadway, 1989). The therapeutic ideal is to support the family's efforts in continued recovery work until the family is stable enough to confront its past.

Strategy With Family Goal Resistance. Individual family members, both parents and children, may need the support and safety of individual therapy in initially coming to grips with the impact of family crises on them. If and when such issues get addressed as a family, grief work is a common focus. Whether the family crisis has been rooted in change or trauma, a significant sense of loss has been felt by family members. A therapist can help guide the family through its own shared journey of grieving and healing. Family rituals are one technique that a therapist might use to help a family on this journey (Imber-Black, Roberts, & Whiting, 1988). The benefit of therapeutic rituals with families is that rituals can symbolize the unspoken and help family members give expression to painful feelings. For example, one mother of a 16-year-old teenage boy who was recovering from substance abuse was becoming increasingly intolerant of her son's "moodiness and laziness" 4 months into his sobriety. She was a widow whose husband had died 6 years earlier. This woman experienced prolonged and unresolved grief and avoided dating again out of being "unfaithful" to her deceased husband. She was highly involved in the family work of her son's early recovery but became less invested in family recovery after her son was sober for about 4 months. In a family therapy session it was disclosed that the 4 months of sobriety coincided with the anniversary of the death of the husband/father. Both the mother's and the son's recent emotional vulnerability were discussed as being related, in part, to the anniversary of the death. Upon further exploration in family therapy, it became apparent that both mother and son were feeling tremendous anger about the husband's/father's death, yet neither believed it was acceptable to openly express this anger. A therapeutic ritual was created whereby both the mother and the son would each write a letter to the husband/father expressing their genuine feelings about him and his death and would read their respective letters out loud to each other. This strategy helped this mother and son to more fully resolve some of their grief issues and continue in recovery.

Stage 4: The Individuation Stage

Family Process. In this fourth and final stage of family recovery, parents and the adolescent-young adult are negotiating the developmentally normative process of separation and individuation. The recovering environment supports the young person's striving toward psychological autonomy, while parents experience the ripple effect of their child's independence.

Family Recovery Crisis. The family recovery crisis in this fourth stage is the crisis of the young person leaving home. As discussed in Chapter 5, the teenager's efforts at separation and individuation can become intertwined with his substance abuse. Consequently, unresolved issues with separation can become reenacted through this family recovery crisis well into young adulthood.

Pittman (1987) offers a succinct summary of leaving-home crises:

> A crisis growing more common than the empty nest occurs in those families in which young adults either don't leave home or fail repeatedly in their efforts at emancipation. Leaving home crises fall into three syndromes: (1) the cozy nest, in which the young adult is at home unemancipated and the parents are comfortable with it; (2) the crowded nest, in which the young adult is at home unemancipated and the parents are uncomfortable with it; and (3) fatal flights, in which the young adult makes a mess of emancipating but won't return home. (p. 208)

Family Goals. The primary family goals of this stage are:

- Support the young person's responsible strides toward creating his own life away from his family
- Support parental efforts to address how their child's independent living impacts on their respective individual functioning and marital functioning

Resistance to Family Goals. Both parents and young persons struggle with their experiences of creating the empty nest (or in the families with younger siblings, the emptier nest). Chronic relapsing well into the recovering person's young adulthood can be indicative of family members protecting themselves from the pain of the empty nest.

Strategy With Family Goal Resistance. Just as in the previous stage of family recovery, both parents and children might benefit from individual therapy or marital therapy in addressing issues with the recovering young person living independently. Conjoint family therapy in this stage can be useful around boundary-making tasks and in creating appropriate distance between parents and their child (Fishman, Stanton, & Rosman, 1982).

Family Recovery Skills

Overview of Family Recovery Skills

Much as the recovering adolescent can grow in sobriety through learning individual recovery skills, so the recovering family can strengthen its functioning with the building of family recovery skills. Family recovery skills are a range of tools about family life and family coping strategies for families dealing with the impact of adolescent substance abuse. Increased awareness and coping strategies such as these can serve to enhance a family's competency in working through the four stages of family recovery.

Categories of Family Recovery Skills

There are three basic categories of family recovery skills:

1. Family addiction awareness
2. Family development awareness
3. Strengthening family dynamics

In helping families to learn family recovery skills, therapists and treatment programs can utilize a variety of modalities. Family therapy, multiple family therapy (O'Shea & Phelps, 1985), parent training (Dishion, Reid, & Patterson, 1988), psychoeducational groups, and the therapeutic elements of parent support groups, such as Families Anonymous, are among the modalities that can integrate the teaching of family recovery skills.

Family Addiction Awareness

This category of family recovery skills pertains to family members learning about addiction as both an individual process for the adolescent and as a system process for the family. Parents and siblings can become enlightened about the teenager's experience with addiction and recovery, including information about the addiction process, chemical dependency, and the unique aspects of adolescent dependency, recovery, and relapse.

Also, family members can assimilate awareness about the family processes involved in addiction and family recovery. The needs of younger siblings in recovering families can be highlighted. Particular attention can be paid to the impact their brother's or sister's substance abuse has had on younger siblings. Issues such as resentment over the chaos and confusion in the family, fear of relapse, confusion over why their sibling got into abusing drugs, and guilt over enabling or not being able to stop their sibling's substance abuse are all family recovery topics.

Grasping understanding about enabling and learning coping strategies for disengaging and empowering are key for parents. Support with developing contracts with their child and gaining effective limit setting and negotiating skills can help to guide parents in these difficult tasks.

In addition, it can be valuable for parents to have an understanding that family recovery is a process, not an event, and that the stages in family recovery help to foster their understanding. Knowing about the pitfalls that can lead to relapse, as well as the accomplishments that can strengthen family functioning, gives parents a realistic idea of what takes place on the road to family recovery.

Family Development Awareness

This category of family recovery skills has two parts: family members learning about adolescence as a distinct stage of psychological development, and family members learning about the stresses of family life during the adolescent phase of the family life cycle and ways of dealing with these stresses.

It is important not to take for granted that parents are attuned to the stresses and challenges of adolescent development. Thus promoting their awareness about adolescent development, including the physical, sexual, cognitive, moral, and emotional changes that their child experiences, can support them in their job as parents.

It can also be a relief for parents to discover how adolescence is a distinctive stage of family life. Knowing about changes in family life during this period, including parental midlife experiences and marital adjustment with adolescent separation, can help to normalize these changes for parents and aid in their dealing with these changes.

Strengthening Family Dynamics

The five dynamics of family functioning that were discussed in Chapter 5 are the focus of this third category of family recovery skills. How these dynamics operate in a family contributes to how organized or disorganized a family is in its functioning. As previously mentioned, most families of adolescent substance abusers experience a fair amount of disorganization with these dynamics. Thus therapeutic attention to these dynamics is strongly indicated.

The following is a summary of suggestions for therapists and treatment programs to keep in mind while helping parents and recovering families with addressing their dynamics:

Leadership Dynamics. Encourage parental teamwork and empowerment. Guide parents in their developing a sense of supportive authority.

Support parental confidence in establishing guidelines for the recovering adolescent's behavior.

Boundary Dynamics. Help parents to be parents and teenagers to be teenagers through encouraging the natural delineation of the generations. Support family members' efforts to create clearly defined and appropriate relationships with one another. Promote emotional separateness among family members without compromising intimacy.

Affect Dynamics. Urge parents to become more accepting of their own feelings and more understanding of their recovering adolescent's feelings. Assist family members with more effective communication of feelings with one another (especially communication with feelings that have been historically avoided in the family).

Communication Dynamics. Help family members to identify more successful ways of discussing issues and feelings within the family. Facilitate family members' awareness of negative communication patterns, such as blaming, that have inhibited successful communication in the past. Nowinski (1990) mentions, in discussing the need for recovering families to strengthen their communication abilities,

> in considering the need for changing roles and old habits within the family, we must look closely at communication. Substance abuse itself represents an attempt to cope with issues and emotions without communicating about them; therefore, communication becomes vital to recovery. (p. 202)

Task/Goal Performing Dynamics. Support family members' efforts to become more proactive and less reactive in negotiating issues within the family. Encourage parents' inclusion of their teenager's input into the process of creating limits and consequences for his behavior. Remind family members of the importance of infusing a sense of renewal and fun into family life.

PEER RELATIONSHIPS IN RECOVERY

Overview of Peer Relationships in Recovery

Teenagers in recovery are faced with the dual challenge of giving up companions who abuse drugs and making new friends with young persons who do not abuse chemicals. This "giving up" companions parallels the experience of giving up drugs. Attempts at recovery, while remaining involved with peers who abuse chemicals, are doomed to relapse. At the same time, recovery does not happen in a vacuum. The recovering adolescent needs to take risks in forming new friendships for his support and social needs.

The work of detaching from chemical use and attaching to recovery-oriented treatment occurs across four stages, as discussed in Chapter 9. Because the recovery work of detaching from chemical-abusing peers and attaching to recovery-supportive peers parallels this process, the recovery work with peer relationships is also discussed according to these four stages of adolescent recovery.

Also, drug use, peer relationships, and sexual behavior are often intertwined. Consequently, sexual issues will need to be addressed along with the teenager's peer relationships in recovery.

Stages of Recovery and Peer Relationships

Stage 1: Shifting

As the adolescent in this first stage denies the impact of chemicals on his functioning, so is he likely to deny the role of his friends in his drug use. The adolescent's resistance to abstinence from chemical use is also a resistance to severing ties with peers who are a lifeline to drugs and a support with a drug-abusing lifestyle. It is all they know. Consequently, giving up these social, albeit unhealthy, ties is very threatening.

Often an adolescent in this stage is closed to forming relationships with new, sober peers. However, some teenagers in this stage might have a nondrug-abusing friend or two within their sphere of friendships. Sometimes, these "clean" peers can be helpful adjuncts to a caring confrontation done to facilitate the substance-abusing adolescent's awareness of the extent of his drug problem. (Selekman, 1991).

Stage 2: Sampling

During this stage of adolescent recovery, many teenagers may still resist the challenge of giving up drugs and peer group as part of the same package. Adolescents in this stage may even be developing a genuine desire to abstain from chemicals, but denial of the role of peers in chemical abuse problems will likely sabotage any efforts at sobriety.

Group therapy can be a powerful resource for helping an adolescent to work through his loyalty binds with drug-involved peers. Within the supportive environment of the group the teenager can: (a) be assisted with openly examining his negative behavioral pattern, and the role of peers with this pattern; (b) have his denial challenged with supportive and reality-based feedback from fellow group members; (c) be a part of the give-and-take of genuinely caring relationships with other adolescents who are similarly wrestling with giving up drugs and drug-using friends (Bratter, 1989).

Meetings of AA and NA can also be helpful to recovering adolescents who feel the dilemma of letting go of negative friendships and beginning new healthy ones. Resistances that many teenagers may experience to meeting sober peers at such meetings include fear of engulfment and fear of failure.

Zweben (1987) discusses this fear of engulfment as the addict's not wanting to lose his identity to the group. The therapeutic task is to help the young person identify what part of his self is disavowing by projecting this fear onto AA or NA members. Understanding his disavowing and projecting might help the young addict to identify with other program members.

Some recovering adolescents may have the desire but not the interpersonal skills to develop new relationships with sober peers. Consequently, they may shy away from even trying to make new friends out of a fear of failure. These recovering adolescents need to learn interpersonal and social skills, such as those discussed in the recovery skills program in Chapter 9. Learning these skills can go a long way toward adolescents creating the kind of peer relationships they need in recovery (Walfish, Massey, & Krone, 1990).

Stage Three: Conversion

During this stage of recovery, in which the young person is openly contending with developmental crises and needs to maintain his commitment to recovery, peer relationships are at a crossroads. This is particularly true with a teenager who is reentering his community and school upon return from a residential, inpatient, or partial hospital program.

In this stage the adolescent is faced with three primary tasks in regard to peer relationships: (a) continue to rely on the network of sober and nonsubstance-abusing peers that he is developing in recovery, (b) make efforts to integrate into the mainstream adolescent culture of his school and community, and (c) maintain clear and firm boundaries when reencountering old drug-abusing friends. All three of these tasks can be sources of peer crisis. Some recovering adolescents have a deep sense of being "all sobered up with no place to go." They may find it very hard to fit in a with mainstream teenage life in their school and feel much alienation. At the same time, their active distancing from drug-involved peers can strike chords of rejection. The hurt, betrayal, ostracism, and loneliness of such peer crisis can be intense.

It is important that the recovering young person have a steady source of peer support during this time of changes in peer relationships. His network of sober peers can be that steady source. AA and NA meetings can continue to be a source for sober peer relationships. In addition, sobriety support groups, not affiliated with 12-step recovery programs, are available to recovering adolescents in many communities.

> There are now many adolescent groups that are especially useful to a recovering teen because they prevent a feeling of isolation and allow the teen to develop a social/recovering peer group. Sobriety that is not fun does not last. (Myers & Anderson, 1991, p. 92)

Stage 4: Coalescing

By the fourth stage of recovery, with the adolescent experiencing progressive successes in sobriety, peer relationships are usually more stable. The teenager has likely made some adaptation to mainstream adolescent peer culture and is experiencing some satisfaction with healthier adolescent socializing. In addition, he has likely had ample opportunities to establish boundaries with, and appropriate distance from, old substance-abusing friends. Ongoing involvement with peers from AA and NA, or other adolescent recovery support groups, can continue to support the teenager's growth with peer relationships in recovery.

Sexual Issues and Peer Relationships in Recovery

Dealing with peer relationships in recovery will inevitably bring about the adolescent's addressing sexual issues in recovery. For many substance-abusing teenagers, their sexual development is problematically entwined with their drug use. Chemical use loosens inhibitions, and, as such, promotes sexual interaction. With adolescents whose sexuality is in a critical period of development, chemically encouraged sexual interactions can create many problems. Among the problems are the following: (a) numbing normal anxieties of sexual awareness during adolescence by using drugs; (b) seeking to enhance sexual performance with chemical use; (c) loss of personal boundaries and engaging in unwanted sex when under the influence of chemicals; (d) unplanned sex and the complications that can result, including sexually transmitted diseases, AIDS, and pregnancy; and (e) becoming physically aggressive under the influence of drugs and forcing sex upon a partner.

With this alarming potential for problems stemming from chemical use and sexual interaction, sexual issues will require intervention during recovery. These interventions include:

1. Helping the teenager to learn healthy ways of dealing with his sexual urges and feelings
2. Facilitating the adolescent's awareness of the difference between more adaptive and maladaptive sexual behaviors
3. Promoting the young person's integration of more satisfactory dating habits during his recovery

Some of these sexual issues might be the result of the adolescent being sexually abused, and require specific interventions during recovery. Treatment issues with recovery adolescents who are also victims of sexual abuse are discussed in Chapter 11.

Dealing With Sexual Feelings

As the adolescent's chemical use is often intertwined with his sexual behavior, sobriety can allow him to experience his sexuality and sexual feelings without chemical contamination. Fuller awareness of sexuality and sexual feelings can be extremely threatening for many young persons in recovery.

> For many teenagers, issues of sexual dependence become overwhelming, as sexual feelings are often a last defense and the strongest attachment against feelings of abandonment, loneliness, isolation, and alienation. Intimacy becomes a major focus in treatment as they struggle with the confusion between sexuality and intimacy. Sexual urges may be strong enough for acting out or leaving treatment. (Chatlos, 1989, p. 199)

It is important that therapists and treatment programs recognize the necessity of working with adolescents around issues related to sexual feelings and urges. Recovering adolescents need understanding and guidance with the identification of, and healthy expression of, myriad feelings that are part of sober sexuality.

The experience of the homosexual adolescent in substance abuse recovery merits particular sensitivity by therapists. Among the issues for gay adolescents are: their awareness of and acceptance of their homosexual feelings, the formation of a personal identity that incorporates their sexual identity, social stigma and the need for a support group, and dealing with family reactions to the disclosure of their sexual identity (Anderson, 1990).

Learning About Adaptive Sexual Behavior

Many recovering adolescents have not had the benefit of a genuine education about sex. Their indoctrination about sex, their feelings about their own sexuality, and their sense of responsibility in sexual relationships is often the result of drug-blurred awareness and expedience. The recovery skills curriculum, discussed in Chapter 9, is one way of helping to promote healthier sexual practices with recovering teenagers. In addition, therapists can take the opportunity to help recovering young persons learn about the importance of birth control, the role of mutually consensual sexual relationships, and other issues pertaining to their sexual development and behavior (Heaslip, Van Dyke, Hogenson, & Vedders, 1989).

Dating and Recovery

A recovering adolescent pursuing dating companions is demonstrating an appropriate developmental need. The therapeutic issue is the appropriate timing of such pursuits. Flights into a relationship, especially during critical junctures in treatment, can be tantamount to the teenager relapsing and avoiding his work in recovery. Therapists need to challenge an adolescent who uses the "thirteenth step" as a substitute for working the 12 steps. A 13th step, whereby the recovering person flees into a relationship and away from his program of recovery, can mirror the instant gratification provided by drugs.

Recovery can also present the adolescent with opportunities to learn dating habits and relational patterns that are more congruent with his recovering lifestyle. Therapists can support the young person in sorting through the feelings, experiences, and risk taking that goes along with normal adolescent dating.

SUMMARY

An individual adolescent's recovery process occurs within a recovery environment. The adolescent's recovery environment is composed of his family and his friends.

This chapter discusses the role of family recovery for the family of the substance-abusing adolescent. Much as with the individual adolescent's recovery, a four-stage model of family recovery is presented paralleling the stages encountered by the adolescent.

Also, just as with the individual adolescent's recovery, recovery skills for the family are discussed. These family recovery skills are a combination of increased awareness about family life and coping strategies for families impacted by adolescent substance abuse.

The recovering adolescent's peer relationships also require attention during the course of treatment. Different dilemmas during the four stages of adolescent recovery arise from the teenager's efforts to detach from substance-abusing friends and forge friendships with sober peers. In addition, because an adolescent's chemical use is so often intertwined with his sexual development, sexual issues with peer relationships will necessitate attention during recovery.

Chapter 11

TREATING VULNERABLE POPULATIONS OF ADOLESCENT SUBSTANCE ABUSERS

INTRODUCTION

Adolescent substance abusers with a concurrent psychological disorder, who are victims of physical or sexual abuse, or who grew up with substance-abusing parents represent three special treatment populations. Such adolescents present a kind of double jeopardy for treatment providers (Rivinus, 1991c). Teenagers grappling with overcoming substance abuse, as well as growing with any of these coexisting developmental impairments, have special treatment needs and command unique attention in treatment.

Young persons in these populations struggle with a kind of developmental eclipse during their teenage years. Treatment seeks to bring awareness, growth, and developmental light into this formative time, so that they may thrive in recovery.

Rationale for Differential Treatment of Vulnerable Populations

There are several reasons for identifying these vulnerable populations of adolescent substance abusers and focusing on their distinctive treatment needs. The first reason is that each of these populations is difficult to engage in substance abuse treatment. The dynamics of denial often serve a dual function for each of these populations. Along with serving to blunt a teenager's awareness of her chemical abuse, denial can also serve to protect the young person from experiencing the full nature of her coexisting psychological disorders, the true pain of her traumatization, or the real impact of her parent's chemical abuse on her life. When denial is serving such a dual function, defenses are more rigid and resistance runs much deeper, thus making the adolescent even more closed to substance abuse treatment.

A second reason for distinguishing these vulnerable populations and their special treatment needs is that once they enter treatment the conditions concurrent with the substance abuse—whether it is a psychological disorder, traumatization, or child of substance-abusing parent (COSAP) experience—can be complicated to assess and diagnose. Substance abuse can mask any of these special conditions, and therapists or treatment teams focusing exclusively on the drug problem run the risk of overlooking an important part of the young person's functioning. The inverse can also be true. Adolescent chemical abusers in treatment systems for a psychological disorder, physical or sexual traumatization, or as the child of a substance abuser, might have each of these respective problems addressed while not receiving treatment for their drug problem. Specialists, such as child psychiatrists and psychologists expert in childhood trauma treatment or clinicians skillful in treating the offspring of addicts, are often needed to help make a differential diagnosis and develop treatment plans for coexisting problems.

An additional reason for giving separate attention to these three vulnerable populations is that the course of treatment and the path of recovery are often more complicated for them. Once the coexisting condition is identified, decisions need to be made by the treatment team as to whether treatment is to be sequenced or if both problems can be treated simultaneously. Also, as discussed in Chapter 2, with adolescent substance abusers a modification of 12-step self-help work needs to be done to make these programs more "adolescent-friendly." Special considerations need to be given to making AA and NA even more accessible for drug-abusing adolescents within these vulnerable populations.

A further concern for these three particular groups of chemically dependent adolescents is that they are at an even higher risk for relapse. If the concurrent problem is not treated or is undertreated, the stresses of this coexisting condition during substance abuse recovery can be overwhelming. Consequently, the newly sober young person can be highly susceptible to resumed chemical use.

A final reason for focusing on the unique treatment needs of these populations is that the interpersonal recovery environment has to be responsive to the more complex treatment needs of the adolescent. Families of these more vulnerable recovering teenagers will also have compounded treatment needs. These families will need to walk down a dual path of family recovery.

Adolescent Substance Abusers
With Multiple Vulnerabilities

As there is much overlap between these three vulnerable populations, some teenagers have the misfortune of belonging to more than one group. If having a substance abuse problem along with a coexisting problem presents a double jeopardy in treatment, then struggling with more than one of these concurrent conditions along with substance abuse presents a "multiple jeopardy."

When a substance-abusing adolescent is vulnerable in a number of these areas, it is as if with each rung up the ladder of recovery, she is striving against the gravitational pull of significant developmental impairment and enormous environmental stress. These teenagers require even more careful consideration and specialized attention in treatment.

CONSIDERATIONS IN TREATING
ADOLESCENT SUBSTANCE ABUSERS
WITH CONCURRENT PSYCHOLOGICAL DISORDERS

General Considerations

Adolescents who are trying to "kick" their chemical habit, as well as overcome the developmental debilitation of a concurrent psychological disorder, represent a specific vulnerable population. As discussed in Chapter 4, psychopathology may be a contributing factor in the development of substance abuse, or substance abuse may play a part in the evolution of a psychological disorder, or both conditions might emanate in some parallel manner from a common set of etiological factors. The exact relationship between adolescent substance abuse and adolescent psychological disorders is complicated and does not lend itself to simple cause and effect understandings.

One common characteristic between substance-abusing adolescents and psychologically disordered adolescents is that both can be understood from a biopsychosocial perspective. Noshpitz and King (1991) and Weiner (1992) are among those who have made comprehensive contributions to the literature on how different categories of adolescent psychological disorders can have biological, psychological, and social determinants. In addition, they offer treatment recommendations for each of these categories of disorders that involve combining biological (such as medication), psychological (such as psychotherapy), and social (such as family intervention) treatments.

In discussing treatment recommendations with this population, one reminder bears mentioning. Substance use disorders are primary conditions, not symptomatic of and secondary to some other disorder. To approach dually diagnosed adolescents as self-medicators whose substance abuse will eventually abate once their psychological disorder is in remission is an erroneous therapeutic assumption. Many adolescents with a concurrent psychological disorder may have been "acting out" with chemicals early on. But the chemical use can eventually "act on" the young person's developing self and a chemical dependency results. Both conditions are intertwined, both are primary, and both deserve focused treatment interventions. Before discussing treatment considerations with specific categories of dually diagnosed adolescents, there are some general treatment considerations with this vulnerable population.

Engagement Issues

Influencing adolescents to enter substance-abuse treatment is a difficult task. The task is even further complicated in the case of the teenager whose chemical abuse is, in part, operating to stabilize or is intertwined with a psychological disorder. Denial of a substance-abuse problem is a warding off of the threat to their perceived intrapsychic lifeline—drugs. The adolescent's defenses will become all the more intensified in protecting themselves from this perceived threat to their psychological survival when denial is confronted.

In one case with an 18-year-old substance-abusing female, who was eventually diagnosed with a coexisting borderline personality disorder, the therapist needed to be highly vigilant in creating a safe therapeutic environment within which to cultivate this teenager's trust. This adolescent was being treated in a dual diagnosis residential program and her primary therapist was persistent with both working at building rapport and processing this teenager's acting out and splitting behavior. In gradually gaining more trust with this adolescent, the therapist was better able to facilitate her openness to receiving feedback about the adverse effects of her chemical use. This teenager's denial of her substance abuse problem subsided, and she was able to work her program of recovery more effectively.

Servicing Issues

Effective assessment and diagnosis of a concurrent psychological disorder often takes clinical acumen and perseverance. Extensive developmental and family history gathering, obtaining collateral data on the teenager's functioning, psychological testing after an appreciable period of sobriety, as well as constant observations of how the young person's psychological functioning changes during recovery may all be necessary for formulating an accurate diagnosis. It is critical not to be premature with a diagnosis and not to allow chemically induced psychological states, including hallucinations, dysphoria, and anxiety, to obscure the true functioning profile of the adolescent.

In diagnosing and treating a concurrent psychological disorder, the contentious issue arises of whether or not medication should be used with the dually diagnosed adolescent. In general, the judicious use of medication with adolescents with severe psychological disorders is indicated. The primary goal is that symptoms of the disorder can be managed and therapeutic issues can be worked on (Gregorius & Smith, 1991). Great caution needs to be used when prescribing medication, particularly mood-altering medication, with dually diagnosed adolescents.

> The use of medications, especially psychotropic, is another point of potential controversy. We absolutely refuse to recommend or condone the use of addictive medications after detoxification. The dangers of cross-addiction and the importance of a chemical-free lifestyle for dual diagnosis clients make this a crucial issue. But we are quite comfortable using other psychotropic medications after a comprehensive evaluation indicates that the client requires this for his or her psychiatric disorder. (Evans & Sullivan, 1990, p. 27)

In electing to prescribe medication for a dually diagnosed adolescent, it is important that the treatment team work through with the adolescent: (a) the difference between appropriate medication and inappropriate self-medication and (b) possible objections to being on medication that are sometimes raised by AA or NA members.

Treatment of both substance abuse and a psychological disorder can be sequenced, or can occur simultaneously. With some teenagers the psychological symptoms need to be addressed prior to dealing with the drug problem. With other teenagers the substance-abuse behavior needs to be managed before treating the psychological disorder. Also, there are times when the adolescent can and should receive dual and concurrent treatments for both disorders. Balanced clinical judgement needs to be exercised in determining how to combine treatments for the dual recovery of the young person. Treatment placement of the teenager along the continuum of care will need to consider programs and therapists who are specifically trained and organized for treating this demanding population.

Recovery Issues

The path of recovery for dually disordered adolescents necessitates flexibility with treatment approach. In early recovery when the dually disordered adolescent's repertoire of denial is firmly entrenched, a caring confrontation therapeutic approach (Chapter 9) is even more strongly indicated. Many psychologically disordered adolescents have very fragile intrapsychic structures, and inattention by therapists to this fragility can be developmentally destructive.

> The imprudent use of confrontation can result in decompensation of psychological and behavioral functioning. The overuse of confrontation can result in the development of an adversarial and nontherapeutic relationship with the patient. It is an unacceptable "trade off" to attain an adolescent's cooperation or acceptance of a substance abuse problem at the expense of their psychological health and well-being. (Singer & White, 1991, p. 22)

As denial subsides and recovery continues with the dually diagnosed young person, if and how to access involvement in a 12-step program needs to be considered. Young persons who are severely cognitively impaired or who are in the throes of a psychotic process will not be able to benefit immediately from attending meetings and participating in the AA or NA program. Each dually disordered adolescent's referral to AA or NA needs to be considered on an individual basis (King & Meeks, 1988).

As the adolescent progresses in recovery and moves to working through developmental crises, long-repressed feelings, impulses, and sensations related in part to his psychological disorder may surface. This intrapsychic activity can threaten the tenuous stability of his chemically free self. The safety and support of further hospitalization or of a residential program may be necessary to stabilize the recovering dually-disordered adolescent at this very crucial stage.

Later stages of recovery entail the teenager with concurrent drug and psychological problems striving to move onto a developmental track more congruent with his healthier instincts. Engaging in reparative developmental work is a process that can provide eventual rewarding results—a chemically free self and healthier psychological functioning.

Recovery Environment Issues

Along with working on family recovery issues, families with dually disordered adolescents also need to attend to family issues specific to the young person's particular psychological disorder. For example, a family with a borderline personality disordered adolescent with antisocial tendencies may need to attend to family structure and boundary concerns. It may need to work on reorganizing the family structure so that the parental hierarchy is optimally functioning and "in charge" of the family. A family with a depressed teenager may need to emphasize support and nurturance patterns more strongly in the family. Such a family may need to work primarily on communication and affect-sharing styles within the family.

Each dually diagnosed adolescent is different, and each family of these teenagers is unique. The distinct needs of each family with a dually diagnosed teenager require attention in treatment as much as the specific needs of the teenager. This is necessary to maximize optimal treatment outcomes.

Considerations in Concurrent Treatment
With Specific Psychological Disorders

Along with identifying some general treatment considerations with adolescent substance abusers with concurrent psychological disorders, it is also important to determine treatment considerations with some categories of dually diagnosed teenagers.

"Dual Diagnosis" is often used in a way that implies homogeneity among this group of patients, as if such an identification will facilitate treatment planning. On the contrary, the typical dual diagnosis patient is a mythical creature. Patients with substance abuse and other psychiatric illness present with a wide variety of clinical problems and require a treatment approach that addresses their specific disorders. (Weiss, Mirin, & Frances, 1992, p. 107)

Among the major psychological disorders that can affect adolescents are anxiety disorders, mood disorders, eating disorders, personality disorders, and schizophrenia. Due to the scope of this book, only a brief discussion of treatment considerations with substance-abusing adolescents who may have one of these five disorders is mentioned here.

Anxiety Disorders

O'Connell (1989) offers some treatment guidelines for substance abusing-anxiety disordered adolescents: "This type of adolescent needs supportive treatment. In addition exploratory therapy may help uncover the causes of the anxiety. These youngsters can also benefit from social skills training, especially assertiveness training focusing on refusal skills" (p. 53).

In addition, treatment should include interventions directed at the young person's experience of his anxiety. Stress management and relaxation training—part of the recovery skills training—can aid the recovering adolescent in his overall anxiety management.

Mood Disorders

The category of mood disorders includes both disorders of depression and bipolar disorders. Once a mood disorder has been diagnosed concurrent with the substance abuse disorder, treatment should concentrate on these dual conditions in the teenager's life. "Treating depression and substance abuse requires a careful targeting of specific individual and social problems. Treatment also must accurately respond to a child's developmental level" (Joshi & Scott, 1988, p. 1356). Because depressed adolescents are at a high risk for suicide, and there appears to be some relationship between depression, chemical use, and suicide with adolescents (Levy & Deykin, 1989), suicidal ideation and impulses will require particularly close monitoring and intervention with this group of recovering adolescents. Depressed adolescents are particularly vulnerable to suicidal impulses in early substance-abuse recovery as intense affective states surge into awareness and drug use to self-medicate is a forbidden option.

Recovering adolescents with a concurrent bipolar disorder require specific treatment interventions aimed at managing their manic phases. As Weiner states in discussing treatment with a bipolar teenager, "Whereas depression calls for guidance, encouragement and reinforcement aimed at helping the person become more active and engaged, mania is best treated by using those techniques to help the person slow down and back off" (Weiner, 1992, p. 148)

Eating Disorders

Anorexia nervosa and bulimia comprise the category of eating disorders. Treatment goals with eating disordered adolescents is summarized by Mishne (1986): "Successful treatment of anorexic and bulimic patients requires appropriate management of food to reinstate normal nutrition for physical well-being and the resolution of the underlying psychological and family problems" (p. 189).

As eating disorders can impact the young person's developing physiology, medical interventions are usually a necessary component to treatment.

Personality Disorders

Adolescents with personality disorders who use chemicals usually do so to self-medicate their feelings of deep emptiness (Miller, 1986). Consequently, treatment with these adolescents needs to be directed at the defensive and self-protective "style" of the disorder.

Adolescents who are more inclined toward an "externalizing" style of functioning turn outward and act out to fill up this experience of emptiness. Supportively confronting this pattern of acting out and facilitating healthy expression of and management of underlying feelings are primary goals for treatment.

Adolescents who have a propensity toward an "internalizing" style of functioning turn inward and usually withdraw into solitary pursuits to deal with their sense of hollowness. Directing these adolescents toward healthy ways of accessing internal life while getting their emotional needs met through supportive relationships are primary treatment goals.

Schizophrenia

In general, therapeutic goals with schizophrenic adolescents should include strengthening their functioning through supplying cognitive structuring, clarifying areas of conflict, encouraging the development of an autonomous identity, supporting more adaptive coping mechanisms and defenses, and facilitating efforts to increase socialization (Weiner, 1992). The fragility of the intrapsychic structure of the schizophrenic young person needs to be respected during his recovery from substance abuse. Confrontation, which can be overwhelming to the point of inducing psychosis, should be eschewed in favor of immediate, supportive, and reality-based feedback, ideally from peers in a group therapy setting (Gregorius & Smith, 1991).

CONSIDERATIONS IN TREATING ADOLESCENT SUBSTANCE ABUSERS WHO ARE VICTIMS OF CHILD ABUSE

General Considerations

Adolescents who are trying to recover from substance abuse as well as heal from the trauma of physical or sexual abuse represent another vulnerable treatment population. As discussed in Chapter 4, a traumatized sense of self may be a determinant in an adolescent's development of chemical dependency.

As clinical populations, there is much overlap between adolescents who are victims of physical abuse and those who are victims of sexual abuse. Frequently adolescents who are victims of one type of abuse are also victims of the other type of abuse (Schmidt, 1991).

In general, treatment of the traumatized substance-abusing adolescent should involve concurrent interventions with both conditions. To attempt to treat the chemical dependency while ignoring the impact of physical or sexual abuse is to set up a high risk for the adolescent to relapse and resume drug use. To attempt treatment of the teenager's physical or sexual trauma while sidestepping the chemical abuse will likely compromise interventions with core issues of the victim. What is a crucial clinical judgement is the timing of treatment interventions with each condition.

Treatment of both conditions can be approached from a biopsychosocial model. Both substance abuse and physical or sexual abuse often present biomedical concerns necessitating attention. In addition, the primary treatment efforts are to promote the young person's reparative developmental work and intrapsychic healing, as well as reparative environmental work with the family and peer relationships.

The following are some specific treatment considerations for adolescent substance abusers who are victims of childhood physical abuse, sexual abuse, or both.

Engagement Issues

Chemically dependent adolescents who are victims of abuse are often difficult to engage in treatment. In addition to denying their drug problem, they are highly self-protective about their victimization. Outside attempts to intrude upon their secret are commonly mistrusted and shunned. Consequently, it is important that clinicians not approach these adolescents in any way that is retraumatizing. Creating optimal therapeutic safety and not replicating dynamics of "overpowering" the adolescent is essential.

Servicing Issues

An adolescent revealing physical or sexual victimization can set in motion a number of case management issues for the therapist or treatment team. Involvement of other systems, including police, child protection services, and the judicial system, may be warranted or mandated for safety, civil, and criminal reasons. "Cooperative intervention" (Sgroi, 1982) between the therapists and these systems, and within these systems, is essential for supporting the adolescent through a painful and possibly explosive period.

In cases where the initial substance abuse assessment or treatment of the adolescent is being conducted and ongoing physical or sexual victimization is disclosed, the safety of the teenager needs to take precedent. The substance abuse concerns have to be put on the back burner until such time that the adolescent's safety has been ensured. For example, one female adolescent who was being assessed for substance abuse at an outpatient clinic revealed to the clinician, upon being interviewed about her developmental history, that she had been sexually abused by an older cousin the previous year. The clinician's priority immediately shifted from the substance abuse assessment to mobilizing to involve appropriate child protection and law enforcement systems to ensure the well-being of this girl. In addition, it was crucial that the clinician served as an emotional support to the girl during this period of individual and family crisis and exercised appropriate judgement as to when to resume directly addressing this girl's substance abuse issues.

Recovery Issues

In recovering from substance abuse and healing from trauma, the chemically dependent adolescent's traumatized sense of self becomes a core issue.

> While alcohol and drugs may play a self-enhancing role in chemical dependence, it appears that for the chemically dependent adolescent, the self-enhancement or self-medicating role of these chemicals is short-lived. In these adolescents the chemical dependence is the first layer of defense; it must be removed before an attempt can be made to work through the repetitive trauma of abuse. (Cavaiola & Schiff, 1989, p. 333)

Abstinence and other recovery crises (Chapter 10) can usher in and restimulate powerful and painful feelings of shame and anger associated with the abuse. These recovering teenagers will need to experience safety and structure in the therapeutic environment in order to progress in recovery and healing.

Recovery Environment Issues

Family recovery issues differ according to whether the abuse of the child is intrafamilial or extrafamilial. The focus in this chapter is primarily with intrafamilial traumatization or victimization of the teen-ager by a parent, other adult relative, or sibling. However, this is not to discount the impact of extrafamilial abuse and the related treatment issues. As Sgroi discusses in instances of extrafamilial child sexual abuse, which also are relevant in cases of child physical abuse, there are two primary family treatment issues (Sgroi, 1982): family members dealing with their sense of failure to protect the child, and family members dealing with their postabuse perceptions of the child.

In cases of intrafamilial abuse of the child, family treatment issues are even more complex. The family may have the hidden agenda of wanting the adolescent to use chemicals so that her substance abuse can be "the problem" and the threat of focusing on abuse issues is lessened. When the abuse becomes disclosed, such families are often involuntary participants in treatment.

Although there is no causal evidence that directly links parental substance abuse with child abuse, there is strong correlative evidence that this is often the case (Lawson, Peterson & Lawson, 1983; Schmidt, 1991). Associations between parental substance abuse and parental violence in the family (O'Sullivan, 1989; Bays, 1990), and parental substance abuse and parental incest (Barnard, 1983, 1990) have been identified. Consequently, individual and family treatment issues related to growing up in a chemically dependent family often need to be addressed in the overall treatment of the victimized adolescent.

Considerations in Concurrent Treatment
With Specific Types of Child Abuse

Physically Traumatized

Treatment considerations with physically abused teenagers begin with seeking to identify and assess the physical abuse if the adolescent has not yet disclosed it. Direct questioning to screen for abuse is strongly indicated for therapists, with an awareness that answering such questions can be extremely painful for the young person.

Once the physical abuse is known to the therapist or treatment team, interventions need to concentrate on how to integrate treatment for his or her traumatization with his or her recovery from substance abuse. Supportive psychotherapy techniques (Chapter 10) can be helpful in treating the teenager's assaulted sense of self.

As violence creates violence, a common treatment issue with this population is its own violent behavior. A syndrome of victims of physical abuse, identification with the aggressor, can result in chemically induced aggression (Cavaiola & Schiff, 1989). Self-management strategies need to be developed in recovery to address violent behaviors.

With cases of intrafamilial physical abuse, family treatment considerations start with recognizing the family dynamics behind the abuse. "Violence in families is usually precipitated by an intrusion of boundaries, an intrusion that leads to helplessness, fear, anger, and confusion, and ultimately to violent expression" (Fishman, 1988, p. 82).

As family treatment progresses and more appropriate boundaries become established between family members, the sense of degradation by both the victim and the victimized will need to be addressed. "Therapy with violent families must deal not only with the system's organization and structure but also with the affective tinge that colors a relationship" (Fishman, 1988, p. 85).

The following are some treatment principles for working with violent families that are also affected by chemical abuse in the family (Potter-Efron & Potter-Efron, 1985):

1. Violence is never an acceptable solution for any family problems and only leads to more violence.
2. The use of alcohol or drugs promotes family violence and cannot be accepted.
3. Secrets keep a family sick; denial of family problems to others, to the family, or to yourself perpetuates the problems.
4. Each member of the family has the right to a decent life, a life free from daily fear, pain, dishonesty, or shame.
5. The entire family has been affected by the use of chemicals or violence by some members. Everyone hurts together and all need to work together to get well.
6. Change is possible, both individually and for the family.

The issues implied in these treatment principles with violent families are not all that need to be dealt with in these families. However, these principles can serve as guidelines when the issues arise in treatment.

Sexually Traumatized

Treatment considerations begin with assessing the adolescent substance abuser for any history of sexual victimization. Screening for sexual abuse by direct inquiry should be a routine part of an intake process. But the victimized teenager, needing to be self-protective, may not reveal any history of being sexually abused. Opportunities may arise during the course of treatment for the adolescent to feel safer and to disclose any experiences of sexual victimization. Hussey and Singer (1989) report on an instrument, the Adolescent Sexual Concern Questionnaire, which can be integrated into the assessment or treatment process and possibly facilitate the young person's trust and comfort with disclosing abuse.

Working with adolescent sexual trauma victims means respecting the individual's integrity and pace in healing from the abuse. It is essential that therapists and treatment teams create a therapeutic climate in which the young person can feel a sense of empowerment and acknowledgement and take an active participation in the setting of treatment goals and priorities. Group therapy, combining both support and education, has been reported to be a useful treatment modality, particularly for female adolescent victims (Homstead & Werthamer, 1989; Hazzard, King & Webb, 1986).

The intertwining shame and dissociative experiences with substance abuse indicate the need for specific types of intervention with these issues during the course of substance abuse recovery. As discussed in Chapter 10, issues related to shame often arise during Stage 3, the conversion stage, of adolescent substance abuse recovery. Psychotherapeutic interventions should be tailored to each sexual trauma victim's unique experience with shame (Nathanson, 1989). Working with the young person's dissociative experiences means creating a therapeutic structure whereby the integration of behavioral, affective, thought, and sensation aspects of the dissociative experiences can be facilitated (Braun, 1989). What is always key is respecting the individual's own pace in therapy, "Abreaction is a painful process that must be done slowly, thoughtfully, and empathetically if the dissociated memories and affects are to be reintegrated successfully" (Coons, Bowman, Pellow, & Schneider, 1989 p. 332).

Family treatment considerations with cases of intrafamilial sexual abuse center on three critical family issues: (a) the failure of family members to protect the victimized child, (b) the failure of boundaries within the family, and (c) the abuse of power by a family member (Sgroi, 1982). A set of orienting premises for working with incestuous families is suggested by Gelinas (1988):

1. Any time there is sexual contact between an adult and a child, it is always the adult's responsibility.
2. A child is intensely loyal to his or her parents, and that loyalty must be explicitly supported in therapy.
3. The adult is held accountable for the incestuous sexual abuse, but the therapist must never scapegoat or allow scapegoating.

Multiple treatment modalities are often necessary in treating incestuous families. As Sgroi states, "Several treatment modalities must be employed simultaneously. Individual, dyad, group, couples, and family therapy can all be used in some combination" (1982, p. 264).

Family treatment can proceed along four phases, as suggested by Gelinas (1988): (a) establishing the therapeutic framework, (b) changing the family structure, (c) offering marital therapy, and (d) effecting a confrontation between the victim and the offender and the family. These four phases of treatment with the incestuous family can overlap the four stages of family recovery with adolescent substance abusers (Chapter 10). The question of when the issues of substance abuse or sexual victimization are addressed in the family is a matter of clinical judgement.

Finally, it is important to mention that male adolescent sexual abuse victims are an often-overlooked and hidden treatment population. (Rohsenow, Corbett, & Devine, 1988). The sexually traumatized adolescent male is at particular risk for developing a substance abuse problem (Harrison, Edwall, Hoffman, & Worthen, 1990).

It is crucial that the treatment needs of both female and male victims of sexual abuse be fully assessed and responded to during the course of substance abuse treatment. Failure to treat, or undertreating the impact of sexual traumatization, may result in the adolescent's "rapid relapse" back into drug abuse (Rohsenow, Corbett, & Devine, 1988).

CONSIDERATIONS IN TREATING ADOLESCENT SUBSTANCE-ABUSING FAMILIES

General Considerations

Adolescent substance abusers from chemically dependent families represent another vulnerable treatment population. They have a developmental vulnerability to substance abuse, just like the other two populations discussed in this chapter, and also are growing up in an environment vulnerable to substance abuse.

Until recently much of the professional literature has dealt specifically with the child of an alcoholic (COA). The COA model for understanding needs serves as a good foundation for working with children of substance-abusing parents (COSAP) (Rivinus, 1991c).

As discussed in Chapter 5, the family with a substance-abusing parent is just one type of dysfunctional family system. The term dysfunctional in this context is the extreme on a continuum of family organization-disorganization. In this extreme of family system disorganization, family dynamics do not provide a safe enough holding environment for the developmental needs of the adolescent. Children with substance-abusing parents are vulnerable to substance abuse for both developmental and environmental reasons.

The COSAP syndrome is a developmentally adaptive response by a teenager for coping with the chronic stress of living with a chemically dependent parent. In short, the COSAP syndrome is a coping style by the young person to psychologically or physically distance himself from the toxic family environment. For some children, their repertoire of coping buffers them from being severely impacted by parental substance abuse. However, for other teenagers the relentless stresses of chemically dependent family life overwhelms their adaptive capacity for coping, leaving them susceptible to maladaptive coping means, such as using drugs.

The environment of the chemically dependent family can also contribute to a child's problem with chemicals. Such families can serve as a precipitating environment for the child's substance abuse by: exposing the child to chemicals; modeling chemical use for the child; and, in instances in which the child strongly identifies with the substance-abusing parent, fostering an imitation of the parent's drug use. These families can also serve as a perpetuating environment for the child's substance abuse by being more prone to enable the adolescent's drug use due to the family's overall disorganization.

Treatment Considerations

The following are some treatment considerations for adolescent substance abusers raised in chemically dependent families.

Engagement Issues

Adolescent substance-abusing COSAPs are often highly resistant to being engaged in substance-abuse treatment. Their denial of their own drug problem is further fueled by having a substance-abusing parent. These teenagers have the added layer of denial of comparing their chemical use to their parent's chemical use. As is often the case, parental chemical abuse is often more entrenched and problematic, thus allowing the adolescent to minimize his use as "not as bad" as his parents. Keeping the adolescent focused on the consequences of his substance abuse and not aligning with his denial-through-comparison is key.

Servicing Issues

In initially assessing and planning treatment with adolescent substance abusers, it is important for therapists not to be led astray by the presence of parental substance abuse. Therapists need to maintain a focus on treatment of the adolescent, at least until the teenager is stable in recovery. "Treatment of an adolescent within a family context often uncovers parental chemical dependency. Other family problems may well be more readily solved when the initial focus is on the adolescent rather than on the alcoholic parent" (Huberty et al., 1987, p. 509).

Recovery Issues

Adolescent recovery issues are how being a COSAP might affect recovery from substance abuse and growing with one's COSAP issues while recovering from substance abuse.

Substance Abuse Recovery Issues. For some COSAP substance abusers the desire to "not be like their parent" can be a strong motivation to work hard in recovery. These teenagers often launch into sobriety and experience a solid period of initial recovery. However, unresolved feelings of loss and anger towards the substance-abusing parent will eventually need to be dealt with in recovery.

For other COSAP substance abusers, especially those who perceive their parents as sober but unhappy (a kind of "dry drunk"), the idea of abstinence and a sober lifestyle is undesirable. These adolescents believe that sobriety doesn't bring happiness and have little faith in the treatment community—including AA and NA. This type of chemical-abusing teenager has additional layers of resistance that need attention in treatment.

There are also those COSAP substance abusers who have a strong positive identification with their actively substance-abusing parent and a kind of invisible loyalty to this parent. For these adolescents, the pain of giving up drugs and, in the process, giving up this chemically anchored identification with the parent is greater than the pain caused by the problems of their own substance abuse. Separation, sense of self, and identity issues are key treatment foci during these adolescents' recovery.

All of these COSAP substance abusers are at risk of relapsing early in recovery, especially if the chronic stress of the chemically dependent family environments remains unresolved. Many of these teenagers need the benefit of a long-term, sober recovery environment, such as a residential program, or, in the case of adolescents who are more stable in their recovery, residing with an alternative "sober family" for a period of time.

COSAP Issues. Drug-abusing adolescents with drug-abusing parents need to be educated about the uniqueness of their experience. Identifying COSAP issues through psychoeducational groups or measures such as the Children of Alcoholics Screening Test (Jaynes & Rugg, 1988) can orient the teenager to some awareness of their experience. Treatment of these COSAP issues can occur throughout the course of an adolescent's substance abuse recovery. What is critical for therapists to be aware of is that dealing with these COSAP issues should enhance the young person's recovery and not deflect from this recovery by overfocusing on the needs of the substance-abusing parent.

The COSAP syndrome needs to be viewed as a continuum—from those adolescents mildly affected by their parents substance abuse, to those teenagers severely impacted by their parent's chemical dependency. There is also a great deal of variability in how each of the COSAP issues is managed by any given adolescent. The major issues of adolescent COSAPs are: trust issues, separation issues, dependent styles or avoidant styles in peer relationships, detachment from feelings, strong feelings of guilt, depression, anxiety, anger and shame, inability to satisfactorily express feelings, learned helplessness, and self-esteem issues (Morehouse, 1984; Rivinus, 1991c).

Group therapy that is both supportive and psychoeducational is an ideal treatment modality for many adolescent COSAPs (Miller, 1983). According to Morehouse (1986), the benefits of such groups for adolescents include: (a) reducing a sense of isolation, (b) learning new ways of coping, (c) receiving positive peer support, (d) practicing sharing feelings, (e) receiving empathetic confrontation when needed, and (f) increasing readiness to participate in Al-Ateen. Al-Ateen meetings can be a powerful adjunctive support for the teenager COSAP, who often feels very alone with the experience of growing up in a chemically dependent family.

Recovery Environment Issues

Family treatment interventions with COSAP substance abusers need to be based on the type of chemically dependent family being treated. The five different types of parental substance abuse introduced in Chapter 5 and reviewed below can have varying influences on the family recovery process. A family can evolve from one type of chemically dependent family to another type during the course of the adolescent's recovery.

Wet-covert chemically dependent families, in which active parental substance is hidden within the family, present closed systems that are difficult to engage in treatment. Sabotage of the adolescent's recovery is common in order to keep the focus on the adolescent as "the problem" and remain detoured from uncovering and dealing with parental substance abuse.

With wet-overt chemically dependent families, in which active parental substance abuse is openly acknowledged within the family and to the outside world, timing is crucial for addressing parental substance abuse. During initial and early recovery, the focus should remain with the adolescent's recovery needs.

> Pursuing the drinking problem in a parent cannot be the main focus in sessions. The therapist needs to warn the family that if the anxiety level gets to be more than they can tolerate, the adolescent who is the problem may have to act out to get the focus back on himself. (Schroeder, 1989, p. 114)

Dry-nonrecovering chemically dependent families, in which parental substance abuse is inactive and there is avoidance of resolving the impact of the parental substance abuse within the family, resemble in some ways the wet-covert families. There is a closed and tense feel to this type of family. If, during the course of the adolescent's recovery, sensitive family issues related to the parental substance abuse surface, the young person may relapse as a way of protecting the sober, but "not recovering" parent. In such an instance the adolescent's flight into relapse to rescue the parent is an unconscious process.

Dry-recovering chemically dependent families, in which parental substance abuse is inactive and there is active effort within and among family members to resolve the impact of the parental substance abuse on the family, present the most workable environment for the adolescent's recovery needs. The openness and striving-to-heal tendencies in this type of family bodes well for the teenager's recovery needs. However, a concern worth mentioning is the parent who is "over-invested" in his or her own recovery (Rivinus, 1991c). In passionately "working his program" and perhaps adopting AA or NA as a kind of "second family," this recovering parent may leave the adolescent with a sense of abandonment—much like the abandonment the adolescent felt when his parent was actively using chemicals. What is key in these families is for parents to balance their own recovery needs with those of their recovering child.

Wet-dry fluctuating chemically dependent families, in which the family experiences a roller coaster ride between periods of active and inactive parental substance abuse, are perhaps the most challenging. The chaotic nature of these families makes it difficult to establish a therapeutic structure. In addition, the affective foundation of these families is continually shifting.

> Variably, during wet or dry phases, parental expressions of love and affection (both genuine and as an expiation of guilt) are directed toward the child but, for the addicted parent, are quickly overridden by the narcissistic necessities dictated by the need for more chemicals of addiction. (Rivinus, 1991c, p. 280)

Unless a stable family holding environment can be created with a wet-dry fluctuating family, facilitating the adolescent's movement to a sober and stable recovery environment is indicated.

The example of one family with an actively alcoholic father and a teenage son in early recovery illustrates how parental substance abuse can impact a child's recovery. The father has twice received treatment for his alcoholism, with limited success of only brief periods of sobriety. This man's drinking problems have been a constant source of conflict between him and his wife for a number of years. The son has had a strong identification with his father. He developed a chemical use problem during his adolescence, and in developing this problem he unconsciously "volunteered" to take his father's place as the source of the family conflict. However, when the teenager eventually received treatment for his own drug problem, the family became unbalanced and returned to having the father's drinking problem as the source of family conflict. The son experienced strong unconscious pulls to rescue his father again from this role, and this teenager was clearly at great risk to relapse. The primary treatment goals at this juncture called for helping the son to become more aware of his family's dynamics, particularly his "rescuing" role with his father, and attempting to directly intervene with the father's ongoing alcohol abuse.

Parental substance abuse and adolescent substance abuse can be a mirroring dynamic in a family. Treatment outcome for the adolescent can, in part, be determined by the substance-abusing parent's own success in recovery. How this translates into a healthy holding environment for the recovering teenager remains vital.

SUMMARY

This chapter concentrated on three distinct populations of adolescent substance abusers—those with concurrent psychological disorders, those who have been physically or sexually abused, and those who have grown up in chemically dependent families. These three groups represent vulnerable treatment populations in that the substance abuse and the coexisting condition present a double jeopardy during recovery. Although these are three distinct vulnerable populations, there is often much overlap as many recovering adolescents are struggling with multiple issues from more than one of these conditions.

Adolescent substance abusers with concurrent psychological disorders are a heterogeneous treatment population. Different categories of adolescent psychological disorders—anxiety disorders, mood disorders, eating disorders, personality disorders, and schizophrenia—were discussed, along with the unique needs of adolescents in "dual recovery."

Adolescent substance abusers who are victims of child abuse—physical, sexual, or both—also regularly appear in substance abuse treatment. Understanding and responding to the special treatment needs of this population is essential for their long-term healing and recovery.

Adolescent substance abusers with substance-abusing parents were also discussed as a vulnerable treatment population. This group of recovering teenagers is developmentally vulnerable in a vulnerable environment. Consequently, treatment interventions aimed at the reparative development work of the adolescent and the reparative environmental work of the family, are key.

Although each of these groups of adolescents is at high risk for developing substance abuse and appear with special needs in treatment, the challenge of treating these teenagers can be met. Due to the condition coexisting with substance abuse, these adolescents are psychologically vulnerable yet developmental reparation and healing is viable.

EPILOGUE

Awareness about addiction and recovery has been growing steadily among helping professionals over the past two decades. The treatment of adolescent substance abusers has been correspondingly emerging as a whole new area of clinical specialty.

The biopsychosocial model is one useful paradigm that can be utilized for understanding and treating addictive disorders. The biopsychosocial model presented in this book is adapted to the specific circumstances pertaining to adolescent substance abusers. This book's model draws from the theoretical diversity of psychodynamic theory, developmental theory, systems theory, and addiction theory, as well as from the therapeutic richness of psychodynamic approaches, cognitive-behavioral approaches, family systems approaches, and 12-step self-help approaches. In essence, this model is a recapitulation of, amplification of, and interweaving of preexisting ideas. Not all theoretical frameworks nor all therapeutic paradigms are included here. In this sense the model offered in this book is only a beginning, and far from the final word on understanding and treating teenagers with drug problems. As new ideas continue to emerge in the mental health and addictions fields, new perspectives will shape the view of and the work with these young people. This book admittedly offers a therapeutic ideal for treating adolescent substance abusers. The reality is that health care reimbursement and public funding pose constraints on the treatment decisions made by clinicians. Nevertheless it is hoped that this ideal will be equitably weighed with other considerations when treatment professionals seek to help drug-involved adolescents and their families.

APPENDIX

THE TWELVE STEPS

1. We admitted we were powerless over _____ , and that our lives had become unmanageable.
2. Came to believe that a power greater than ourselves could restore us to sanity.
3. Made a decision to turn our will and our lives over to the care of God, *as we understood God.*
4. Made a searching and fearless moral inventory of ourselves.
5. Admitted to God, to ourselves, and to another human being the exact nature of our wrongs.
6. Were entirely ready to have God remove all these defects of character.
7. Humbly asked God to remove our shortcomings.
8. Made a list of all persons we had harmed, and became willing to make amends to them all.
9. Made direct amends to such people wherever possible, except when to do so would injure them or others.
10. Continued to take personal inventory and when we were wrong promptly admitted it.
11. Sought through prayer and meditation to improve our conscious contact with God *as we understood God*, praying only for knowledge of God's will for us and the power to carry that out.
12. Having had a spiritual awakening as the result of these steps, we tried to carry this message to _____ , and to practice these principles in all our affairs.

THE TWELVE STEPS OF ALCOHOLICS ANONYMOUS

1. We admitted we were powerless over alcohol—that our lives had become unmanageable.

2. Came to believe that a Power greater than ourselves could restore us to sanity.

3. Made a decision to turn our will and our lives over to the care of God *as we understood Him.*

4. Made a searching and fearless moral inventory of ourselves.

5. Admitted to God, to ourselves, and to another human being the exact nature of our wrongs.

6. Were entirely ready to have God remove all these defects of character.

7. Humbly asked Him to remove our shortcomings.

8. Made a list of all persons we had harmed, and became willing to make amends to them all.

9. Made direct amends to such people wherever possible, except when to do so would injure them or others.

10. Continued to take personal inventory and when we were wrong promptly admitted it.

11. Sought through prayer and meditation to improve our conscious contact with God, *as we understood Him*, praying only for knowledge of His will for us and the power to carry that out.

12. Having had a spiritual awakening as the result of these steps, we tried to carry this message to alcoholics, and to practice these principles in all our affairs.

The Twelve Steps are reprinted with permission of Alcoholics Anonymous World Services, Inc. Permission to reprint and adapt the Twelve Steps does not mean that AA has reviewed or approved the contents of this publication nor that AA agrees with the views expressed herein. AA is a program of recovery from alcoholism—use of the Twelve Steps in connection with programs and activities that are patterned after AA, but which address other problems, does not imply otherwise.

THE TWELVE STEPS OF NARCOTICS ANONYMOUS

1. We admitted that we were powerless over our addiction, that our lives had become unmanageable.

2. We came to believe that a Power greater than ourselves could restore us to sanity.

3. We made a decision to turn our will and our lives over to the care of God *as we understood Him.*

4. We made a searching and fearless moral inventory of ourselves.

5. We admitted to God, to ourselves, and to another human being the exact nature of our wrongs.

6. We were entirely ready to have God remove all these defects of character.

7. We humbly asked Him to remove our shortcomings.

8. We made a list of all persons we had harmed, and became willing to make amends to them all.

9. We made direct amends to such people wherever possible, except when to do so would injure them or others.

10. We continued to take personal inventory and when we were wrong promptly admitted it.

11. We sought through prayer and meditation to improve our conscious contact with God *as we understood Him,* praying only for knowledge of His will for us and the power to carry that out.

12. Having had a spiritual awakening as a result of these steps, we tried to carry this message to addicts, and to practice these principles in all our affairs.

REFERENCES

Adler, T. (1990, July). Alcoholism gene study is controversial. *APA Monitor*, p. 8.

Alibrandi, L. A. (1985). The folk psychotherapy of Alcoholics Anonymous. In S. Zimberg, J. Wallace, & S. B. Blume (Eds.), *Practical approaches to alcoholism psychotherapy* (pp. 239-256). New York: Plenum.

American Psychiatric Association. (1987). *Diagnostic and statistical manual of mental disorders* (rev. ed.). Washington, DC: Author.

American Society of Addiction Medicine. (1991). *Patient placement criteria for the treatment of psychoactive substance use disorders.* Washington, DC: Author.

Anderson, D. (1990). Homosexuality in adolescence. In M. Sugar (Ed.), *Atypical adolescence and sexuality* (pp. 181-200). New York: Norton.

Anderson, G. L. (1987). *When chemicals come to school: The student assistance program model.* Greenfield, WI: Community Recovery Press.

Anderson, C., & Stewart, S. (1983). *Mastering resistance: A practical guide to family therapy.* New York: Guilford.

Anderson, S. C., & Henderson, D. C. (1984). Family therapy in the treatment of alcoholism. *Social Work in Health Care, 8*(4), 79-94.

Anglin, T. M. (1987). Interviewing guidelines for the clinical evaluation of adolescent substance abuse. *Pediatric Clinics of North America, 34,* 381-398.

Azima, F. J. Cramer, & Richmond, L. H. (1989). *Adolescent group psychotherapy.* Madison, CT: International Universities.

Bailey, G. (1989). Current perspectives on substance abuse in youth. *Journal of the American Academy of Child and Adolescent Psychiatry, 28,* 151-162.

Barnard, C. P. (1983). Alcoholism and incest: Improving diagnostic comprehensiveness. *International Journal of Family Therapy, 5,* 136-144.

Barnard, C. P. (1990). Alcoholism and sex abuse in the family: Incest and marital rape. *Journal of Chemical Dependency Treatment, 3,*(1), 131-144.

Barnes, G. M., Farrell, M. P., & Cairnes, A. (1986). Parental socialization factors and adolescent drinking behaviors. *Journal of Marriage and the Family, 48,* 27-36.

Barnes, G. M., & Windle, M. (1987). Family factors in adolescent alcohol and drug abuse. *Pediatrician, 14,* 13-18.

Barnhill, L., Squires, M. F., & Gibson, G. (1982). The epidemiology of violence in a CMHC setting: A violence epidemic? In J. C. Hansen & L. R. Barnhill (Eds.), *Clinical approaches to family violence* (pp. 21-33). Rockville, MD: Aspen.

Baumrind, D., & Moselle, K. (1985). A developmental perspective on adolescent drug abuse. In Stimmel, B. (Ed.), Brock, J., Lettieri, D., & Brook, D. (Guest Eds.), *Alcohol and substance abuse in adolescence* (pp. 41-67). New York: Haworth.

Bays, J. (1990). Substance abuse and child abuse: Impact of addiction on the child. *Pediatric Clinics of North America, 37,* 881-904.

Black, C. (1981). *It will never happen to me! Children of alcoholics: As youngsters-adolescents-adults.* Denver, CO: Medical Administration Corp.

Blos, P. (1962). *On adolescence: A psychoanalytic interpretation.* New York: Free Press.

Blos, P. (1967). The second individuation process of adolescence. *The Psychoanalytic Study of the Child, 22,* 162-186.

Blum, K. (1984). *Handbook of abusable drugs.* New York: Gardner.

Blum, K., Noble, E. P., Sheridan, P. J., Montgomery, A., Ritchie, T., Jagadesswaran, P., Nogami, H., Briggs, A. H., & Cohn, J. B. (1990). Allelic association of human dopamine D2 receptor gene in alcoholism. *Journal of the American Medical Association, 263,* 2055-2060.

Blum, R. W. (1987). Adolescent substance abuse: Diagnostic and treatment issues. *Pediatric Clinics of North America, 34,* 523-537.

Botvin, G. J., & Tortu, S. (1988). Peer relationships, social competence, and substance abuse prevention: Implications for the family. In Coombs, R. H. (Ed.), *The family context of adolescent drug use* (pp. 245-273). New York: Haworth.

Bratter, T. E. (1971). Treating adolescent drug abusers in a community-based interaction group program. *Journal of Drug Issues, 1,* 237-252.

Bratter, T. E. (1989). Group psychotherapy with alcohol and drug addicted adolescents: Special clinical concerns and challenges. In F. J. Cramer Azima & L. H. Richmond (Eds.), *Adolescent group psychotherapy* (pp. 163-189). Madison, CT: International Universities.

Braun, B. G. (1989). Psychotherapy of the survivor of incest with a dissociative disorder. *Psychiatric Clinics of North America, 12,* 307-324.

Brook, J. S., Nomura, C., & Cohen, P. (1989). A network of influences on adolescent drug involvement: Neighborhood, school, peer, and family. *Genetic, Social, and General Psychology Monographs, 115,* 125-145.

Brook, J. S., Whiteman, M., & Gordon, A. S. (1983). Stages of drug use in adolescence: Personality, peer, and family correlates. *Developmental Psychology, 19,* 269-277.

Brown, J. A., Vik, P. W., & Creamer, V. A. (1989). Characteristics of relapse following adolescent substance abuse treatment. *Addictive Behaviors, 14,* 291-300.

Bukstein, O. G., Brent, D. A., & Kaminer, Y. (1989). Comorbidity of substance abuse and other psychiatric disorders in adolescents. *American Journal of Psychiatry, 146,* 1131-1141.

Bush, B., Shaw, S., Cleary, P., Delbanco, T. L., Aronson, M. D. (1987). Screening for alcohol abuse using the CAGE questionnaire. *Brown University Digest of Addiction Therapy and Application, 6*(3), 7-12.

Campbell, E. J. M., Scadding, J. G., & Roberts, R. S. (1979). The concept of disease. *British Medical Journal, 2,* 757-762.

Carroll, J. F. X. (1986). Secondary prevention: A pragmatic approach to the problem of substance abuse among adolescents. In G. Beschner & A. S. Friedman (Eds.), *Teen drug use* (pp.163-184). Lexington, MA: Lexington Books.

Carter, E. A., & McGoldrick, M. (1980). The family life cycle and family therapy: An overview. In E. A. Carter & M. McGoldrick (Eds.), *The family life cycle: A framework for family therapy* (pp. 3-20). New York: Gardner.

Cavaiola, A. A., & Schiff, M. (1989). Self-esteem in abused, chemically dependent adolescents. *Child Abuse and Neglect, 13*, 327-334.

Chassin, L. (1984). Adolescent substance use and abuse. *Advances in Child Behavioral Analysis and Therapy, 3*, 99-152.

Chatlos, J. C. (1989). Adolescent dual diagnosis: A 12-step transformational model. *Journal of Psychoactive Drugs, 21*, 189-201.

Chemical Dependent Anonymous (CDA). (1990). Severna Park, MD: Chemical Dependency Anonymous Communications, Inc., General Service Office.

Cohen, J. (1985). Learning disabilities and adolescence: Developmental considerations. *Adolescent Psychiatry, 12*, 177-196.

Cohen, P. R. (1989). Promoting recovery and preventing relapse in chemically dependent adolescents. In P. B. Henry (Ed.), *Practical approaches in treating adolescent chemical dependency: A guide to clinical assessment and intervention* (pp. 205-238). New York: Haworth.

Cohen, P. R. (1991). *Helping your chemically dependent teenager recover: A guide for parents and other concerned adults.* Minneapolis, MN: Johnson Institute.

Cohen, S. (1988). *The chemical brain: The neurochemistry of addictive disorders.* Irvine, CA: Care Institute.

Coleman, P. (1989). [Letter to the editor]. *Journal of the American Medical Association, 261*(13), 1879-1880.

Coleman, S. B. (1979). Siblings in session. In E. Kaufman & P. Kaufman (Eds.), *Family therapy of alcohol and drug abuse* (pp. 131-143). New York: Gardener.

Coombs, R. H., & Coombs, K. (1988). Developmental stages in drug use: Changing family involvements. In R. H. Coombs (Ed.), *The family context of adolescent drug use* (pp. 73-98). New York: Haworth.

Coombs, R. H., Paulson, M. J., & Palley, R. (1988). The institutionalization of drug use in America: Hazardous adolescence, challenging parenthood. In R. H. Coombs (Ed.), *The family context of adolescent drug use* (pp. 9-37). New York: Haworth.

Coons, P. M., Bowman, E. S., Pellow, T. A., & Schneider, P. (1989). Post-traumatic aspects of the treatment of victims of sexual abuse and incest. *Psychiatric Clinics of North America, 12*(2), 325-335.

Davis, M. & Raffe, I. H. (1985). The holding environment in the inpatient treatment of adolescents. *Adolescent Psychiatry, 12*, 434-443.

Dembo, R., Williams, L., Wish, E. D., Dertke, M., Berry, E., Getreu, A., Washburn, M., & Schmeidler, J. (1988). The relationship between physical and sexual abuse and illicit drug use: A replication among a new sample of youths entering a juvenile detention center. *The International Journal of the Addictions, 23*, 1101-1123.

de Shazer, S., (1985). *Keys to solution in brief therapy.* New York: Norton.

Dishion, T. J., Reid, J. B., & Patterson, G. R. (1988). Empirical guidelines for a family intervention for adolescent drug use. In R. H. Coombs (Ed.), *The family context of adolescent drug use* (pp. 189-224). New York: Haworth.

Donovan, D. M. (1988). Assessment of addictive behaviors: Implications of an emerging biopsychosocial model. In D. M. Donovan & G. A. Marlatt (Eds.), *Assessment of addictive behaviors* (pp. 3-48). New York: Guilford.

Doweiko, H. E. (1990). *Concepts of chemical dependency.* Pacific Grove, CA: Brooks Cole.

Dulcan, M. K., & Popper, C. W. (1991). *Concise guide to child and adolescent psychiatry.* Washington, DC: American Psychiatric Press.

DuPont, R. L. (1988). The counselor's dilemma: Treating chemical dependence at college. In T. Rivinus (Ed.), *Alcoholism/chemical dependency and the college student* (pp. 41-61). New York: Haworth.

DuPont, R. L., & McGovern, J. P. (1991). The growing impact of the children-of-alcoholics movement on medicine: A revolution in our midst. In T. Rivinus (Ed.), *Children of chemically dependent parents: Multiperspectives from the cutting edge* (pp. 313-329). New York: Brunner/Mazel.

Easson, W. M. (1979). The early manifestations of adolescent thought disorder. *Journal of Clinical Psychiatry, 40*(11), 469-475.

Ehrlich, P. (1987). 12-step principles and adolescent chemical dependence treatment. *Journal of Psychoactive Drugs, 19,* 311-317.

Elkind, D. (1984). *All grown up and no place to go: Teenagers in crisis.* Reading, MA: Addison/Wesley.

Elkind, D. (1991). Teenagers in the postmodern world. In A. Pedersen & P. O'Meara (Eds.), *Teens: A fresh look* (pp. 34-50). Santa Fe, NM: John Muir Publications.

Erikson, E. H. (1956). The concept of ego identity. *The Journal of the American Psychoanalytic Association, 4,* 56-121.

Erikson, E. H. (1968). *Identity: Youth and crisis.* New York: Norton.

Esman, A. H. (1985). A developmental approach to the psychotherapy of adolescents. *Adolescent Psychiatry, 12,* 119-133.

Evans, K., & Sullivan, J. M. (1990). *Dual Diagnosis: Counseling the mentally ill substance abuser.* New York: Guilford.

Everstine, D. S., & Everstine, L. (1989). *Sexual trauma in children and adolescents: Dynamics and treatment.* New York: Brunner/Mazel.

Ewing, C. P. (1978). *Crisis intervention as psychotherapy.* New York: Oxford University Press.

Famularo, R., Stone, K., & Popper, C. (1985). Preadolescent alcohol abuse and dependence. *American Journal of Psychiatry, 142,* 1187-1189.

Fatis, M., & Konewko, P. J. (1983). Written contracts as adjuncts in family therapy. *Social Work, 28,* 161-163.

Feigelman, W. (1987). Day-care treatment for multiple drug abusing adolescents: Social factors linked with completing. *Journal of Psychoactive Drugs, 19,* 335-344.

Fischer, J. (1985). Psychotherapy of adolescent alcohol abusers. In S. Zimber, J. Wallace, & S. B. Blume (Eds.), *Practical approaches to alcoholism psychotherapy* (pp. 295-313). New York: Plenum.

Fishman, H. C. (1988). *Treating troubled adolescents: A family therapy approach.* New York: Basic Books.

Fishman, H. C., Stanton, M. D., & Rosman, B. L. (1982). Treating families of adolescent drug abusers. In M. D. Stanton & T. C. Todd (Eds.), *The family therapy of drug abuse and addiction* (pp. 335-357). New York: Guilford.

Flanzer, J. P., & Sturkie, K. (1987). *Alcohol and adolescent abuse: The Alcan family services treatment model*. Holmes Beach, FL: Learning Publications.

Fleck, S. (1980). Family functioning and family pathology. *Psychiatric Annals, 10,* 46-57.

Flores, P. J. (1988). *Group psychotherapy with addicted populations*. New York: Haworth.

Freudenberger, H. J., & Carbone, J. (1984). The reentry process of adolescents. *Journal of Psychoactive Drugs, 16,* 95-99.

Friedman, A. S. (1985). Referral and diagnosis of adolescent substance abusers. In A. S. Friedman & G. M. Beschner, (Eds.), *Treatment services for adolescent substance abusers* (pp. 66-79). Rockville, MD: National Institute on Drug Abuse.

Friedman, A. S. (1990). The adolescent drug abuser and the family. In A. S. Friedman & S. Granick (Eds.), *Family therapy for adolescent drug abuse* (pp. 3-22). Lexington, MA: Lexington Books.

Friedman, A. S., & Utada, A. (1989). A method for diagnosing and planning the treatment of adolescent drug abusers: The adolescent drug abuse diagnosis (ADAD) instrument. *Journal of Drug Education, 19,* 285-312.

Gelinas, D. J. (1988). Family therapy: Characteristic family consellation and basic therapeutic stance. In S. M. Sgroi (Ed.), *Vulnerable populations: Vol. 1. Evaluation and treatment of sexually abused children and adult survivors* (pp. 25-49). Lexington, MA: Lexington Books.

Gifford, P. D. (1989). AA and NA for adolescents. In P. B. Henry (Ed.), *Practical approaches in treating adolescent chemical dependency: A guide to clinical assessment and intervention* (pp. 265-284). New York: Haworth.

Gold, M. S., & Dackis, C. A. (1986). Role of the laboratory in the evaluation of suspected drug abuse. *Journal of Clinical Psychiatry, 47,* 17-23.

Goldstein, A. P. (1989). Refusal skills: Learning to be positively negative. *Journal of Drug Education, 19,* 271-283.

Goodwin, D. W. (1983/Summer). The genetics of alcoholism: Implications for youth. *Alcohol Health & Research World,* pp. 59-63.

Gorski, T. T., & Miller, M. (1982). *Counseling for relapse prevention*. Independence, MO: Herald House.

Greenspan, S. I. (1977). Substance abuse: An understanding from psychoanalytic developmental and learning perspectives. *National Institute on Drug Abuse Research Monograph Series, 12,* 73-87.

Gregorius, H. H., & Smith, T. S. (1991). The adolescent mentally ill chemical abusers: Special considerations in dual diagnosis. *Journal of Adolescent Chemical Dependency, 1*(4), 79-113.

Griswold-Ezekoye, S. (1986). The multicultural model in chemical abuse prevention and intervention. In S. Griswold-Ezekoye, K. L. Kumpfer, & W. J. Bukoski (Eds.), *Childhood and chemical abuse: Prevention and intervention* (pp. 203-229). New York: Haworth.

Harrison, P. A., Edwall, G. E., Hoffman, N. G., & Worthen, M. D. (1990). Correlates of sexual abuse among boys in treatment for chemical dependency. *Journal of Adolescent Chemical Dependency, 1*(1), 53-67.

Hartman, D. (1969). Drug-taking adolescents. *Psychoanalytic Study of the Child, 24,* 384-398.

Hazzard, A., King, H. E., & Webb, C. (1986). Group therapy with sexually abused adolescent girls. *American Journal of Psychotherapy, 40,* 213-223.

Heaslip, J., Van Dyke, D., Hogenson, D., & Vedders, L. (1989). *Young people and drugs: Evaluation and treatment.* Center City, MN: Hazelden.

Hersch, P. (1990, July/August). The resounding silence. *The Family Therapy Networker,* pp. 18-29.

Hodgman, C. H. (1983). Current issues in adolescent psychiatry. *Hospital and Community Psychiatry, 34,* 514-521.

Homstead, K. C., & Werthamer, L. (1989). Time-limited group therapy for adolescent victims of child sexual abuse. In S. M. Sgroi (Ed.), *Vulnerable populations: Vol. 2. Sexual abuse treatment for children, adult survivors, offenders, and persons with mental retardation* (pp. 65-84). Lexington, MA: Lexington Books.

Huberty, D. J., & Huberty, C. E. (1984). Helping the parents to survive: A family systems approach to adolescent alcoholism. In E. Kaufman (Ed.), *Power to change: Family case studies in the treatment of alcoholism* (pp. 131-176). New York: Gardner.

Huberty, D. J., Huberty, C. E., Flanagan-Hobday, K., & Blackmore, G. (1987). Families issues in working with chemically dependent adolescents. *Pediatric Clinics of North America, 34,* 507-521.

Hussey, D., & Singer, M. (1989). Innovations in the assessment and treatment of sexually abused adolescents: An inpatient model. In S. M. Sgroi (Ed.), *Vulnerable populations: Vol. 2. Sexual abuse treatment for children, adult survivors, offenders, and persons with mental retardation* (pp. 43-64). Lexington, MA: Lexington Books.

Imber-Black, E., Roberts, J., & Whiting, R. (1988). *Rituals in families and family therapy.* New York: Norton.

Inaba, D. S. (1990, February/March). Drug challenges of the 1990s. *Adolescent Counselor,* pp. 30-31.

Jaynes, J. H., & Rugg, C. A. (1988). *Adolescents, alcohol, and drugs: A practical guide for those who work with young people.* Springfield, IL: Charles C Thomas.

Jellinek, E. M. (1960). *The disease concept of alcoholism.* New Haven, CT: Hillhouse.

Johnson, V. E. (1973). *I'll quit tomorrow.* New York: Harper & Row.

Johnson, V., & Pandina, R. J. (1991). Effects of the family environment on adolescent substance use, delinquency, and coping styles. *American Journal of Drug and Alcohol Abuse, 17,* 71-88.

Joshi, N. P., & Scott, M. (1988). Drug use, depression, and adolescents. *Pediatric Clinics of North America, 35,* 1349-1364.

Jurich, A. P., Polson, C. J., Jurich, J. A., & Bates, R. A. (1985). Family factors in the lives of drugs users and abusers. *Adolescence, 20,* 143-159.

Kandel, D. (1975). Stages in adolescent involvement in drug use. *Science, 190,* 912-914.

Kandel, D. B., & Raveis, V. H. (1989). Cessation of illicit drug use in young adulthood. *Archives of General Psychiatry, 46,* 109-116.

Karpman, S. B. (1968). Script drama analysis. *Transactional Analysis Bulletin, 7,* 39-43.

Kaufman, E. (1980). Myth and reality in the family patterns and treatment of substance abusers. *American Journal of Drug and Alcohol Abuse, 7,* 257-279.

Kaufman, E. (1985). Adolescent substance abuse and family therapy. In M. P. Mirkin & S. L. Koman (Eds.), *Handbook of adolescents and family therapy* (pp. 245-271). New York: Gardner.

Kaufman, E., & Borders, L. (1988). Ethnic family differences in adolescent substance use. In R. H. Coombs (Ed.), *The family context of adolescent drug use* (pp. 99-121). New York: Haworth.

Kaufman, E., & Kaufmann, P. (1979). From a psychodynamic orientation to a structural family approach in the treatment of drug dependency. In E. Kaufman & P. Kaufmann (Eds.), *Family therapy of drug and alcohol abuse* (pp. 43-54). New York: Gardner.

Kaufmann, P. (1979). Family therapy with adolescent substance abusers. In E. Kaufman & P. Kaufmann (Eds.), *Family therapy of drug and alcohol abuse* (pp. 71-79). New York: Gardner.

King, J. W., & Meeks, J. E. (1988). Hospital programs for psychiatrically disturbed, drug-abusing adolescents. *Adolescent Psychiatry, 15,* 522-534.

Klimek, D., & Anderson, M. (1988). *Inner world, outer world: Understanding the struggles of adolescence.* Ann Arbor, MI: ERIC/CAPS.

Kohut, H. (1971). The analysis of the self. New York: *International Universities.*

Kohut, H. (1987). Building psychic structure that regulates self-esteem. In M. Elson (Ed.), *The Kohut seminars on self psychology and psychotherapy with adolescents and young adults* (pp. 61-76). New York: Norton.

Kreilkamp, T. (1989). *Time-limited intermittent therapy with children and families.* New York: Brunner/Mazel.

Kusnetz, S. (1986). Services for adolescent substance abusers. In G. Beschner & A. S. Friedman, *Teen Drug Use* (pp. 123-153). Lexington, MA: Lexington Books.

LaFountain, W. L. (1987). *Parents in crisis: How Families Anonymous can help.* Center City, MN: Hazelden.

Lawson, G. W. (1992). A biopsychosocial model of adolescent substance abuse. In G. W. Lawson & A. M. Lawson (Eds.), *Adolescent substance abuse: Etiology, treatment, and prevention* (pp. 3-10). Gaithersburg, MD: Aspen.

Lawson, G., Peterson, J. S., & Lawson, A. (1983). *Alcoholism and the family: A guide to treatment and prevention.* Rockville, MD: Aspen.

Lettieri, D. L. (1985). Drug abuse: A review of explanations and models of explanation. In B. Stimmel, J. Brook, D. Lettieri, & D. W. Brook (Eds.), *Alcohol and substance abuse in adolescence* (pp. 9-40). New York: Haworth.

Levine, K. G. (1991). *When good kids do bad things: A survival guide for parents.* New York: Norton.

Levoy, D., Rivinus, T. M., Matzko, M., & McGuire, J. (1991). Children in search of a diagnosis: Chronic trauma disorder of childhood. In T. M. Rivinus (Ed.), *Children of chemically dependent parents: Multiperspectives from the cutting edge* (pp. 153-170). New York: Brunner/Mazel.

Levy, J. C., & Deykin, E. Y. (1989). Suicidality, depression, and substance abuse in adolescence. *American Journal of Psychiatry, 146,* 1462-1467.

Lidz, T. (1983). *The person: His and her development throughout the life cycle.* New York: Basic Books.

Macdonald, D. I. (1984). Drugs, drinking, and adolescence. *American Journal of Diseases of Children, 138,* 117-125.

Macdonald, D. I., & Newton, M. (1981). The clinical syndrome of adolescent drug abuse. *Advances in Pediatrics, 28,* 1-25.

MacKenzie, R. G., Cheng, M., & Haftel, A. (1987). The clinical utility and evaluation of drug screening techniques. *Pediatric Clinics of North America, 34,* 423-436.

McDermott, D. (1984). The relationship of parental drug use and parents' attitude concerning adolescent drug use to adolescent drug use. *Adolescence, 19,* 89-97.

McHolland, J. D. (1985). Strategies for dealing with resistant adolescents. *Adolescence, 20,* 349-368.

McHugh, M. J. (1987). The abuse of volatile substances. *Pediatric Clinics of North America, 34*, 333-340.

McPeake, J. D., Kennedy, B., Grossman, J., & Beaulieu, L. (1991). Innovative adolescent chemical dependency treatment and its outcome: A model based on outward bound programming. *Journal of Adolescent Chemical Depedency, 2*(1), 29-57.

Maddahian, E., Newcomb, M. D., Bentler, P. M. (1988). Risk factors for substance use: Ethnic differences among adolescents. *Journal of Substance Abuse, 1,* 11-23.

Mandel, J., & Feldman, H. W. (1986). The social history of teenage drug use. In G. Beschner & A. S. Friedman (Eds.), *Teen drug use* (pp. 19-42). Lexington, MA: Lexington Books.

Marlatt, G. A., & Gordon, J. R. (1985). *Relapse prevention: Maintenance strategies in the treatment of addictive behaviors.* New York: Guilford.

Masterson, J., & Strodbleck, P. (1972). *Treatment of the borderline adolescent: A developmental approach.* New York: John Wiley.

Meeks, J. E. (1988). Adolescent chemical dependency. *Adolescent Psychiatry, 15,* 509-521.

Meyer, R. E. (1986). How to understand the relationship between psychopathology and addictive disorders: Another example of the chicken and the egg. In R. E. Meyer (Ed.), *Psychopathology and addictive disorders* (pp. 3-16). New York: Guilford.

Miller, D. (1973). The drug-dependent adolescent. *Adolescent Psychiatry, 2,* 70-97.

Miller, D. (1986). *Attack on the self: Adolescent behavioral disturbances and their treatment.* Northvale, NJ: Jason Aronson.

Miller, N. (1983). Group psychotherapy in a school setting for adolescent children of alcoholics. *Groups, 7*(1), 34-40.

Miller, N. S., & Gold, M. S. (1989). Suggestions for changes in DSM-III-R criteria for substance use disorders. *American Journal of Drug and Alcohol Abuse, 15,* 223-230.

Minuchin, S. (1974). *Families and family therapy.* Cambridge, MA: Harvard University Press.

Mirkin, M. P., & Koman, S. L. (1985). *Handbook of adolescents and family therapy.* New York: Gardner.

Mishne, J. M. (1986). *Clinical work with adolescents.* New York: Free Press.

Moberg, D. P. (1983). Identifying adolescents with alcohol problems: A field test of the adolescent alcohol involvement scale. *Journal of Studies on Alcohol, 44,* 701-722.

Moberg, D. P., & Hahn, L. (1991). The adolescent drug involvement scale. *Journal of Adolescent Chemical Dependency, 2*(1), 75-88.

Morehouse, E. R. (1984). Working with alcohol-abusing children of alcoholics. *Alcohol Health and Research World, 8*(4), 14-19.

Morehouse, E. (1986). Counseling adolescent children of alcoholics in groups. In R. J. Ackerman (Ed.), *Growing in the shadow: Children of alcoholics* (pp. 125-142). Pompano Beach, FL: Health Communications.

Morgan, P., Wallack, L., & Buchanan, D. (1989). Waging drug wars: Prevention strategy or politics as usual. In B. Segal (Ed.), *Perspectives on adolescent drug abuse* (pp. 99-124). New York: Haworth.

Muldoon, J. A., & Crowley, J. F. (1986). *One step ahead: Early-intervention strategies for adolescent drug problems.* Minneapolis, MN: Community Intervention.

Musto, D. (1987). *The American disease: Origins of narcotic control.* New York: Oxford University Press.

Myers, D. P., & Andersen, A. R. (1991). Adolescent addiction: Assessment and identification. *Journal of Pediatric Health Care, 5*(2), 86-93.

Nakken, J. M. (1989). Issues in adolescent chemical dependency assessment. In P. B. Henry (Ed.), *Practical approaches in treating adolescent chemical dependency: A guide to clinical assessment and intervention* (pp. 71-93). New York: Haworth.

Narcotics Anonymous. (1982). Van Nuys, CA: Narcotics Anonymous World Service Office.

Nathanson, D. L. (1989). Understanding what is hidden: Shame in sexual abuse. *Psychiatric Clinics of North America, 12,* 381-388.

National Institute of Drug Abuse (1989). *The adolescent assessment/referral system manual.* Rockville, MD: Author.

Needle, R., McCubbin, H., Wilson, M., Reineck, R., Lazar, A., & Mederer, H. (1986). Interpersonal influences in adolescent drug use—The role of older siblings, parents, and peers. *The International Journal of the Addictions, 21,* 739-766.

Neuhaus, C. (1991). [Book Review of "Diseasing of America: Addiction treatment out of control" by S. Peele]. *Journal of Psychoactive Drugs, 23,* 87-88.

Newcomb, M., Bentler, P., & Collins, C. (1986). Alcohol use and dissatisfaction with self and life: A longitudinal analysis of young adults. *The Journal of Drug Issues, 16,* 479-494.

Newton, M. (1981). *Gone way down: Teenage drug use is a disease.* Chicago, IL: American Studies Press.

Noshpitz, J. D., & King, R. A. (1991). *Essentials of child psychiatry: Vol. 1. Pathways of growth.* New York: John Wiley.

Nowinski, J. (1990). *Substance abuse in adolescents and young adults: A guide to treatment.* New York: Norton.

Obermeier, G. E., & Henry, P. B. (1989). Adolescent inpatient treatment. In P. B. Henry (Ed.), *Practical approaches in treating adolescent chemical dependency: A guide to clinical assessment and intervention* (pp. 163-182). New York: Haworth.

O'Brien, R., & Cohen, S. (1984). *The encyclopedia of drug abuse.* New York: Facts on File.

O'Connell, D. F. (1989). Treating the high risk adolescent: A survey of effective programs and interventions. In P. B. Henry (Ed.), *Practical approaches in treating adolescent chemical dependency: A guide to clinical assessment and intervention* (pp. 49-69). New York: Haworth.

Oetting, E. R., & Beauvais, F. (1986). Peer cluster theory: Drugs and the adolescent. *Journal of Counseling and Development, 65,* 17-22.

Offer, D., Ostrov, E., & Howard, K. I. (1981). The mental health professional's concept of the normal adolescent. *Archives of General Psychiatry, 38,* 149-152.

Olson, P. H., Portner, J., & Bell, R. (1982). *FACES-II.* Duluth: University of Minnesota Department of Family Social Science.

O'Shea, M. D., & Phelps, R. (1985). Multiple family therapy: Current status and critical appraisal. *Family Process, 24,* 555-582.

Oster, G. D., & Caro, J. E. (1990). *Understanding and treating depressed adolescents and their families.* New York: John Wiley.

O'Sullivan, C. M. (1989). Alcoholism and abuse: The twin family secrets. In G. W. Lawson & A. W. Lawson (Eds.), *Alcoholism and substance abuse in special populations* (pp. 273-303). Rockville, MD: Aspen.

Page, R. M., & Cole, G. E. (1991). Loneliness and alcoholism risk in late adolescence: A comparative study of adults and adolescents. *Adolescence, 26,* 925-930.

Peele, S. (1989). Diseasing of America: Addiction treatment out of control. Lexington, MA: Lexington Books.

Peele, S., & Brodsky, A. (1991). *The truth about addiction and recovery: The life process program for outgrowing destructive habits.* New York: Simon & Schuster.

Petchers, M. K., & Singer, M. I. (1990). Clinical applicability of a substance abuse screening instrument. *Journal of Adolescent Chemical Dependency, 1*(2), 47-56.

Piaget, J. P. (1975). The intellectual development of the adolescent. In A. H. Esman (Ed.), *The psychology of adolescence: Essential readings* (pp. 104-108). Madison, CT: International Universities.

Piercy, F. P., Volk, R. J., Trepper, T., Sprenkle, D. H., & Lewis, R. (1991). The relationship of family factors to patterns of adolescent substance abuse. *Family Dynamics of Addiction Quarterly, 1*(1), 41-54.

Pittman, F. S., (1987). *Turning points: Treating families in transition and crisis.* New York: Norton.

Potter-Efron, R. T., & Potter-Efron, P. J. (1985). Family violence as a treatment issue with chemically dependent adolescents. *Alcoholism Treatment Quarterly, 2*(2), 1-16.

Prall, R. C. (1990). The neurotic adolescent. In M. H. Etezady (Ed.), *The neurotic child and adolescent* (pp. 241-302). Northvale, NJ: Jason Aronson.

Preto, N. G., & Travis, N. (1985). The adolescent phase of the family life cycle. In M. P. Mirkin & S. L. Koman (Eds.), *Handbook of adolescents and family therapy* (pp. 21-38). New York: Gardner.

Quinn, W. H., Kuehl, B. P., Thomas, F. N., & Joanning, H. (1988). Families of adolescent drug abusers: Systematic interventions to attain drug-free behavior. *American Journal of Drug and Alcohol Abuse, 14,* 65-87.

Rachman, A. W., & Raubolt, R. R. (1985). The clinical practice of group psychotherapy with adolescent substance abusers. In T. E. Bratter & G. G. Forrest (Eds.), *Alcoholism and substance abuse: Strategies for clinical intervention* (pp. 349-375). New York: Free Press.

Raubolt, R. R. (1983). Brief, problem-focused group psychotherapy with adolescents. *American Journal of Orthopsychiatry, 53,* 157-165.

Raubolt, R. R., & Bratter, T. E. (1974). Games addicts play: Implications for group treatment. *Corrective and Social Psychiatry, 1974, 20*(4), 3-10.

Reilly, D. M., (1978). Family factors in the etiology and treatment of youthful drug abuse. *Family Therapy, 2,* 149-171.

Rinsley, D. B., (1988). The dipsas revisited: Comments on addiction and personality. *Journal of Substance Abuse Treatment, 5,* 1-7.

Rivinus, T. M. (1991a). Introduction. In T. M. Rivinus (Ed.), *Children of chemically dependent parents: Multiperspectives from the cutting edge* (pp. xv-xx). New York: Brunner/Mazel.

Rivinus, T. M. (1991b). Psychoanalytic theory and children of chemically dependent parents: Ships passing in the night? In T. M. Rivinus (Ed.), *Children of chemically dependent parents: Multiperspectives from the cutting edge* (pp. 103-127). New York: Brunner/Mazel.

Rivinus, T. M. (1991c). Treatment of children of substance-abusing parents: Selected developmental, diagnostic, and treatment issues. In T. M. Rivinus (Ed.), *Children of chemically dependent parents: Multiperspectives from the cutting edge* (pp. 263-287). New York: Brunner/Mazel.

Robak, R. (1991). *A primer for today's substance abuse counselor.* Lexington, MA: Lexington Books.

Robinson, L. H. (1990). In defense of parents. *Adolescent Psychiatry, 17,* 36-50.

Robinson, D., & Greene, J. (1988). The adolescent alcohol and drug problem: A pratical approach. *Pediatric Nursing, 14,* 305-310.

Rohsenow, D. J., Corbett, R., & Devine, D. (1988). Molested as children: A hidden contribution to substance abuse? *Journal of Substance Abuse Treatment, 5,* 13-18.

Sarrel, L. J., & Sarrel, P. M. (1990). Sexual unfolding in adolescents. In M. Sugar (Ed.), *Atypical adolescence and sexuality* (pp. 18-43). New York: Norton.

Sarri, R. (1991). [Book Review of "Diseasing of America: addiction treatment out of control" by S. Peele]. *Social Work, 36,* 91-92.

Savage, M., & Stickles, J. (1990). Adolescent and counselor preference for recovering vs non-recovering alcoholism counselors. *Journal of Adolescent Chemical Dependency, 1*(2), 117-138.

Schaefer, D. (1987). *Choices and consequences: What to do when a teenager uses alcohol/drugs.* Minneapolis, MN: Johnson Institute.

Schave, D., & Schave, B. (1989). *Early adolescence and the search for self: A developmental perspective.* New York: Praeger.

Schiff, M. M., & Cavaiola, A. A. (1989). Adolescents at risk for chemical dependency: Identification and prevention issues. In P. B. Henry (Ed.), *Practical approaches in treating adolescent chemical dependency: A guide to clinical asessment and intervention* (pp. 25-47). New York: Haworth.

Schiff, M. M., & Cavaiola, A. A. (1990). Teenage chemical dependence and the prevalence of psychiatric disorders: Issues for prevention. *Journal of Adolescent Chemical Dependency, 1*(2), pp. 35-46.

Schinke, S. P., Botvin, G. J., & Orlandi, M. A. (1991). *Substance abuse in children and adolescents: Education and intervention.* Newbury Park, CA: Sage.

Schmidt, M. (1991). Problems of child abuse with adolescents in chemically dependent families. *Journal of Adolescent Chemical Dependency, 1*(4), 9-24.

Schroeder, E. (1989). Therapy for the chemically dependent family. In P. B. Henry (Ed.), *Practical approaches in treating adolescent chemical dependency: A guide to clinical assessment and intervention* (pp. 95-129). New York: Haworth.

Schuckit, M. A. (1989). *Drug and alcohol abuse: A clinical guide to diagnosis and treatment.* New York: Plenum.

Schwartz, G. E. (1982). Testing the biopsychosocial model. The ultimate challenge facing behavioral medicine? *Journal of Consulting and Clinical Psychology, 50,* 1040-1053.

Selekman, M. (1991). "With a little help from my friends": The use of peers in the family therapy of adolescent substance abusers. *Family Dynamics of Addiction Quarterly, 1*(1), 69-76.

Seymour, R., Smith, D., Inaba, D., & Landry, M. (1989). *The new drugs: Look-alikes, drugs of deception, and designer drugs.* Center City, MN: Hazelden.

Sgroi, S. M. (1982). Family treatment. In S. M. Sgroi (Ed.), *Handbook of clinical intervention in child sexual abuse* (pp. 241-267). Lexington, MA: Lexington Books.

Shaffer, H. J. (1985). The disease controversy: Of metaphors, maps, and menus. *Journal of Psychoactive Drugs, 17*(2), 65-76.

Shelder, J., & Block. J. (1990). Adolescent drug use and psychological health: A longitudinal inquiry. *American Psychologist, 45,* 612-630.

Shelton, C. (1989). *Adolescent spirituality: Pastoral ministry for high school and college youth.* New York: Crossroad.

Shilts, L. (1991). The relationship of early adolescent substance use to extracurricular activities, peer influence, and personal attitudes. *Adolescence, 26,* 613-617.

Singer, M. I., & White, W. J. (1991). Addressing substance abuse problems among psychiatrically hospitalized adolescents. *Journal of Adolescent Chemical Dependency, 2*(1), 13-27.

Skagen, R., & Fisher, D. G. (1989). Substance use among high school students in relation to school characteristics. *Addictive Behaviors, 14,* 129-138.

Skinner, H. (1981). Assessment of alcohol problems. In Y. Israel (Ed.), *Research advances in alcohol and drug problems* (pp. 319-369). New York: Plenum.

Smith, T. E. (1984). Reviewing adolescent marijuana abuse. *Social Work, 29,* 17-21.

Smith, T. E. (1985). Groupwork with adolescent drug abusers. *Social Work with Groups, 8*(1), 55-64.

Stanton, M. D., Todd, T. C., Heard, D. B., Kirschner, S., Kleiman, J. I., Mowatt, D. T., Riley, P., Scott, S. M., & van Deusen, J. M. (1978). Heroin addiction as a family phenomenon: A new conceptual model. *American Journal of Drug and Alcohol Abuse, 5,* 125-150.

Stanton, M. D., & Todd, T. C. (1982). The therapy model. In M. D. Stanton & T. C. Todd (Eds.), *The family therapy of drug abuse and addiction* (pp. 109-153). New York: Guilford.

Steiner, C. S. (1971). *Games alcoholics play.* New York: Ballantine Books.

Steinglass, P. (1979). Family therapy with alcoholics: A review. In E. Kaufman & P. Kaufmann (Eds.), *Family therapy of drug and alcohol abuse* (pp. 147-186). New York: Gardner.

Steinglass, P. (1980). A life history model of the alcoholic family. *Family Process, 19,* 211-225.

Stolberg, V. B., & DeValve, D. (1991). Eating disorders and chemical dependency among students. *Journal of Adolescent Chemical Dependency, 1*(4), 49-78.

Suchman, D., & Broghton, E. (1988). Treatment alternatives for university students with substance use/abuse problems. In T. Rivinus (Ed.), *Alcoholism/chemical dependency and the college student* (pp. 131-146). New York: Haworth.

Sugar, M. (Ed.). (1975). *The adolescent in group and family therapy.* New York: Brunner/Mazel.

Sunderwirth, S. G. (1990). Harnessing brain chemicals: The influence of molecules on mind, mood, and behavior. In H. B. Milkman & L. I. Sederer (Eds.), *Treatment choices for alcoholism and substance abuse* (pp. 25-41). Lexington, MA: Lexington Books.

Suski, P. J. (1992). Responding to substance abuse and its related issues. *Journal of Adolescent Chemical Dependency, 2*(2), 45-57.

Tarter, R. E. (1990). Evaluation and treatment of adolescent substance abuse: A decision tree method. *American Journal of Drug and Alcohol Abuse, 16,* 1-46.

Todd, T. C. (1985). Anorexia nervosa and bulimia: Expanding the structural model. In M. P. Mirkin & S. L. Koman (Eds.), *Handbook of adolescents and family therapy* (pp. 223-243). New York: Gardner.

Treadway, D. C. (1989). *Before it's too late: Working with substance abuse in the family.* New York: Norton.

Treece, C., & Khantzian, E. J. (1986). Psychodynamic factors in the development of drug dependence. *Psychiatric Clinics of North America, 9,* 399-412.

Ungerleider, J. T., & Siegel, N. J. (1990). The drug abusing adolescent: Clinical issues. *Psychiatric Clinics of North America, 13,* 435-442.

University of Michigan Institute for Social Research (1992). *The national high school senior survey: 1992.* Ann Arbor: Author.

Van Meter, W., & Rioux, D. (1990). The case for shorter residential alcohol and other drug abuse treatment of adolescents. *Journal of Psychoactive Drugs, 22,* 87-88.

Vicary, J. R., & Lerner, J. V. (1986). Parental attributes and adolescent drug use. *Journal of Adolescence, 9,* 115-122.

Walfish, S., Massey, R., & Krone, A. (1990). Interpersonal relationships of adolescent substance abusers. *Journal of Adolescent Chemical Dependency, 1*(2), 5-13.

Wallace, J. (1984). Myths and misconceptions about Alcoholics Anonymous. *About AA.* New York: AA World Services.

Wallace J. (1985). Working with the preferred defense structure of the recovering alcoholic. In S. Zimberg, J. Wallace, & S. B. Blume (Eds.), *Practical approaches to alcoholism psychotherapy* (pp. 23-36). New York: Plenum.

Wallace, J. (1989). *On the new disease model of alcoholism.* Newport, RI: Edgehill.

Washton, A. M., Stone, N. S., & Hendrickson, E. C. (1988). Cocaine abuse. In D. M. Donovan & G. A. Marlatt (Eds.), *Assessment of addictive behaviors* (pp. 364-389). New York: Guilford.

Wegscheider, S. (1981). *Another chance: Hope and health for the alcoholic family.* Palo Alto, CA: Science and Behavior Books.

Weidman, A. A. (1983). Adolescent substance abuse: Family dynamics. *Family Therapy, 10,* 47-55.

Weidman, A. A. (1985). Engaging the families of substance abusing adolescents in family therapy. *Journal of Substance Abuse Treatment, 2,* 97-105.

Weiner, I. B. (1992). *Psychological disturbance in adolescence (2nd ed.).* New York: John Wiley.

Weiss R. D., Mirin, S. M., & Frances, R. J. (1992). The myth of the typical dual diagnosis patient. *Hospital and Community Psychiatry, 43,* 107-108.

Wexler, D. B. (1991). *The adolescent self: Strategies for self-management, self-soothing, and self-esteem in adolescents.* New York: Norton.

Wheeler, K., & Malmquist, J. (1987). Treatment approaches in adolescent chemical dependency. *Pediatric Clinics of North America, 34,* 437-447.

White, H. R., & Labouvie, E. W. (1989). Towards the assessment of adolescent problem drinking. *Journal of Studies on Alcohol, 50,* 30-37.

Wieder, H., & Kaplan, E. (1969). Drug use in adolescents: Psychodynamic meaning and parmacogenic effect. *Psychoanalytic Study of the Child, 24,* 399-431.

Wight, J. C. (1990). Family systems theory and adolescent substance abuse: A proposal for expanding the role of the school. *Journal of Adolescent Chemical Dependency, 1*(2), 57-76.

Williams, F. S. (1986). The psychoanalyst as both parent and interpreter for adolescent patients. *Adolescent Psychiatry, 13,* 164-177.

Winnicott, D. W. (1965). *The maturational process and the facilitating environment: Studies in the theory of emotional development.* New York: International Universities.

Winters, K. C. (1990). Clinical considerations in the assessment of adolescent chemical dependency. *Journal of Adolescent Chemical Dependency, 1*(1), 31-52.

Winters, K. C. (1992). *Personal Experience Screening Questionnaire.* Los Angeles, CA: Western Psychological Services.

Winters, K. C., & Henly, G. A. (1989). *Personal Experience Inventory.* Los Angeles, CA: Western Psychological Services.

Winters, K. C. & Henly, G. A. (1992). *Adolscent Diagnostic Interview.* Los Angeles, CA: Western Psychological Services.

Woody, G. E., McLellan, A. T., Lubursky, L., & O'Brien, C. P. (1986). Psychotherapy for substance abuse. *Psychiatric Clinics of North America, 9,* 547-562.

Wurmser, L. (1977). Mr. Pecksniff's horse? (Psychodynamics in compulsive drug use). *National Institute on Drug Abuse Research Monograph Series, 12,* 37-72.

Wurmser, L. (1987). Flight from conscience: Experiences with the psychoanalytic treatment of complusive drug abusers. *Journal of Substance Abuse Treatment, 4,* 157-179.

York, P., York, D., & Wachtel, T. (1982). *Tough Love.* New York: Bantam.

Zarek, D., Hawkins, J. D., & Rogers, P. D. (1987). Risk factors for adolescent substance abuse. *Pediatric Clinics of North America, 34,* 481-493.

Zucker, R. A., & Lisansky Gomberg, E. S. (1986). Etiology of alcoholism reconsidered: The case for a biopsychosocial process. *American Psychologist, 41,* 783-793.

Zweben, J. E. (1987). Recovery-oriented psychotherapy: Facilitating the use of 12-step programs. *Journal of Psychoactive Drugs, 19,* 243-251.

Zweben, J. E. (1989). Recovery-oriented psychotherapy: Patient resistances and therapist dilemmas. *Journal of Substance Abuse Treatment, 6,* 123-132.

AUTHOR INDEX

SUBJECT INDEX

Abstinence contract:
  goals in using, 142
  guidelines for, 142-143
  time-limited intermittent treatment
    (TLIT) and, 143-144
Addiction:
  as multifaceted disorder, xv
  criteria of compulsion in definition of,
    19
  phenomenon of denial in definition of,
    19
  tendency to relapse in definition of, 19
  understanding of with adolescents,
    18-22
  working definition of, 18-19
Addiction dynamics:
  biopsychosocial expressions of, 52-56
  compulsion, 53, 57
  denial, 54-56, 57
  relapse, 53-54, 57
Addiction theory, 220
Addictive disease concept, 20-22, 23
  alcoholism as prototype of, 20, 22
  arguments supporting, 20, 21
  benefits of, 22
  challenges to, 20, 21
  history of, 20
Addictive disorders, unity of, xvi
Adolescent addiction stages, 19-20

Adolescent Alcohol Involvement Scale,
  125
Adolescent Assessment/Referral System
  (AARS), 120, 121
Adolescent Chemical Use Experience
  (ACUE) continuum, 4-8, 26, 27,
  145
  dependent use stage of (Stage 4), 8, 9,
    12, 19, 25, 26, 29, 146, 147
  experimental use stage of (Stage 1), 5,
    9, 11, 29, 138, 146
  mood swings and, 4
  movement along, 8-9
  operational use stage of (Stage 3),
    6-7, 9, 12, 25, 29, 146, 147
  social use stage of (Stage 2), 5-6, 9,
    11, 26, 29, 138, 146
  stages of, 5-8, 23
Adolescent Chemical Use Problem
  (ACUP) Index, 10-11, 12, 14-15,
  54, 113, 120, 121, 132, 134, 155,
  171, 174
  assessment using, 121-131, 132
  developing treatment plan using,
    134-135
  problem domains of, 10-11, 121
Adolescent Diagnostic Interview, 123
Adolescent Drug Abuse Diagnosis
  Instrument, 125

ABOUT THE AUTHOR

PHILIP P. MUISENER is a clinical social worker with the Glastonbury Youth and Family Services, Glastonbury, Connecticut. He specializes in the treatment of substance abusing adolescents and has been working with adolescents and their families for more than 12 years. Mr. Muisener holds an M.S.W. from the University of Connecticut School of Social Work, an M.S. in Counseling from Central Connecticut State University, and has been a Certified Alcohol and Drug Counselor for 8 years. He has practiced as a therapist in a variety of treatment settings. In addition, he has provided consultation and training in assessing and treating adolescent substance abuse to school systems, hospitals, and child guidance clinics.